S0-DJW-507

NEURAL NETWORKS
Advances and Applications

NEURAL NETWORKS
Advances and Applications

Edited by

Erol GELENBE
Ministère de l'Education Nationale
Université René Descartes
Ecole des Hautes Etudes en Informatique
Paris, France

1991

NORTH-HOLLAND
AMSTERDAM • NEW YORK • OXFORD • TOKYO

QA
76.87
N478
1991

ELSEVIER SCIENCE PUBLISHERS B.V.
Sara Burgerhartstraat 25
P.O. Box 211, 1000 AE Amsterdam, The Netherlands

Distributors for the United States and Canada:
ELSEVIER SCIENCE PUBLISHING COMPANY, INC.
655 Avenue of the Americas
New York, N.Y. 10010, U.S.A.

ISBN: 0 444 88533 1

© ELSEVIER SCIENCE PUBLISHERS B.V., 1991

All rights reserved. No part of this publication may be reproduced, stored in a retrieval system, or transmitted, in any form or by any means, electronic, mechanical, photocopying, recording or otherwise, without the prior written permission of the publisher, Elsevier Science Publishers B.V./Physical Sciences and Engineering Division, P.O. Box 103, 1000 AC Amsterdam, The Netherlands.

Special regulations for readers in the U.S.A. - This publication has been registered with the Copyright Clearance Center Inc. (CCC), Salem, Massachusetts. Information can be obtained from the CCC about conditions under which photocopies of parts of this publication may be made in the U.S.A. All other copyright questions, including photocopying outside of the U.S.A., should be referred to the copyright owner, Elsevier Science Publishers B.V., unless otherwise specified.

No responsibility is assumed by the publisher for any injury and/or damage to persons or property as a matter of products liability, negligence or otherwise, or from any use or operation of any methods, products, instructions or ideas contained in the material herein.

Printed in The Netherlands

PREFACE

The area of Artificial Neural Networks, or Connexionism, has received renewed attention in the last five years.

In the scientific community, many computer scientists have felt that this attention has been excessive both with respect to the new ideas which were being proposed and with respect to the potential for real applications. Indeed, some of the enthusiasm which was being expressed was not based on realistic expectations or on proven applications. Thus there are good reasons to take a sceptical view of the area.

On the other hand, the numerous attempts to relate Neural Networks with problems in combinatorial optimization, pattern recognition, image processing, artificial intelligence, or control systems, the introduction of some new "learning" algorithms such as back-propagation, and the intrinsic parallelism of these models which make them particularly attractive for a parallel processing implementation, justify (in my opinion) some moderate optimism about the future of this area. Indeed, it is reasonable to expect that Neural Networks will find their niche among the methods and techniques which computer scientists use for intrinsically difficult problems.

Recently links have been also established between these models and theoretical computer science via a new area known as learning theory. An additional attraction of Neural Networks is the dialog they establish between computer science, biology, physics, psychology, numerical and non-linear analysis, and other areas. In the future, we may discover that neural networks are useful for the computationally fast and approximate solution of certain decision problems which are based on simultaneously acting diverse criteria with information of different forms.

The major shortcoming of the Neural Networks area is the lack of an operational and solid theory for their design and analysis. In my opinion this should be the major thrust area for research in the near future.

This book attempts to provide a snapshot of academic and industrial research in Neural Network theory and of its major applications, written by active contributors to the field. The contributors are computer scientists, electrical engineers and physicists, and this diversity is willingly entertained in this volume. We hope to provide the reader with a pertinent and objective view of recent research and of relevant applications in an open and impartial manner.

Erol Gelenbe
Ecole des Hautes Etudes en Informatique
Paris, June 1990

CONTENTS

NEURAL NETWORKS: Advances and Applications
E. Gelenbe (Editor)
© Elsevier Science Publishers B.V. (North-Holland), 1991

Theory of the Random Neural Network Model [1])

by

Erol Gelenbe

Ecole des Hautes Etudes en Informatique,
Université René Descartes (Paris V)
45 rue des Saints-Pères
75006 Paris

Abstract   The purpose of this article is to survey results concerning a new neural network model, the random network, which we have introduced in [1] and extended and generalized in [2,3]. In this model "negative" or "positive" signals circulate, modelling inhibitory and excitatory signals. These signals can arrive either from other neurons or from the outside world, they are summed at the input of each neuron and constitute its signal potential. The state of each neuron in this model is its signal potential, while the network state is the vector of signal potentials at each neuron. If its potential is positive, a neuron fires, and sends out signals to the other neurons of the network or to the outside world. As it does so its signal potential is depleted. We have shown [1] that in the Markovian case, this model has product form, i.e. the steady-state probability distribution of its potential vector is the product of the marginal probabilities of the potential at each neuron. The signal flow equations of the network, which describe the rate at which positive or negative signals arrive to each neuron, are non-linear, so that their existence and uniqueness is not easily established except for the case of feedforward (or backpropagation) networks. In [2], the relationship betwen this model and the usual connectionist (formal) model of neural networks is discussed, and two sub-classes of networks are examined: balanced and damped networks, and stability conditions are examined in each case. In practical terms, these stability conditions guarantee that the unique solution can be found to the signal flow equations and therefore that the network has a well-defined steady-state behaviour. In [3] the model is extended to the case of "multiple signal classes" dealing with networks in which each neuron processes several streams of signals simultaneously. We also indicate how the random network can be used to implement the well-

---

[1]) This research was supported by the Distributed Algorithms Section of C3-CNRS (French National Program on Parallelism and Concurrency).

known XOR neural network with a hidden layer, and discuss its use for the approximate solution solve of hard combinatorial optimization problems. We finally suggest a hardware implementation of the model.

1. Introduction

We consider a network of n neurons in which <u>positive and negative</u> signals circulate. Each neuron accumulates signals as they arrive, and can fire if its total signal count at a given instant of time is positive. Firing then occurs at random according to an exponential distribution of constant rate, and it sends signals out to other neurons or to the outside of the network. In this model, each neuron i of the network is represented at any time t by its input signal potential $k_i(t)$, which we shall simply call the potential.

Positive and negative signals have different roles in the network; positive signals represent excitation, while negative signals represent inhibition. A negative signal <u>reduces by 1</u> the potential of the neuron to which it arrives (i.e. it "cancels" an existing signal) or has no effect on the signal potential if it is already zero, while an arriving positive or signal <u>adds 1</u> to the neuron potential. The potential at a neuron is constituted only by positive signals which have accumulated, which have not yet been cancelled by negative signals, and which have not yet been sent out by the neuron as it fires.

Consider the representation of biophysical neuron output behaviour which is shown schematically in the diagram given below (see for instance [5] or [7]). At time t=0 a neuron is excited; at time T (typically T may be of the order of 50 milliseconds) it fires a train of impulses along its axone. Each of these impulses is practically of identical amplitude (represented in our random model by 1). Some time later (say around $t = T + \tau$) the neuron may fire another train of impulses, as a result of the same excitation, though the second train of impulses will usually contain a smaller number. Even when the neuron is not excited, it may send out impulses at random, though much less frequently (i.e. at a slower rate) than when it is excited.

Our model represents the firing pattern of an excited neuron by a train of impulses or unit signals; the +1 or -1 value is tied to the interpretation (excitation or inhibition) given to the arriving signal at the receiving neuron.

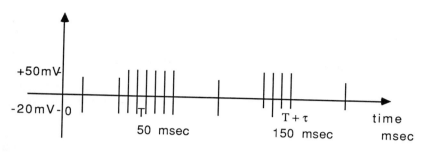

Representation of biophysical neuron

output signal after excitation

at time t = 0

Signals can either arrive to a neuron from the outside of the network (exogenous signals) or from other neurons. Each time a neuron fires, a signal leaves it depleting the total input potential of the neuron. A signal which leaves neuron i heads for neuron j with probability $p^+(i,j)$ as a positive (or normal) signal, or as a negative signal with probability $p^-(i,j)$, or it departs from the network with probability $d(i)$. Let $p(i,j)=p^+(i,j)+p^-(i,j)$; it is the transition probability of a Markov chain representing the movement of signals between neurons.

We shall assume that $p^+(i,i)=0$ and $p^-(i,i)=0$; though the former assumption is not essential we insist on the fact that the latter indeed is to our model; this assumption excludes the possibility of a neuron sending a signal directly to itself. Clearly we shall have

$$\Sigma_j \, p(i,j) + d(i) = 1 \text{ for } 1 \le i \le n \ .$$

A neuron is capable of firing and emitting signals if its potential is strictly positive.

We assume that exogenous signals arrive to each neuron in Poisson streams of positive or negative signals.

In [1] we show that the purely Markovian version of this network, with positive signals which arrive to the i-th neuron according to a Poisson process of rate $\Lambda(i)$, negative customers which arrive to the i-th neuron according to a Poisson process of rate $\lambda(i)$, iid exponential neuron firing times with rates r(1), ... , r(n), and Markovian movements of signals between neurons, has a product form solution. That is, the open network's stationary probability distribution can be written as the product of the marginal probabilities of the state of each neuron.

Thus <u>in steady-state the network's neurons are seemingly independent, though they are in fact coupled</u> via the signals which move from one neuron to the other in the network.

The model we propose has a certain number of interesting features:

- it appears to represent more closely the manner in which signals are transmitted in a biophysical neural network where they travel as voltage spikes rather than as fixed signal levels,
- it is computationally efficient in the feed-forward case, and whenever network stability can be shown,
- it is easy to simulate, since each neuron is simply represented by a counter; this may lead to a simple hardware implementation which is described in Section 6,
- it is closely related to the connexionist model and it is possible to go from one model to the other easily,
- it represents neuron potential and therefore the level of excitation as an integer, rather as a binary variable, which leads to more detailed information on system state; furthermore the neuron is interpreted as being in the "firing state" if its potential is positive.

As one may expect from existing models of neural networks [2], the signal flow equations which yield the rate of signal arrival and hence the rate of firing of each neuron in steady-state are non-linear . Thus in [1] we were able to establish their existence (and also a method for computing them) only in the case of feed-forward networks, i.e. in networks where a signal cannot return eventually to a neuron which it has already visited either in negative or positive form. This of course covers the case of back-propagation ornetworks [4]. In this paper we establish existence and uniqueness of solutions [2] for so-called "balanced and quasi-balanced" networks as well as for the class of "dissipative" networks, and uniqueness of the solution in the general case whenever the solution exists.

In this paper we shall first recall briefly the main results proved in [1] concerning the <u>random neural network model.</u>

We discuss the relation of the model to the usual connexionist network. We illustrate it with two examples, a dissipative network in which neurons only influence each other via inhibition, and a network which computes the exclusive OR (XOR) function. We then present briefly the manner in which the random network model can be used to solve approximately some hard combinatorial problems.

Two special classes of networks [2] which have internal feedback and for which we are able to provide stability results and compute the network state are then characterized. These are the balanced networks, and the quasi-damped networks. The first class includes all networks for which the steady-state behaviour of each neuron is the same. The second class includes all networks in which the positive signal flow rates to neurons are small enough that the network would be stable even if internal negative signals are removed. The generalization of the model to "multiple class signals" [3] is also discussed; in this new development, it is suggested that neural neworks which process simultaneously several different activities be considered. Finally we present a simple hardware realization of random networks.

2. General properties of the random network model

In this section we shall recall the main theoretical result concerning the random network model.

The following property states that the steady-state probability distribution of network state can always be expressed as the product of the probabilities of the states of each neuron. Thus the network is seemingly composed of independent neurons, though this is obviously not the case. Let $k(t)$ be the vector of signal potentials at time t, and $k = (k_1, ..., k_n)$ be a particular value of the vector. We are obviously interested in the quantity $p(k,t) = \text{Prob} [k(t) = k]$.

Let $p(k)$ denote the stationary probability distribution

$$p(k) = \lim_{t->\infty} \text{Prob} [k(t) = k]$$

if it exists.

Theorem 1 [1] Let

(1) $$q_i = \lambda^+(i)/[r(i) + \lambda^-(i)],$$

where the $\lambda^+(i)$, $\lambda^-(i)$ for $i = 1, \dots, n$ satisfy the following system of non-linear simultaneous equations:

(2) $\quad \lambda^+(i) = \Sigma_j \, q_j r(j) p^+(j,i) + \Lambda(i), \quad \lambda^-(i) = \Sigma_j \, q_j r(j) p^-(j,i) + \lambda(i)$

If a unique non-negative solution $\{\lambda^+(i), \lambda^-(i)\}$ exists to equations (1),(2) such that each $q_i < 1$, then:

(3) $$p(k) = \prod_{i=1}^{n} [1-q_i] \, q_i^{k_i}$$

We omit the proof, which can be found elsewhere [1,2]. Since $\{ k(t) : t \geq 0 \}$ is a continuous time Markov chain it satisfies the usual Chapman-Kolmogorov equations; thus in steady-state it can be seen that $p(k)$ must satisfy the following global balance equations:

(4) $p(k) \, \Sigma_i \, [\, \Lambda(i) + (\lambda(i) + r(i)) \mathbf{1}[k_i > 0] \,]$

$\quad = \Sigma_i \, [p(k^+_i) r(i) d(i) + p(k^-_i) \Lambda(i) \mathbf{1}[k_i > 0] + p(k^+_i) \lambda(i)$

$\quad + \Sigma_j \, \{ \, p(k^{+-}_{ij}) r(i) p^+(i,j) \mathbf{1}[k_j > 0] + p(k^{++}_{ij}) r(i) p^-(i,j) \,)$

$\quad + p(k^+_i) r(i) p^-(i,j) \mathbf{1}[k_j = 0] \, \} \,]$

where the vectors used in (4) are defined as follows:

$$k^+_i = (k_1, \dots, k_i+1, \dots, k_n)$$
$$k^-_i = (k_1, \dots, k_i-1, \dots, k_n)$$
$$k^{+-}_{ij} = (k_1, \dots, k_i+1, \dots, k_j-1, \dots, k_n)$$
$$k^{++}_{ij} = (k_1, \dots, k_i+1, \dots, k_j+1, \dots, k_n)$$

and $\mathbf{1}[\, X \,]$ is the usual characteristic function which takes the value 1 if X is true and 0 otherwise. Theorem 1 is proved by showing that (3) satisfies this system of equations.

The computational simplicity of this result is illustrated by the useful consequence indicated below.

Corollary 1.1 The probability that neuron i is firing in steady-state is simply given by q_i and the average neuron potential in steady-state is simply $A_i = q_i/[1-q_i]$.

By Theorem 1 we are guaranteed a stationary solution of product form provided the non-linear signal flow equations have a non-negative solution. The following result can be easily established (though this was not done in [1]).

Theorem 2 If the solutions to (1), (2) exist with $q_i<1$, then they are unique.

Proof Since { k(t) : $t\geq0$ } is an irreducible and aperiodic Markov chain, if a positive stationary solution p(k) exists, then it is unique. By Theorem 1, if the $0 < q_i<1$ solution to (1),(2) exist for i=1,...,n, then p(k) is given by (3) and is clearly positive for all k. Suppose now that for some i there are two different q_i ,q'_i satisfying (1),(2). But this implies that for all k_j , $\lim_{t->\infty}P[k_i(t)= 0]$ has two different values [1-q_i] and [1-q'_i] , which contradicts the uniqueness of p(k); hence the result.

Let us now turn to the existence and uniqueness of the solutions $\lambda^+(i)$, $\lambda^-(i)$, $1\leq i\leq n$ to equations (1),(2) which represent the average arrival rate of positive and negative signals to each neuron in the network. An important class of models is covered by the following result concerning feedforward networks.

We say that a network is feedforward if for any sequence $i_1,...$,$i_s,$ ... , i_r, ... , i_m of neurons, $i_s=i_r$ for r>s implies

$$\prod_{v=1}^{m-1} p(i_v,i_{v+1}) = 0$$

Theorem 3 [1] If the network is feedforward, then the solutions $\lambda^+(i)$, $\lambda^-(i)$ to equations (1), (2) exist and are unique.

Let us now examine the similarity relationship of our model with the usual connexionist model [4].

2.1 Analogy with classical connexionist networks

A connexionist network [4] is a set of n neurons each of which computes its state y(i) using a sigmoid function y(i) = f(x(i)) where x(i) = (Σ_j $w_{ji}y(j)$- θ_i) is the input signal composed of the weighted sums of the states y(j) of the other neurons of the network; the w_{ji} are the weights and θ_i is the threshold. In its simplest form $f(\ )$ is the unit step function. The set of weights and the set of thresholds completely characterise the network.

An analogy between the usual model of neural networks and the model introduced in this paper, <u>the random network</u>, can be constructed.

Each neuron is represented by a neuron of the random network. The threshold of neuron i is represented by a flow of negative signals to the neuron so that $\lambda(i) = \theta_i$.

Consider the non-output neuron i ; it is represented by the random neuron i whose parameters are chosen as follows:

(5) $d(i) = 0$,　$r(i)p^+(i,j) = w_{ij}$ if $w_{ij} > 0$ and $r(i)p^-(i,j) = |w_{ij}|$ if $w_{ij} < 0$

Summing over all j, the firing rate $r(i)$ of the non-output "random" neuron i is chosen :

(6) $$r(i) = \Sigma_j |w_{ij}|$$

Finally, for each output random neuron i set $d(i) = 1$, and assign some appropriate value to $r(i)$.

To introduce into the random network the external parameters or inputs to the neural network we use the arrival rates of positive signals $\Lambda(i)$.

Assume that the external signals to the formal neural network are binary. If the input signal to neuron i is 0 or if neuron i is not connected to an external signal we set $\Lambda(i) = 0$. If the external signal to neuron i has the value 1, we set $\Lambda(i) = \Lambda$. Here Λ can be chosen so as to obtain the desired effect at the output neurons .

All the parameters of the random network are chosen from those of the formal network, except for the firing rates of the output neurons, and the input rate of positive signals.

The state $Y = (y_1, \dots , y_n)$ of the formal neural network, where y_i is 0 or 1, is simulated by the state probabilities q_i of the random neurons.

Consider $\lim_{t->oo} P[k_i(t)>0]$ which (as a consequence of Corollary 1.1) is simply q_i; we associate y_i to q_i. Thus we have for some "cut-point" $1- \alpha$,

(7) $[y_i = 0] <=> q_i < 1- \alpha$; $[y_i = 1] <=> q_i \geq 1- \alpha$.

A finer (i.e. more detailed) way of differentiating between highly excited and relatively unexcited neurons is via the average neuron potential $A_i = q_i/[1-q_i]$ .as will be seen in the example given below.

In an arbitrary neural network, i.e. one which does not have the feedforward structure, this procedure could also be used for establishing the random network. We could also use the d(i) at each neuron i in order to represent the loss currents which are known to exist in biological neural systems [5], and take r(i)d(i) to be the rate of loss of electric potential at a neuron if we wish to include this effect in the model.

Example 1 A simple example often given to illustrate the behaviour of formal neural networks is the network for the XOR (exclusive OR) function [2]. We shall present the equivalent random model representation for this network. In Figure 1(a) we show a formal neural network which receives two binary inputs x_1, x_2 and which produces $y(x_1, x_2)$ the boolean function XOR. It is composed of four neurons; each neuron is numbered (1 to 4) and the synaptic weights are indicated on arcs between neurons. The threshold of each neuron is assumed to be 0.

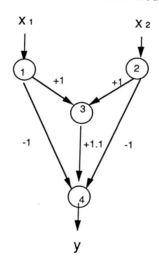

Figure 1(a) A connexionist network for the boolean XOR function

On Figure 1(b) we show the random network analog corresponding to Figure 1(a). According to the rules we have given for constructing the random network analog, we have:

- $\lambda(i) = 0$ for $i=1,..,4$ because all thresholds are 0;
- $r(1) = r(2) = 2$, $r(3) = 1.1$, $r(4) = r$, as yet undetermined;
- $p^+(1,3) = p^+(2,3) = 0.5$, $p^-(1,4) = p^-(2,4) = 0.5$, $p^+(3,4) = 1$;
- $d(1) = d(2) = d(3) = 0$, $d(4) = 1$.

Recall that according to the rules proposed in Section 3, we choose a value $\Lambda(i) = \Lambda$ to represent $x_i = 1$, and $\Lambda(i)=0$ to represent $x_i = 0$. Set Λ large enough to saturate neurons 1 and 2, i.e. any $\Lambda > 2$.

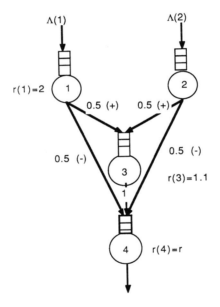

Figure 1(b) The random network analog of the formal neural shown in Figure 1; here $p^+(1,3)=p^+(2,3)=0.5$, $p^+(3,4)=1$, and $p^-(1,4)=p^-(2,4)=0.5$.

q_4 is the analog of the output y of the connexionist network of Figure 1(a). Notice that:

$$
\begin{aligned}
&\quad\quad\quad 0, \text{ if } \Lambda(1)=L(2)=0,\\
(8)\quad\quad q_4 = &\quad 1.1/[r+2] \text{ if } \Lambda(1)=\Lambda(2)=\Lambda >2,\\
&\quad 1/[r+1] \text{ if } \Lambda(1)=\Lambda, \ \Lambda(2)=0 \text{ or vice-versa.}
\end{aligned}
$$

Setting $\alpha = 0.85$ and $r = 0.1$ we see that we obtain the XOR function with this network., since we have $q_4 = 0.909$ when $\Lambda(1)=\Lambda$, $\Lambda(2)=0$ or vice-versa, and $q_4 = 0.5238$ if $\Lambda(1)=\Lambda(2)=\Lambda$ for any $\Lambda>2$. n fact we may choose any $1-\alpha$ such that $1.1/[r+2] < 1-\alpha < 1/[r+1]$. The capacity of the network to represent the XOR function becomes even more apparent if we consider the average potential of neuron 4; we then have $A_4 = 11.222$ when $\Lambda(1)=2$, $\Lambda(2)=0$ or vice-versa, and $A_4 = 1.0999$ if $\Lambda(1)=\Lambda(2)=\Lambda$ for any $\Lambda>2$. Thus average neuron potential can also be used very effectively to discriminate between the output states of the neural network since we have a ratio greater than 10 between the average potential of neuron 4 of the input equivalent to (0,1) or (1,0) and the input equivalent to (1,1).

Example 2 (A dissipative feedback network which recognizes (0,1) or (1,0)) The next example is composed of two neurons shown in Figure 2 . Each neuron receives flows of positive signals of rates $\Lambda(1),\Lambda(2)$ into neurons 1 and 2. A signal leaving neuron 1 enters neuron 2 as a negative signal and a signal leaving neuron 2 enters neuron 1 as a negative signal:

$$
p^-(1,2)=p^-(2,1)=1.
$$

This network may be said to be "dissipative" because only negative signals move from one neuron to another even though exogenous signals are positive.

Let $k = (k_1,k_2) \geq (0,0)$ be the joint signal potential vector at the two neurons. The Chapman-Kolmogorov equations in steady-state are:

$$
p(k) [\Lambda(1) + \Lambda(2) + r(1)\mathbf{1}[k_1>0] + r(2)\mathbf{1}[k_2>0]]
$$

$$
= p(k_1+1,k_2+1)[r(1) + r(2)] + \Lambda(1)p(k_1-1,k_2) + \Lambda(2)p(k_1,k_2-1)
$$

where vectors k with negative elements are to be ignored and $\mathbf{1}[X]$ takes the value 1 if X is true and 0 otherwise.

The unique solution to these equations is:

$$p(k) = (1-u)(1-v)u^{k_1}.v^{k_2},$$

if u<1,v<1, where

- u = $\Lambda(1)/[r(1) + \lambda^-(1)]$, v= $\Lambda(2)/[r(2) + \lambda^-(2)]$, with
- $\lambda^-(2)$= ur(1), $\lambda^-(1)$=vr(2).

This is a special case of Theorem 1. For instance when $\Lambda(1)=\Lambda(2)=1$, r(1)=r(2)=1.1 we obtain $\lambda^-(1)=\lambda^-(2)= 0.5[5^{1/2} - 1]$, so that u,v in the expression for p(k) become u=v= $2/[1+5^{1/2}]$ = 0.617, so that the average potential at each neuron is 1.611. Now if we set $\Lambda(1)=1$, $\Lambda(2)=0$, with the same values of r(1)=r(2)=1, we see that neuron 1 saturates (its average potential becomes infinite), while the second neuron's input potential is zero, and vice-versa if we set $\Lambda(1)=0$, $\Lambda(2)=1$. Thus this network recognizes the inputs (0,1) and (1,0).

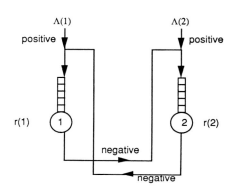

Figure 2 The neural network with positive and negative signals examined in Example 2.

2.2 Random networks for combinatorial optimization problems

Several authors have suggested the use of neural networks as tools to provide approximate solutions to combinatorial optimization problems such as graph matching, the traveling salesman problem, task placement in a distributed system, etc. (see for instance [8,9,10]). The basic idea is often the following. A neural network is constructed in which a neuron is affected to each element of the problem solution; for instance a neuron is affected to each (**city,position**) pair for the traveling salesman problem. If a neuron is "on", this implies that the corresponding city should be in the given position in the "approximately optimal" solution. Then strongly inhibitory links are established between neurons which represent incompatible elements of the solution; e.g. a city may not be in two different positions, and a position may not be occupied by two different cities. Furthermore, inhibitory links are placed between neurons in a manner which represents cost; e.g. for the traveling salesman problem, the intensity of inhibitory links can represent the distance between cities when placed contiguously on a route. Once the model is set up, it is allowed to relax dynamically to a steady-state which should be of "minimum energy" representing a quasi-minimal cost solution.

The random network is well adapted for handling this kind of problem. The neural model for such problems is set up in much the same way described above. However, once the model is specified it is solved numerically using Theorem 1, rather than simulated, leading to a considerable gain in time compared to existing techniques based on the Boltzmann machine or on Hopfield-Tank networks [8,9]. Results in this area are reported elsewhere [10].

3. Balanced neural networks

We now consider a class of networks whose signal flow equations have a particularly simple solution. We shall say that a network with negative and positive signals is balanced if the ratio

$$(9) \quad \delta_i = [\Sigma_j \, q_j r(j) p^+(j,i) + \Lambda(i)] / [\Sigma_j \, q_j r(j) p^-(j,i) + \lambda(i) + r(i)]$$

is identical for any $i=1,...,n$. This in effect means that all the q_i are identical.

Theorem 4 The signal flow equations (1),(2) have a (unique) solution if the network is balanced.

Proof From (1),(2) we write

$$(10) \quad q_i = [\Sigma_j \, q_j r(j) p^+(j,i) + \Lambda(i)] / [\Sigma_j \, q_j r(j) p^-(j,i) + \lambda(i) + r(i)]$$

If the system is balanced, $q_i = q_j$ for all i,j. From (10) we then have that the common $q = q_i$ satisfies the quadratic equation:

(11) $\qquad q^2 R^-(i) + q[\lambda(i) + r(i) - R^+(i)] - \Lambda(i) = 0$

where $R^-(i) = \Sigma_j \, r(j)p^-(j,i)$, $R^+(i) = \Sigma_j \, r(j)p^+(j,i)$. The positive root of this quadratic equation, which will be independent of i, is the solution of interest:

$$q = \left\{(R^+(i) - \lambda(i) - r(i)) + [(R^+(i) - \lambda(i) - r(i))^2 + 4 \, R^-(i)\Lambda(i) \,]^{1/2}\right\}/2R^-(i)$$

QED.

4. Damped and Dissipative networks

We say that a network with negative and positive signals is <u>dissipative</u> if $p^+(j,i) = 0$ for all i,j.

Notice that a dissipative network will, in general, have some positive exogenous signal arrivals to be of any interest. However in such a network a neuron may only send negative signals to another neuron. A dissipative network will, in general, have some positive exogenous signal arrivals in order to be of any interest.

Theorem 5 If the network is dissipative and $r(i) + \lambda(i) > \Lambda(i)$ then the signal flow equations (1), (2) have an unique solution with $q_i < 1$.

In fact such networks are a special case of damped networks which will be discussed below.

We shall say that a network is <u>damped</u> if $p^+(j,i) \geq 0$,
$p^-(j,i) \geq 0$ with the following property : $r(i) + \lambda(i) > \Lambda(i) + \Sigma_j r(j)p^+(j,i)$
for all $i=1, \dots ,n$.

Theorem 6 [2] If the network is damped then the customer flow equations (1), (2) always have an unique solution with $q_i < 1$.

Proof The proof is by construction of the n-dimensional vector homotopy [6] function $H(q,x)$ for a real number $0 \leq x < 1$. Let us define the following n-vectors:

$$q = (q_1, \dots , q_n), \quad F(q) = (F_1(q), \dots , F_n(q))$$

where

$$F_i(q) = [\Sigma_j \, q_j r(j)p^+(j,i) + \Lambda(i) \,] / [\Sigma_j \, q_j r(j)p^-(j,i) + \lambda(i) + r(i)]$$

Clearly, the equation we are interested in is $q = F(q)$ which, when it has a solution in $D = [0,1]^n$, yields the appropriate values of the q_i for Theorem 1 to be applicable in order to compute the stationary solution of the network. Notice that $F(q) : R^n \to R^n$. Notice also that $F(q) \, \varepsilon \, C^2$. Consider the mappings $F(q) : D \to R^n$. Clearly, we are interested in the interior points of D since we seek solutions $0 < q_i < 1$. Write $D = D^o \cup \delta D$ where δD stands for the boundary of D, and D^o is the set of interior points. Let $y = (y_1, \ldots, y_n)$ where

$$y_i = [\Sigma_j \, r(j)p^+(j,i) + \Lambda(i) \,] / [\lambda(i) + r(i)]$$

By assumption $y_i < 1$ for all $i = 1,..,n$. Now define

$$H(q,x) = (1-x)(q-y) + x(q-F(q)), \; 0 \le x < 1.$$

Clearly $H(q,0) = q-y$ and $H(q,1) = q-F(q)$. Consider the set

$$H^{-1} = \{q : q \, \varepsilon \, D, \, H(q,x)=0 \text{ and } 0 \le x < 1\}$$

We can show that H^{-1} and δD have an empty intersection, i.e. as x is varied from 0 towards 1 the solution of $H(q,x)$ is it exists does not touch the boundary of D. To do this assume the contrary; this implies that for some $x = x^*$ there exists some $q = q^*$ for which $H(q^*,x^*) = 0$ and such that $q_i^* = 0$ or 1. If $q_i^* = 0$ we can write

$$- (1-x^*)y_i - x^* F_i(q^*) = 0, \text{ or } x^*/(1-x^*) = -y_i/F_i(q^*) < 0 \Rightarrow x^* < 0,$$

which contradicts the assumption about x. If on the other hand $q_i^* = 1$, then we can write

$$-(1-x^*)(1-y_i) - x^*(1-F_i(q^*)) = 0, \text{ or } x^*/(1-x^*) = -(1-y_i)/(1-F_i(q^*)) < 0 \Rightarrow$$
$$x^* < 0$$

because $(1-y_i) > 0$ and $0 < F_i(q^*) < y_i$ so that $(1-F_i(q^*)) > 0$, contradicting again the assumption about x. Thus $H(q,x) = 0$ cannot have a solution on the boundary δD for any $0 \le x < 1$. As a consequence, applying Theorem 3.3.1

of [6] (which is a Leray-Schauder form of the fixed-point theorem), it follows that $F(q)=q$ has at least one solution in D^o ; it is therefore a unique solution as a consequence of Theorem 4.

5. Multiple class networks

Consider a neural network which generalises the model presented in [1,2]. It is composed of n neurons and receives exogenous positive (excitatory) and negative (inhibitory) signals, as well as endogenous signals exchanged by the neurons. As in [1,2] excitatory or inhibitory signals ar sent by excited neurons to other neurons in the network, or to the outside world. The arrival of an excitatory signal increases the potential of a neuron by 1, while an inhibitory signal's arrival decreases it by one. A neuron is excited if its potential is positive; it then fires at exponentially distributed intervals sending excitatory signals of different classes, or inhibitory signals, to other neurons or to the outside of the network. This model has been introduced in [3]. It represents a neural network which processes several streams of information in parallel, which appears to be a sensible generalization of existing mode.

Positive signals may belong to several <u>classes</u>. In this model, the potential at a neuron is represented by the vector $\underline{k}_i = (k_{i1}, ..., k_{iC})$ where k_{ic} is the value of the "class c potential" of neuron i, or its "excitation level in terms of class c signals" . The total potential of neuron i is $k_i = \Sigma_{c=1,C} k_{ic}$.

Exogenous positive signals of class c arrive to neuron i in a Poisson stream of rate $\Lambda(i,c)$, while exogenous negative signals arrive to it according to a Poisson process of rate $\lambda(i)$. Thus negative signals belong to a single class. When a positive signal of class c arrives to a neuron, it merely increases k_{ic} by 1. When a negative signal arrives to it, if $k_i > 0$ the potential is reduced by 1, and the class of the potential to be reduced is chosen at random: with probability k_{ic}/k_i it is of class c for any c = 1, ... , C. As with single class networks discussed above, a negative signal arriving to a neuron whose potential is zero has no effect on its potential.

When its potential is positive ($k_i > 0$), neuron i can fire; the potential depleted is of class c with probability k_{ic}/k_i in which case the neuron fires at rate $r(i,c) > 0$. In the interval $[t, t+\Delta t[$, neuron fires, depletes by 1 its class c potential, and sends to neuron j a class ξ positive signal with probability:

$$r(i,c)(k_{ic}/k_i)p^+(i,c;j,\xi)\Delta t + o(\Delta t)$$

or a negative signal with probability :

$$r(i,c)(k_{ic}/k_i)p^-(i,c;j)\Delta t + o(\Delta t)$$

On the other hand, the probability that the depleted signal is sent out of the network, or that it is "lost" is

$$r(i,c)(k_{ic}/k_i)d(i,c)\Delta t + o(\Delta t)$$

The $\{p^+(i,c;j,\xi), p^-(i,c;j), d(i,c)\}$ are the transition probabilities of a Markov chain with state-space $\{1, \ldots, n\} \times \{1, \ldots, C\} \times \{+,-\}$ representing the movement of signals in the network, and for (i,c), $1 \leq i \leq n$, $1 \leq c \leq C$:

$$\sum_{(j,\xi)} p^+(i,c;j,\xi) + \sum_j p^-(i,c;j) + d(i,c) = 1.$$

Notice that if the network only contains a single class of positive signals $(C=1)$ then we simply have the model presented previously in [1,2].

The complete state of the network is represented by the vector (of vectors) $\underline{k} = (\underline{k}_1, \ldots, \underline{k}_n)$. Under the above assumptions, the process $\{ \underline{k}(t), t \geq 0 \}$ is Markovian, and we shall denote by $p(\underline{k},t) = P[\underline{k}(t) = \underline{k}]$ the probability distribution of its state. Its behaviour is then described by the Chapman-Kolmogorov equations:

$$
\begin{aligned}
dp(\underline{k},t)/dt = &- p(\underline{k},t)\Sigma_{(i,c)} [\Lambda(i,c) + (\lambda(i) + r(i,c))(k_{ic}/k_i)] \\
&+ \Sigma_{(i,c)} \{ p(\underline{k}+e_{ic},t)r(i,c)((k_{ic}+1)/(k_i+1))d(i,c) + \\
&+ p(\underline{k}-e_{ic},t)\Lambda(i,c)1[k_{ic}>0] + p(\underline{k}+e_{ic},t)\lambda(i)((k_{ic}+1)/(k_i+1)) + \\
&+ \Sigma_{(j,\xi)} (p(\underline{k}+e_{ic}-e_{j\xi},t)r(i,c)((k_{ic}+1)/(k_i+1))p^+(i,c;j,\xi)1[k_{j\xi}>0] \\
&+ p(\underline{k}+e_{ic},t)r(i,c)((k_{ic}+1)/(k_i+1))p^-(i,c;j)1[k_j=0] \\
&+ p(\underline{k}+e_{ic}+e_{j\xi},t)r(i,c)((k_{ic}+1)/(k_i+1))((k_{jc}+1)/(k_j+1))p^-(i,c;j))\}
\end{aligned}
$$

where we have used the notation:

$$\underline{k} + e_{ic} = (\underline{k}_1, \ldots, (k_{i1}, \ldots, k_{ic} + 1, \ldots, k_{iC}), \ldots, \underline{k}_n)$$
$$\underline{k} + e_{jc} = (\underline{k}_1, \ldots, (k_{j1}, \ldots, k_{jc} + 1, \ldots, k_{jC}), \ldots, \underline{k}_n)$$
$$\underline{k} + e_{ic} - e_{j\xi} = (\underline{k}_1, \ldots, (k_{i1}, \ldots, k_i + 1, \ldots, k_{iC}), \ldots, (k_{j1}, \ldots, k_\xi - 1, \ldots, k_{iC}), \ldots, \underline{k}_n)$$
$$\underline{k} + e_{ic} + e_{j\xi} = (\underline{k}_1, \ldots, (k_{i1}, \ldots, k_i + 1, \ldots, k_{iC}), \ldots, (k_{j1}, \ldots, k_\xi + 1, \ldots, k_{iC}), \ldots, \underline{k}_n)$$

These vectors are defined only if there elements are non-negative.

The stationary solution of the model described above has product form, i.e. that its steady-state probability distribution is the product of the marginal probabilities of each neuron.

Theorem 7 [3] Let $\underline{k}(t)$ be the vector representing the state of the neural network at time t, and let $\{q_{ic}\}$ with $0 < \Sigma_{(i,c)} \, q_{ic} < 1$, be the solution of the system of non-linear equations:

(1) $$q_{ic} = \lambda + (i,c) \, /[r(i,c) + \lambda^-(i)] \, ,$$

(2) $$\lambda + (i,c) = \Sigma_{(j,\xi)} \, q_{j\xi} \, r(j,\xi) p^+(j,\xi;i,c) + \Lambda(i,c),$$
$$\lambda^-(i) = \Sigma_{(j,\xi)} \, q_{j\xi} \, r(j,\xi) p^-(j,\xi;i) + \lambda(i),$$

then the stationary solution $p(\underline{k}) \equiv \lim_{t->oo} P[\underline{k}(t) = \underline{k}]$ exists and is given by:

(3) $$p(\underline{k}) = \prod_{i=1}^{n} (k_i!) G_i \prod_{c=1}^{C} [(q_{ic})^{k_{ic}}/k_{ic}!] \, ,$$

where the G_i are appropriate normalising constants.

6. A simple hardware implementation of random networks

In addition to being an analytical tool for the study of neural networks via the results provided in Theorems 1 to 6, random networks can also be implemented in hardware as shown in Figure 3.

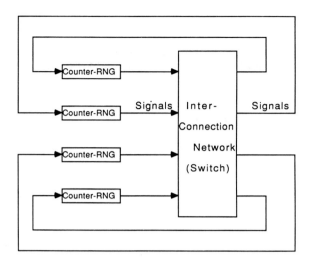

Figure 3   A possible hardware implementation of a Random Network

Each neuron is simulated using a Counter and a Random Number Generator (RNG). The latter is used to simulate the exponential delays associated with the signal emission process, as well as to handle the signal routing probabilities. The interconnection network receives signals, which can be viewed as short packets of data containing the signal's polarity and its destination, and routes the signal to the appropriate output line connected to the neuron to which it is addressed. Alternatively, all routing information and signal polarity (including the random generation of the destination) can be handled by the interconnection network. This network can be programmable so as to represent different networks. External signal sources can be implemented simply as permanently activated counters which constantly generate signals at their output. Obviously, as with any highly parallel machine implementation, the complexity of the system is concealed in the interconnection network.

Acknowledgements   The author gratefully acknowledges the partial support for this research of Pôle Algorithmique Répartie, C3 CNRS, the French National Program in Distributed Computing.

References

1. Gelenbe, E. "Random neural networks with negative and positive signals and product form solution", <u>Neural Computation,</u> Vol. 1, No. 4, 1989.

2. Gelenbe, E. "Stability of the random neural network model", accepted for publication in <u>Neural Computation</u>.

3. Fourneau, J.M., Gelenbe, E. "Random neural networks with multiple classes of signals", submitted for publication in <u>Neural Computation</u>.

4. Rumelhart, D.E., McClelland, J.L. and the PDP Research Group "Parallel distributed processing Vols. I and II", Bradford Books and MIT Press, Cambridge, Mass., 1986.

5. Kandel, E.C., Schwartz, J.H. "Principles of neural science", Elsevier, Amsterdam, 1985.

6. Garcia, C.D., Zangwill, W.I. "Pathways to Solutions, Fixed Points, and Equilibria," Prentice Hall, Englewood Cliffs, N.J. (1981).

7. Sejnowski, J.T. "Skeleton fields in the brain", in Hinton, G.E., Anderson, J.A. Ed. Parallel Models of Associative Memory", Lawrence Elbaum Associates Publishers, Hillsdale, N.J., 1981.

8. Hérault, L., Niez, J.-J., "Neural networks and combinatorial optimization: a survey of NP-complete graph problems" this volume.

9. Hopfield, J., Tank, D. "Neural computation of decsions in optimization problems", Biological Cybernetics, Vol. 52, pp 141 ff, 1985.

10. Gelenbe, E., Koubi, V., Mokhtari, M. "Random networks for associative memory and combinatorial optimization", in preparation.

NEURAL NETWORKS: Advances and Applications
E. Gelenbe (Editor)
© Elsevier Science Publishers B.V. (North-Holland), 1991

ABSTRACTION HIERARCHY IN NEURAL NETWORKS :
A RIGOROUS TREATMENT

R. Hong Tuan
Laboratoire de Physique Théorique et Hautes Energies*
Université de Paris XI, bâtiment 211, 91405 Orsay Cedex

Abstract Treating neural networks as Boltzmann systems and using an action proposed earlier which make them equivalent to electric networks we are able to discuss rigorously the final internal states of these networks once input- and output-states are given. These final states are (connected or disconnected) trees joining the excited nodes of the network, as we have earlier argued using a heuristic mechanical analogy with a rubber sheet. These trees are crucial to define concepts as vertices of the trees and have a hierarchy among them according to the number of vertices necessary to cross to attain one of them starting from the excited boundary (or input-output) nodes.

1. Introduction

The reason why networks have become popular is that they can learn through training. The networks we are considering here have a boundary on which sit input and output nodes. These nodes support potential variables X_{j_o} which take values (during the training) representing the couples of input and output states one want the network to associate. Inside the network are internal nodes and links supporting respectively potential variables X_j and link variables w_{ij}. Usually, there is a function f determining the value of a X_j on a node j from the values of the X_k's of the nodes k linked to j and from the w_{jk}'s of the links jk. In a feed-forward network (which is the type of network we will use), given input-variables values $(X_{j_o})_{in} = (V_{j_o})_{in}$, all the values of the variables on

---

* Laboratoire associé au Centre National de la Recherche Scientifique.

the other nodes (internal ones and output ones) are determined by repeated use of that function. However, the internal state and output state can also be determined from the input state by an action principle, where the action is a function of the potentials X_j, X_k and w_{jk} which has to be minimized in order to fix the values of these variables. This is what we call a Boltzmann approach to networks. In the usual approach (using the function f) an algorithm called a back-propagation algorithm[1] is used to adjust the w_{ij}'s in order to produce values of $(X_{j_o})_{out}$ as close as possible to the wanted $(V_{j_o})_{out}$.

In a recent article[2] we have proposed an action principle (taking a Boltzmann approach to neural networks) which allows one to train networks without the use of a back-propagation algorithm[1]. The advantages of an action principle are crucial as we now recall.

i) In order to implement a back-propagation algorithm, we have, in fact, to analytically perform the evaluation and the derivation of an energy function E (measuring the discrepancy between the desired values $(V_{j_o})_{out}$ of output variables and their actual values $(X_{j_o})_{out}$) with respect to a large number of variables, i.e. weight variables w_{ij} attached to the links ij relating the nodes of the network. In practice, if we have a layered network, where one layer of nodes is linked only to a precedent and a following layer of nodes, this calculation starts by evaluating

$$\partial E\Big(\big\{X_k\big\},\big\{w_{ij}\big\}\Big)\big/\partial\, w_{ij}$$

in the output layer, then, in the layer one step inside the network, and then, in the next preceding layer until one comes back to the first input-layer. Hence, the "back-propagation" name of this algorithm. Also, the dependence of E on the node-variables X_k of one layer is needed to calculate E as a function of the X_k's of the next layer. We thus have to know E as a function of the sets $\{X_k\}$ and $\{w_{ij}\}$ of all node-variables and weights of the network in order to minimize this quantity. This is what we call a highly non-local calculation. The more variables there will be, the more cumbersome and error-prone will be the implementation of this algorithm.

What we have proposed is to replace this analytical minimization through gradient-descent by a simulated annealing using for instance the well-known Metropolis[3] algorithm. A partition function is written for the network, minus the logarithm of its integrand being an action A (playing the role of the above energy E) with

$$(1) \qquad A = \sum_{i<j} \alpha_{ij} \left(X_i - X_j \right)^2 \ , \ \alpha_{ij} > 0 \ ,$$

α_{ij} being equal to the weight w_{ij} when two nodes i and j are linked and equal to zero when there is no link ij (X_j and X_i are node-variables). We have chosen α_{ij} to be positive in order to provide a ground-state for the network. This is an essential property shared by all physical systems. Without any ground-state the minimization of A would take, a priori, an infinite time because then, A could become infinitely negative. Inhibition between neighbour-nodes can be achieved by taking potentials or node-variables of opposite signs. Now, if a node is connected to only a few neighbour-nodes the minimization of A can be performed by independent evaluations of

$$A_i = \sum_{j} \alpha_{ij} \left(X_i - X_j \right)^2$$

on far away nodes, thus considerably accelerating the calculation (parallel processing is then easy to implement). We also remind the reader that threshold effects can be mimicked by adding a certain level of noise to A_i.(A noise for the X_j's will prevent $|X_j - X_i|$ from becoming too small. Therefore an X_j will only vary if its neighbours X_i have values such that $|X_j - X_i|$ is superior to the noise. Remember that an excitation propagates in our network by putting potentials equal or approximately equal). The condition that only neighbour-nodes are to be linked is what we call a <u>locality property</u> of the action A. It is then straightforward to show that our system is an <u>electric network</u> with conductances α_{ij} and potentials X_k.

Of course, we need to have constraints on the way A is minimized because, otherwise, taking all α_{ij}'s equal to zero would put A equal to zero immediately, and this would completely forbid any correlation between $(X_{i_o})_{in}$ variables and $(X_{j_o})_{out}$ variables we want to associate : we would have a completely isolating medium. Thus, in practice, the X_k's should be varied first, materializing equipotential domains on the network. The α_{ij}'s would be varied in a second step (as well as the X_k's) becoming rapidly infinitesimal outside equipotential regions. (On an equipotential, $(X_i - X_j)^2 = 0$, so there is no need to vary the corresponding α_{ij}'s in order to minimize A). This second step minimization "wires" the networks in a definite way and creates the memory it will have of the association $(X_{i_o})_{in} \Leftrightarrow (X_{j_o})_{out}$ we want.

ii) It was argued that the equipotentials relating boundary- (i.e. input- and output-) nodes would form simple patterns which could be either <u>simple paths</u> or <u>trees with vertices which we called "working-nodes"</u>. Then, the wiring mechanism described above (letting α_{ij}'s evolve) put all α_{ij}'s equal to zero outside these trees of equipotentials. This means that there is conductivity only along these trees. Consequently if one excites some boundary nodes at the ends of a tree of equipotentials, because of the non-zero conductivity all potentials X_j along the tree will also be excited, and in particular the nodes of the tree, the working-nodes. This was done using a mechanical analogue (a rubber sheet). Also, an abstraction hierarchy among working-nodes was defined. The more working-nodes one has to cross going from the boundary of the network to a given working-node, the higher the abstraction level of this node.

So, a big advantage of the electric representation of the network is that, with it, one can begin <u>to understand</u> how memory of associations appears and how an emergent property like abstraction can exist.

Our purpose, here, is to demonstrate, using a rigorous mathematical apparatus, that the simple image of network operation we just described can be recovered. Remember that we had to use the mechanical analogue of a rubber-sheet (therefore using an heuristic argument) to explain how trees would appear as conducting wires when boundary nodes were excited and the minimization described above was applied. The fundamental object here is the partition function

$$(2) \quad P = \int_0^{\infty} \prod_{\{ij\}} d\,\alpha_{ij} \int_{-\infty}^{+\infty} \prod_{\{k\}} d\,X_k \, \exp(-A) \prod_{i_o \in \partial N} \delta\left(X_{i_o} - V_{i_o}\right)$$

$(\partial N = \text{boundary of the network})$

which is a sum over all possible configurations weighted by $\exp(-A)$ (V_{i_o} are the values imposed for the variables X_{i_o} at the input- and output-nodes i_o). However, the minimization of A will correspond to a selection of only a few ground-state configurations as we will show later on. These configurations are trees which link input- and output-nodes together.

2. Finding the dominant contributions to the partition function

As we can see immediately by looking at expression (2), we have an integral the value of which is equal, up to some irrelevant factor, to the value of its integrand when A is minimum (using a saddle-point approximation, for instance). To this minimum will be associated configurations (i.e. values of α_{ij} and X_k) which will dominate over others (in the sense of being more likely to be found) and will represent the state of the network once learning is achieved, or the ground-state attained. An essential assumption we will now make is that we have a planar connection pattern among nodes. This is, in fact, almost equivalent to requiring that only a few neighbour nodes are linked to a given node. Let us denote by A_{ij}

$$(3) \qquad P = c^{st} \int_0^\infty \prod_{\{ij\}} d\alpha_{ij} \left[\det (D - A) \right]^{-1/2} \quad .$$

$$\exp\left[-1/2 \sum_{jk\ell_o m_o} \left(A_c \right)_{\ell_o j}^T (D-A)^{-1} \left(A_c \right)_{km_o} \left(V_{\ell_o} - V_{m_o} \right)^2 \right]$$

where c^{st} stands for some constant, the value of which is irrelevant for us, here. <u>Let us suppose that all excited nodes on the border have the same value V_o for their potentials X_{k_o}</u>. Then, (3) reduces

to

$$(4) \qquad P = c^{st} \int_0^\infty \prod_{\{ij\}} d\alpha_{ij} \left[\det (D - A) \right]^{-1/2} \quad .$$

Now, it can be shown that the determinant $\det(D - A)$ has a very peculiar geometrical interpretation : <u>it is the sum of the products</u> $\prod_{tree} \alpha_{ij}$ <u>over all trees passing through all the nodes of the network</u> <u>and having all their ends on all border-nodes</u>, or

$$(5) \qquad \det (D - A) = \sum_{\{trees\}} \prod_{tree} \alpha_{ij} \quad .$$

The trees in the ensemble of all trees {tree} may have several disconnected components, as long as the ensemble of all component-trees of a tree pass through all nodes of the network and have ends on all border-nodes of the network. It is easy to see that the maximum number of component-trees if $n_o/2$ if we have n_o border-nodes. If n_o is even, these $n_o/2$ component-trees are simply open paths on the network. On a regular network (when every inner node has six neighbours linked to it) or, more generally, <u>on a</u> <u>triangulation covering a surface</u>, <u>as opposed to a tree-like network</u>, the node-node incidence matrix with elements $A_{ij} = \alpha_{ij}$ (which are zero when the nodes i and j are not connected by any link) and let $D_{ii} = \sum_k \alpha_{ik}$ be a diagonal matrix ($D_{ij} = 0$ if $i \neq j$). $(A_c)_{km_o}$ will denote the matrix connecting internal nodes k to border-nodes m_o.

Input- and output-nodes will, in the following, be treated on the same footing and we will call them border-nodes.

Then, the partition function P given in (2) is[4] the Feynman amplitude for the graph dual (in the sense of graph theory, i.e. its vertices being in the center of the faces of the original graph and its links across the links of this original graph and in one-to-one correspondence with them) to the one having the incidence matrix A_{ij}. In field theory, this amplitude is useful to calculate transition probabilities from input-states with $X_{i_o} = V_{i_o}$ to output-states with $X_{j_o} = V_{j_o}$.

Here, the variables X_k have only one component, but field theory deals with vectors X_k^μ ($\mu = 1, 2, \ldots, d$) which correspond to an euclidean d-dimensional space. Hence, the partition function P in (2) is a Feynman-graph amplitude in a one-dimensional space. If a vertex (in a planar graph) has a maximum number of neighbours linked to it, the graph becomes a triangulation of the surface on which it is drawn and the corresponding field theory is a ϕ^3-field theory[4].

The dependence on the potential variables X_k being gaussian, we can analytically perform the integrals over them. This integration which is, in fact, a sum over all possible $\{X_k\}$ configurations, selects the most likely to appear because of the exponential weight $\exp(-A) = \exp[-\sum_{i<j} \alpha_{ij}(X_i - X_j)^2]$. The result of this integration is

the number of possible trees, as defined above, g r o w s exponentially[5] with the number n of nodes

(6) $\det \left(D - A \right) \sim a^n \, (\bar{\alpha})^n$

if $\bar{\alpha}$ is mean-value for the link-variables α_{ij} and a^n ($a \approx 5.03$ for a regular triangulation[5]) the total number of trees (up to some power of n). As det(D - A) occurs with the power – 1/2 in the integrand of expression (4) for P, we immediately notice that $[\det(D - A)]^{-1/2}$ will be (for surface-like networks) an exponentially decreasing function of the number n of internal nodes.

As can be seen in (5), if all α_{ij} are zero, det $(D - A)^{-1/2}$ will be infinite. Because – 1/2 is a small power, however the integral (4) would still be convergent. So, in practice one should not have to worry about problems due to divergent integrals (at least when the dimension d stays equal to one. For higher d, we would have to care about divergencies). Nevertheless, we introduced some noise for the potential variables X_j. Here we will do the same for the link variables α_{ij} because, minimizing $\alpha_{ij} \, (X_i - X_j)^2$ we don't want to let $(X_i - X_j)^2$ grow indefinitely (which it would if the α_{ij}'s were zero). So, we will assume here that $\alpha_{ij} > \varepsilon$, ε being a small ($\varepsilon \ll 1$) quantity. Of course, we don't want the extreme situation to happen where all α_{ij}'s become equal to their minimum value ε because, as stressed earlier in the introduction, this would forbid any memory of mutual excitation among border-nodes to remain. Hence, the minimization of A, the action, has to be made in two steps, the first one consisting in letting only potentials X_k to be varied, the α_{ij}'s staying fixed[2]. During this first step, minimization domains on the network connecting excited border-nodes will be created where potentials are nearly equal.

However, once this is done, on the domains where $(X_i - X_j)^2$ has been minimized, α_{ij} can take finite values (i.e. values much larger than ε) without affecting the value of A and P. Of course, this is true as long as $(X_i - X_j)^2$ stays small on those domains. Fluctuations may (in the second step minimization where α_{ij} and X_k variables are both allowed to vary) tend to destroy afterwards these equipotential domains by letting $(X_i - X_j)^2$ grow and the associated α_{ij} decrease. However, it is legitimate to think, that everything being equal otherwise, <u>it would take a much longer time for this erasing process to happen than for the α_{ij}'s on the other links to become equal to ε</u>. Now, if all links incident with a node i_r have $\alpha_{i_r j}$'s equal to ε, <u>the situation will be the same as if one considered a network with this node i_r removed</u>, their corresponding contributions $\alpha_{i_r j} (X_i - X_j)^2$ to the action being very small and hence negligeable. This can be checked on expression (5) where the only remaining trees (i.e. those with a sizeable contribution) would cover a network deprived of this node i_r. This phenomenon of effective node suppression occurs everywhere on the network where $(X_i - X_j)^2$ is not already small (i.e. $<< 1$) from the first step minimization. So we are left with a network effectively deprived of all nodes except on equipotential domains. However, we can go even further : <u>rapidly, only one tree will be selected with nodes related by links on which α_{ij}'s are larger than one.</u> (Of course, this tree may be one of a few trees differing only by small deformations) . The reason why this happens comes from the following fact : if α_{ij}'s stay finite (≥ 1, i.e. non-infinitesimal) on a surface-like domain, the number of contributing trees to the sum in expression (5) will be exponentially big and

(7)
$$[\det(D - A)]^{-1/2} \sim [a\,\alpha]^{-n/2}$$

will be exponentially small (see (6)). Therefore, regions in the integration domain $\int_\varepsilon^\infty \prod_{\{ij\}} d\,\alpha_{ij}$ where this exponential suppression does not occur are favored, i.e. tree-like domains on the network. This is exactly what we argued[2] would happen using a more heuristic mechanical analogy with a rubber sheet. Therefore, tree-like configurations (on which $\alpha_{ij} \geq 1$) make up the dominant part of the integration in (4) and are precisely the configurations we were looking for which minimize the action A. Briefly speaking, one-dimensional patterns are favored over surface-like ones because of the exponential number of trees existing on surface-like domains. The reason why these one-dimensional patterns are trees is that, in the first step, $(X_i - X_j)^2$ has been minimized on domains connecting excited border-nodes of the network, which, naturally have a tree shape or topology. First step equipotential domains then serve as seeds which in the second step are thinned out to trees.

In fact, at the end of the minimization process, for a given border-nodes excitation we may have a set of different solutions, each one corresponding to a tree of a different topology (two trees being indeformable into each other by a continuous deformation if they don't have the same topology).

Each tree (of fixed topology) will then correspond to an isolated minimum of A and it may be difficult to go from one tree to another one in a smooth way, i.e. without imposing additional constraints on the way minima are reached. For instance, we may progressively change the input-output configurations in different ways, reaching the same input-output configuration after many two-step minimization cycles. Depending on the way this final configuration is attained, different tree configurations on the network may arise. Using a current-life analogy, we may learn the same lesson using different concepts or different knowledge representations. Here concepts would be represented in the network by nodes which are at vertices of trees. Then, concepts would be defined by the association they make between border-nodes if they are "simple" concepts. A vertex-node related only through other vertex-nodes (or working-nodes[2]) to border-nodes would be an "abstracted concept". The degree[2] of abstraction of a vertex-node (or working-node) is then defined as the number of vertex-nodes or working-nodes necessary to cross to go from it to the boundary- nodes.

3. Conclusion

Developing a physical analogy between neural networks and electrical networks we are able to understand how the first ones are able to spontaneously construct a memory associating excited input- and output-nodes (or border-nodes).

Using a two-step minimization algorithm, where in the first step only potential or node-variables are varied, we create seeds which are equipotential domains on which the link-variables stay finite ($\alpha_{ij} \geq 1$) ; later on, after the second step, the only domains where the α_{ij} stays finite are trees which connect all excited border-nodes. These trees (tree means no circuit, i.e. closed path is left) may have several disconnected components. In fact, if there are n_0 excited border-nodes, the presence of $n_0/2$ trees (if n_0 is even) means that these trees are simply open paths (without any vertex having more than two branches).

The fact that only trees are left is consistent with our previous conclusion using a more heuristic derivation[2] based on a mechanical analogy with a rubber sheet which was deformed on its border. However, our present argument is much more rigorous since it is quantitative.

Of course, we always need a practical computation (this meaning extended numerical computations) in order to see if there is any loophole in our argument. Nevertheless, we think that if our results are numerically confirmed, it would lead us to conclude that we really understand how an abstraction hierarchy (i.e. a hierarchy of more and more abstract concepts) is a natural emergent property of networks treated as Boltzmann machines.

References

1. Rumelhart, D.E., Hinton, G.E. and Williams, R.J., Nature 323, 533-536, 1986.

2. Hong Tuan, R. "A local action for neural networks", preprint LPTHE Orsay 88/55, 1988.

3. Metropolis, N., Rosenbluth, A.W., Rosenbluth, M.N., Teller, A.H. and Teller, E., Journal of Chemical Physics 6, 1087, 1953.

4. Hong Tuan, R. "Logarithmic correction to the local equivalence of planar field theories and string theories", preprint LPTHE Orsay 88/34, 1988.

5. Boulatov, D.V., Kazakov, V.A., Kostov, I.K. and Migdal, A.A., Nucl. Phys. B275 [FS17] 641, 1986.

NEURAL NETWORKS: Advances and Applications
E. Gelenbe (Editor)
© Elsevier Science Publishers B.V. (North-Holland), 1991

Recent Applications of Competitive Activation Mechanisms

by

James A. Reggia*, Yun Peng*, and Paul Bourret**

*Dept. of Computer Science
University of Maryland
College Park, MD 20742
USA

**ONERA-CERT
2 Avenue Edouard Belin
31055 Toulouse CEDEX
France

Abstract: Inhibitory interactions in neural/connectionist models have traditionally been implemented using inhibitory connections. Recently an alternative approach based on competitive activation mechanisms has been proposed. This paper describes the use of competitive activation mechanisms for a variety of tasks: print-to-sound transformation, diagnostic inference, minimal vertex covering, communication scheduling and device control. In addition to whatever usefulness these systems may find, the results obtained with them are important because they provide the first demonstration that competitive activation mechanisms can function usefully in meaningful applications.

1. Introduction

Recently, a new approach to producing "competitive" or inhibitory effects in connectionist models has been proposed [Reggia, 1985, 1987]. Rather than implementing competitive/inhibitory interactions directly through explicit structural features (inhibitory connections) of a network, they are produced indirectly by the functional mechanism or rule used by nodes to control the spread of activation. With this approach the nodes in a network "compete" for any externally applied activation, and for this reason are said to use a *competitive activation mechanism*. Models using competitive activation mechanisms have a number of advantages over those using traditional methods, e.g., they require substantially fewer connections in some applications.

Initial computer simulations with small, simple networks using competitive activation mechanisms [Reggia, 1987] and subsequent mathematical analysis [Wang et al, 1988; Benaim & Samuelides, 1989] were encouraging and demonstrated the basic validity of this idea. However, this initial work did not provide any indication of whether such an approach could function meaningfully in the large, complex networks that might be encountered in real-world applications. In particular, two significant barriers to effective use of competitive activation mechanisms seemed evident initially. First, different versions of competitive activation mechanisms can exhibit quantitative and even qualitative differences in behavior. It is not obvious in general how one should go about devising a specific competitive activation mechanism for individual applications. Second, in contrast to more conventional activation mechanisms, no learning methods exist that have been studied in connectionist models which use a competitive activation mechanism.

This paper focuses on efforts to address the first of these two issues. During the last three years we have studied a number of applications of competitive activation mechanisms relevant to cognitive science, artificial intelligence, and control applications. In this paper some of these applications and the methodological concepts that have emerged in the context of their development are presented. The material is divided into two sections. First, the basic idea of a competitive activation mechanism is briefly described. Second, several examples of deriving specific competitive activation mechanisms for a variety of applications are presented. These applications include a model of converting printed text to spoken form, diagnostic hypothesis generation, minimum vertex covering, scheduling communications, and dynamic device control. The effectiveness of the competitive activation rules used in these models has been confirmed by computer simulations which demonstrate that the models perform well, in some cases with complex networks of appreciable size. The paper ends by describing some implications of this work, efforts to overcome the second barrier to more widespread use of competitive activation methods mentioned above by developing new learning methods, and other ongoing research.

2. Competitive Interactions in Connectionist Models

In the following, each node n_i in the network of a connectionist model is viewed as having an activation level $a_i(t)$ at time t, and the pattern of activation over the entire network is represented as a time-varying vector $\mathbf{a} = [a_1, a_2, ..., a_n]$. Each node receives activation from other nodes over weighted connections, where weight w_{ij} designates the weight on the connection directed to node n_i from node n_j. Note that with weights as well as other double subscripted quantities the receiving/destination node index is first, e.g., w_{ij} is a weight on a connection *to* node n_j. Incoming activation over n_i's input connections as well as any externally applied input to node n_i forms a resultant input $in_i(t)$. Each node can be viewed as following an *activation rule/mechanism*, a local function/procedure which the node uses to update its activation level as a function of its input and current activation level.

Two nodes in a connectionist model are said to be *competitors* if the gain of one occurs at the expense of the other, i.e., if their functional relationships are inhibitory in nature. For example, models using continuous time and activation levels where the ith node follows an activation rule

$$(1) \qquad \frac{da_i}{dt} = f_i(\mathbf{a}),$$

can be said to involve *competitive interactions* between nodes i and j if $\frac{\partial f_i}{\partial a_j} < 0$ when $i \neq j$ [Grossberg, 1982; Hirsch, 1987]. Note that this definition of competition indicates inhibitory interactions but says nothing about the underlying mechanisms involved in producing those inhibitory interactions.

It is critical to the following to appreciate that the *mechanism* by which competition (inhibitory interactions) occurs can vary from situation to situation. *Direct* or *antagonistic competition* occurs when entity i directly interacts with rival entity j in a fashion that suppresses j's activity (wrestling match; predator-prey relations). *Indirect* or *allocational competition* occurs when two rivals require and/or consume the same limited resource, the consumption by one rival resulting in less for the other to consume (animal populations sharing a common limited food source; businesses selling in the same market). These two mechanisms for producing competition are not mutually exclusive.

Given the distinction between the antagonistic and allocational mechanisms that can underly competitive (inhibitory) interactions, one can inquire how previous connectionist modelling efforts have used these two mechanisms. Previous activation mechanisms developed in connectionist modelling have been based on the assumption that competitive/inhibitory effects during spread of activation are brought about solely by antagonistic mechanisms [Amari & Arbib, 1982; Feldman & Ballard, 1982; Grossberg, 1982; Reggia & Sutton, 1988]. In other words, two "competing nodes" have direct inhibitory connections to one another. The inhibitory connections used in these models are often intended to produce a *winner-takes-all situation* in which an equilibrium is achieved with one node maximally activated and the other nodes having zero activation (e.g., [Feldman & Ballard, 1982, p. 218]). The use of inhibitory connections is not limited to such situations, however.

As will be seen below, many formulations of competitive activation mechanisms are possible. For illustrative convenience, we assume that $a_k(t)$ and w_{ji} are restricted to the interval [0, 1] unless specifically noted otherwise (this restriction is *not* an essential property of a competitive activation mechanism). Typically, competitive activation mechanisms are implemented by letting the flow of activation from n_i to n_j be a time-varying function of a_j, the destination node activation level. As a specific example, the amount of activation $out_{ji}(t)$ flowing from node n_i to node n_j can be given by

(2)
$$out_{ji}(t) = \frac{a_j(t)\, w_{ji}}{\sum_k a_k(t) w_{ki}} \cdot a_i(t)$$

where the summation is over all nodes k to which node n_i sends connections. Here the output from node n_i going to node n_j depends not only on a_i and the constant w_{ji}, but also on receiving node n_j's activation level a_j (as well as the sum in the denominator). Stated otherwise, the total output $out_i(t)$ from node n_i is $a_i(t)$; the fraction of this going to node n_j is proportional to $a_j w_{ji}$, according to equation (2). The key feature here is that node i divides its output among the nodes that it sends output to; if node k gets more of node i's output, then other nodes (such as j) must get less. This approach to implementing competitive interactions can be contrasted with that used in more traditional connectionist models. For example, with a non-competitive activation mechanism the value

(3)
$$out_{ji}(t) = w_{ji}\, a_i(t)$$

might be used so that $out_{ji}(t)$ is not influenced by the activation $a_j(t)$ of the node n_j receiving node n_i's output.

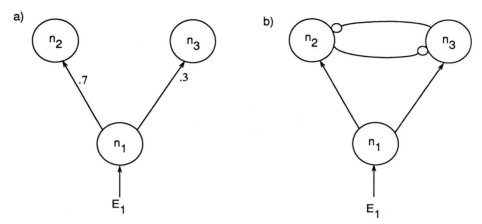

Figure 1. a) Three node network in which external input E_1 activates node n_1. Weights $w_{21} = 0.7$ and $w_{31} = 0.3$ are associated with the links. A competitive activation mechanism is assumed. b) Architecture of similar network when a more traditional non-competitive activation mechanism is used. The only difference between the two networks is the two inhibitory links (end with small circles) between n_2 and n_3. In the general case, it is not known how to transform a network without inhibitory connections and using a competitive activation mechanism into an equivalent network with inhibitory connections and a non-competitive activation.

The dynamics of connectionist models using competitive activation mechanisms can be most easily appreciated from example simulations. Consider the simple network in Figure 1a; there are no inhibitory connections in this network. A single external input E_1 activates node n_1, which in turn connects to and activates nodes n_2 and n_3. Note the larger weight 0.7 on the connection from n_1 to n_2. Suppose that each node here follows the activation rule

(4)
$$\frac{da_i}{dt} = (in_i - a_i)(1 - a_i)$$

where

$$in_1(t) = E_1(t),$$

$$in_2(t) = out_{21}(t),$$

$$in_3(t) = out_{31}(t),$$

and $out_{ji}(t)$ is given by equation (2). Assume all $a_i(0) = 0.0$, and let $E_1(t) = 1$ for $t > 0$. At $t = 0$ in this simulation, both the numerator and denominator in equation (2) are 0. We define $out_{ji}(t) = w_{ji} \cdot a_i(t)$ to hold whenever this is the case. Numerical simulation of this system exhibits the behavior given in Table 1. Node n_1 quickly becomes activated. Initially, activation levels a_2 and a_3 both grow, but eventually $a_2 \rightarrow 1$ and $a_3 \rightarrow 0$. This is an example of *winner-takes-all* or *choice* behavior in that an activation pattern over a set of nodes (n_2 and n_3) reaches equilibrium with one node fully activated and other nodes fully inactive.

Table 1: Node Activations Over Time			
Time	a_1	a_2	a_3
0	0	0	0
0.2	0.18	0.007	0.003
1	0.55	0.200	0.012
2	0.77	0.434	0.011
4	0.95	0.690	0.005
6	0.99	0.801	0.002

Figure 1b shows a similar network that exhibits the same behavior when a traditional non-competitive activation mechanism is used. The difference is that the two competing nodes n_2 and n_3 now have inhibitory connections to each other (indicated by connections with circular terminators). With this second network, as n_2 becomes more active than n_3, it directly suppresses activation of n_3 via its inhibitory connection ($w_{32} < 0$).

Using competitive activation mechanisms rather than inhibitory links between competing nodes is desirable from the perspective of developing connectionist models directly from existing associative networks in artificial intelligence and cognitive science. Such networks do not need to incorporate inhibitory links, and in many cases it is neither desirable nor feasible to introduce them. There are several reasons that this is the case. First, most connections/links in semantic networks correspond to empirical associations with at least theoretically measurable frequencies of occurrence. In contrast to this well-defined correspondence between model components (excitatory connections) and the entities being modelled (measurable associations), there is no generally recognized analogous real-world correspondence to inhibitory connections in AI/cognitive psychology theory. This is very different than the situation one encounters with connectionist models of neural circuitry in the brain (inhibitory connections between neurons are common).

Another reason for desiring to minimize inhibitory connections in networks is that it is preferable to minimize connections in general. For example, if there are n nodes in a set of competing nodes and they must directly inhibit one another to produce a winner-takes-all phenomenon, then close to n^2 inhibitory connections would be required. For example, 1000 nodes would require almost 1,000,000 inhibitory connections. There are ways to minimize such connections without using competitive activation mechanisms requiring on the order of 3n connections [Touretzky & Hinton, 1988], but their generality remains to be established and they do not address multiple "winners" situations as in the following paragraph. Hierarchical structuring of networks might also be used to reduce the number of required inhibitory connections in some applications. Nevertheless, scaling up to large networks while using explicit inhibitory links in this fashion would clearly require a large number of inhibitory connections (at least $O(n)$). Preliminary experiments on parallel computers suggest that an important element in achieving speed-up in such a framework is the maximum fanout of nodes [Tagamets & Reggia, 1989]. This implies that a competition-based activation mechanism may have significant advantages over implementing competition directly via explicit inhibitory links, even on parallel architectures.

Furthermore, implementing direct competition via inhibitory links is at best problematic in situations where multiple simultaneous "winners" are desired (see diagnosis model below). If a set of competing nodes with direct, mutually-inhibitory links tries to sustain multiple winners simultaneously, these winners will tend to extinguish each others' activations. Further, in some situations, two nodes may be considered to be in competition, while in other situations the same two nodes may not be competitors and may actually "cooperate" to formulate a solution to a problem [Peng & Reggia, 1989]. Allocational competition appears to provide a clean solution for determining such relationships dynamically.

Finally, there is a fundamental difference that arises when a competitive rather than a non-competitive activation mechanism is used. This difference is always present but is best illustrated with feed-forward networks. Consider a feed-forward network composed of several layers of nodes and using a *non*-competitive activation mechanism. In this case, output node activations cannot influence one another (they are not directly connected to each other in a feedforward-only network; e.g., n_2 and n_3 in Figure 1a). In contrast, with a competitive activation mechanism, even though a "feed-forward network" is involved, activation levels of nodes in one layer are used in a retrograde (feedback) fashion to guide the forward flow of activation from the preceding layer. This occurs because $out_{ji}(t)$ is a function of the destination node n_j's activation level. Thus, as the output nodes' activation levels stabilize, they have exerted a powerful indirect influence on each others values.

Initial simulations [Reggia, 1987] with small, very simple networks and theoretical analyses [Wang et al, 1988; Benaim & Samuelides, 1989; Benaim, 1990] have demonstrated that the basic concept of a competitive activation mechanism is sound and have shed light on some of their properties. Additional theoretical analysis with large networks is currently underway [Reggia & Edwards, 1990]. Models using a suitable formulation of this approach generally reach equilibrium states where the network activation forms a circumscribed pattern. Clear cut, context-sensitive winner-takes-all behavior can be produced. For example, had there been an additional, small input to n_3 in the earlier example (Figure 1a and Table 1), then node n_3 would have emerged as the "winner" in its competition with node n_2. It is in this sense that determination of a "winning node" is context sensitive. All of these features make competitive activation methods an attractive new connectionist modelling method, particularly if the two current limitations of competitive activation methods stated earlier (lack of general methodology for creating application-specific methods, lack of learning rules that work with competitive activation methods) can be overcome.

Recent work has focused effort on the first of these issues: developing the methods needed to apply this approach in larger, more complex networks. Several exploratory applications, representative of this effort, are now described. These examples deal with print-to-sound conversion, diagnostic problem-solving, minimum vertex covering, scheduling communications, and dynamic device control. The implementation of many of these applications was achieved using a general-purpose software environment called MIRRORS [D'Autrechy et al, 1988]. This environment supports a very-high-level, non-procedural language for specifying nodes, their connections, and the details of specific experimental simulations.

3. Print-to-Sound Transformation

Print-to-sound transformation (reading aloud a single printed word) was selected as the first large-scale test of competitive activation mechanisms because it provides a challenging but relatively circumscribed problem. The print-to-sound transformation is challenging in that the existence of two hypothesized "routes" by which information flows through the underlying associative network implies that nodes serving as outputs for the model might receive conflicting information about what their activation levels should be. Such conflicts must be resolved by these nodes based on locally-available information as node activations approach equilibrium. On the other hand, compared to many other cognitive tasks involving associative memory (e.g., natural language processing at the semantic level), the underlying network is relatively circumscribed; hence a fairly significant subset of it can be captured in a model. There is also a relatively large amount of empirically-derived information upon which to base network structure, assignment of weights to connections, and analysis of simulation results.

In reading a word aloud, a sequence of printed graphemes is transformed into a sequence of spoken phonemes. A *grapheme* is defined to be one or a few printed characters serving as the written representation of a phoneme (speech sound). For typographic convenience, phonemes will be represented by lower-case letters between slanted lines, graphemes by upper-case letters, and word/morphemes by double-quote marks. For example, the word "onion" consists of five graphemes, O N I O N, which correspond to five phonemes, $/uh^+$ n y uh- n/.

The cognitive task of word naming or reading aloud is often thought of as information flow and transformation through two routes [Ellis,

1984]. Figure 2 illustrates the two routes by which information flows as it is transformed from written to spoken form in our connectionist model. Circles are *sets* of nodes (G_i = graphemes, P_i = phonemes, W = words) and arrows are *sets* of connections in this figure. One route is the *grapheme-phoneme correspondence or GPC route* (bottom of Figure 2). Reading aloud via this route involves mapping graphemes onto their corresponding phonemes. The second route is the *lexical route* (top of Figure 2). Reading aloud via this route involves the mapping of graphemes onto morphemes/words via the visual word recognition system and then onto their phonemic representation. The "dual-route model" of reading is strongly supported by evidence from empirical studies of both normal skilled readers and individuals with acquired dyslexia.

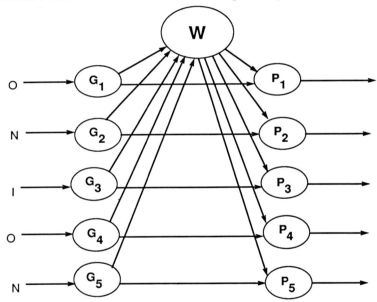

Figure 2. Structure of the network in the print-to-sound model. Each circle is a set of nodes (G_1 = graphemes, P_1 = phonemes, W = words). When the five graphemes of the word "onion" serve as input, there are five position-specific copies of each set of grapheme and phoneme nodes.

The network in the connectionist model of print-to-sound transformation uses a local representation of information. Nodes represent graphemes, phonemes and words, while connections represent positively-weighted associations between these entities. Running a simulation involves selective application of an externally-supplied source of input to the appropriate grapheme nodes, thereby driving up their activation levels. Activation then spreads from grapheme nodes to phoneme nodes (via the GPC route), and from grapheme nodes to "hidden" word nodes to phoneme nodes (via the lexical route). The activation levels of phoneme nodes represent the network's output.

Since each word node in the network connects to multiple grapheme/phoneme nodes occurring in specific positions, there are actually multiple copies or *instances* of grapheme and phoneme node sets in any simulation. The exact number of instances of grapheme and phoneme node sets is determined by the number of graphemes that are designated as input. If a specific simulation involves the presentation of a sequence of n graphemes as input, this is implemented in the model by dynamically constructing n copies of the grapheme nodes prior to initiating the simulation. Each set of grapheme nodes corresponds to one input position, where positions are numbered from 1 (initial position) to n (final position). For each set of grapheme nodes so constructed, a corresponding set of phoneme nodes is generated (recall that a grapheme is defined as the orthographic representation of a single phoneme) along with all relevant connections from graphemes to phonemes in one position. Thus, for an input sequence of n graphemes, counting the set of word nodes there are 2n + 1 interconnected sets of nodes present. Figure 2 illustrates the specific example where the connectionist model is presented with five graphemes (O, N, I, O, and N) as input. The network contains five sets of grapheme nodes and five sets of phoneme nodes.

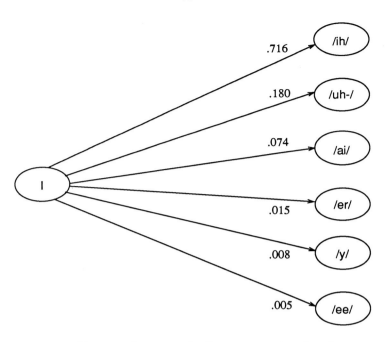

Figure 3. The grapheme node I connects to six phoneme nodes. Weights on the connections are conditional probabilities.

There are 48 phonemes and 168 graphemes represented as nodes in *each* position-specific set in the print-to-sound model's associative network. These nodes and their connections, which form the GPC route, are based on published data [Berndt et al, 1987]. An example of a single grapheme node I and its connections to phoneme nodes in a path of the GPC route is illustrated in Figure 3. Each grapheme node also sends connections to word nodes. Each phoneme node receives additional incoming connections from other grapheme nodes, as well as connections from appropriate word nodes, that are not shown here. Each numeric weight in Figure 3 represents the conditional probability that the grapheme I will be pronounced as the corresponding phoneme. The set of word nodes contains over 1000 two-syllable words with a wide range of frequencies that were not preselected on the basis of orthographic or phonetic structure.

Each grapheme node in the ith grapheme set is connected to all word nodes in which that grapheme appeared in the ith position. The weight on each link from a grapheme node to its word nodes is 1/n, where n is the total number of words to which that grapheme connected. Each word node has forward connections to phoneme nodes in the appropriate position-specific phoneme sets. The word node for "onion," for example, has a connection to /y/ in the third set P_3 of phoneme nodes. With the exception of 17 words with common multiple pronunciations, a word node has one connection with a weight of 1.0 to a single phoneme node in each phoneme set (or no connections to some phoneme sets if the number of phoneme sets exceeded the number of phonemes in the word).

In summary, the associative network in the print-to-sound model consists of numerous positively weighted, forward connections forming multiple, position-specific paths through two routes (Figure 2). There are no reverse connections (phonemes to words or graphemes, words to graphemes), no inhibitory connections, and no connections between any two phonemes, any two graphemes, or any two words. The complete network involved in a simulation is relatively large. For example, for the input graphemes O N I O N, there are a total of 2110 nodes (5 times 168 grapheme nodes, plus 5 times 48 phoneme nodes, plus 1030 word nodes) and roughly 12,000 forward connections. The use of a competitive activation mechanism however, avoids the need for more than a million lateral inhibitory connections that would normally be required to produce winner-take-all behavior among word nodes and among each position-specific set of phoneme nodes.

The method used to derive the competitive activation mechanism for the print-to-sound model was a computer-assisted, heuristic search process. The competitive activation mechanisms derived through this search process and subsequently used in the print-to-sound connectionist model can be summarized as follows. Calculation of $in_i(t)$ for each node n_i is arranged so that $0 \leq in_i(t) \leq 1$. This is achieved using

$$(5) \qquad in_i(t) = 1 - \prod_k (1 - out_{ik}(t))$$

where $out_{ik}(t)$ is the output from node n_k arriving at node n_i at time t as given by equation (2), or is an external input to n_i. As long as each out_{ik} value satisfies $0 \leq out_{ik} \leq 1$, equation (5) guarantees that the resultant in_i is also restricted to this range. Equation (5) can be viewed as combining individual inputs out_{ik} in a non-linear, accumulative fashion. According to equation (5), in_i is a monotonically increasing function of every out_{ik}, and can be viewed as a numerical version of a logical OR operation. Input to all nodes is based on equation (5), but the details of how this was done depends on whether the node involved is a grapheme, phoneme or word node [Reggia et al, 1988].

Starting with $a_i(0) = 0.0$, each node in the print-to-sound model uses equations (2) and (5) and the following rule to update its activation level:

$$(6) \qquad \frac{da_i}{dt} = k_i \cdot [in_i - 2a_i (1 - in_i)] (1 - a_i).$$

The first non-constant factor here, $in_i - 2a_i (1 - in_i)$, can be positive or negative. This factor causes a_i to increase whenever $in_i > 2a_i (1 - in_i)$, to decrease whenever $in_i < 2a_i(1 - in_i)$, and insures that $a_i \geq 0$. The second factor, $1 - a_i$, insures that a_i has 1.0 as a maximum value. The constant k_i is 1.0 for phoneme and grapheme nodes. For word nodes, the value of k_i is a logarithmic function of p_i, a node's prior probability. We introduced k_i to allow analysis of word frequency effects.

To demonstrate that the equations (2), (5) and (6) provide an effective competitive activation mechanism, it is necessary to show that the print-to-sound connectionist model using this activation mechanism exhibits interesting behavior. Does the competitive activation mechanism described above, when used with the complex print-to-sound network, produce suitable winner-takes-all behavior among word nodes and phoneme nodes in the absence of lateral inhibitory connections? In particular, it was not obvious a *priori* that competitive activation mechanisms could work well in the context of conflicting input signals to phoneme nodes arriving over two separate routes.

A single brief example of a representative simulation with the print-to-sound model is given here to illustrate its ability to activate correctly word and phoneme nodes with a sharply defined winner-takes-all performance. The sequence of five graphemes, O N I O N, representing an irregular word serves as input to the model. Table 2 gives activation levels as a function of time for selected nodes in the network. The symbol "-" means "inactive" ($a_i < .001$) and the symbol "****" means saturated" ($a_i > .99$). Each 10 iterations (first column) represents one unit of simulated time.

Table 2: Example Simulation with Print-to-Sound Model						
Itera- tions	Graph- eme	Words		Phonemes		
		"onion"	"union"	/ih/$_3$	/y/$_3$	/n/$_5$
0	-	-	-	-	-	-
10	.651	.063	.134	.001	-	.029
20	.878	.211	.164	.001	-	.166
30	.958	.383	.097	-	-	.360
40	****	.657	.023	-	.253	.613
50	****	.884	.002	-	.658	.803
60	****	.967	-	-	.875	.942
70	****	****	-	-	.956	.979
80	****	****	-	-	.985	****
90	****	****	-	-	****	****

Grapheme nodes quickly become saturated (second column). While a fair number of word nodes are activated early in the simulation, activation levels are given for only the target word "onion" and one of its orthographic neighbors, "union", which has four of five graphemes in common with the target word. These are the most highly activated word nodes during this simulation. Early in the simulation, the node representing the orthographic neighbor "union" is *more* activated than the node for "onion". However, eventually "onion" dominates and becomes fully activated, while activation of all other word nodes (both those shown here and all others) dies out. The clear-cut winner-takes-all behavior arises completely through allocational competition, with "onion" eventually dominating because of its perfect match with the input graphemes in this case. The larger early activation of the node representing the orthographic neighbor "union" arises primarily as a word frequency effect.

The rightmost columns in Table 2 illustrate activation levels of selected phoneme nodes. Allocational competition results in clear-cut, winner-takes-all activation of exactly those phoneme nodes representing the correct pronunciation of the word "onion". Activation of phoneme nodes is slower than that of word nodes because, especially early on, their activation depends on receiving significant input from *both* the lexical and GPC routes. The rightmost column illustrates the mapping of grapheme N_5 to phoneme /n/$_5$ in the fifth position. In this case, the GPC route connection $N_5 \rightarrow /n/_5$ in the final position has the large weight .975. Further, the most highly active word nodes ("onion," and "union") both have a $/n/_5$ in their phonemic realization. Thus, $/n/_5$ receives reinforcing input simultaneously from the lexical and GPC routes, and rapidly activates with little significant competition. In contrast, in the third position grapheme I_3 connects to six phonemes (Figure 3). Activation levels for two of these phonemes, $/ih/_3$ and $/y/_3$, are given in Table 2. Weights on the GPC route connections are .716 for $I_3 \rightarrow /ih/_3$ and .008 for $I_3 \rightarrow /y/_3$, the latter being the correct phonemic realization of I_3 in "onion." The very low weight on the GPC connection to $/y/_3$ and support for $/ih/_3$ from the word route (e.g., from "prison", "exist", etc, in this case) result in the slow activation of $/y/_3$ relative to $/n/_5$; see Table 2. However, a clean winner-takes-all activation of $/y/_3$ still eventually occurs.

To examine word frequency and regularity effects on the model's performance, data consisting of four sets of words with 16 words per set were used to test the model [Reggia et al, 1988]. Words for each of these sets were selected from those in the associative network's lexicon based on word frequency (high vs. low) and regularity (very regular vs. very irregular). In all 64 runs where a word contained in the model's lexicon was introduced as input, the correct set of phonemes eventually attained a 1.0 activation level, and all remaining phoneme nodes in each of the phoneme sets had a 0.0 activation level. Thus, clear-cut winner-takes-all behavior for the correct phoneme node always occurred with these simulations in a fashion similar to that demonstrated with "onion" above (Table 2). Measurements were recorded with the print-to-sound model of the time t_5 required for the correct set of phoneme nodes in each of the 64 words to attain a 0.50 activation level. These data were averaged for the 16 words in each data set and are given in columns 3-4 of Table 3 for each of the four sets of test words where k_i is based on word frequency. Phonemes for low-frequency irregular words had a delayed activation rate compared to phonemes in the other three sets of words.

The performance of the print-to-sound model was also tested using non-words as input. The set of non-words consisted of arbitrarily selected, 2-syllable words which were not contained in the model's lexicon. For ten non-words for which winner-takes-all behavior was attained for all phonemes, the mean $t_{.5}$ value for phonemes was 66.6 (see bottom row, Table 3). This was a significantly greater $t_{.5}$ value than for the four sets of test words.

Table 3: Simulation Results (Print-to-Sound Model) $t_{.5} \pm$ sd			
Word Group	n	phonemes	word
1. High Freq. Reg.	16	27.9 ± 0.73	18.8 ± 1.29
2. High Freq. Irreg.	16	30.6 ± 2.39	18.9 ± .89
3. Low Freq. Reg.	16	33.3 ± 2.50	26.1 ± 4.06
4. Low Freq. Irreg.	16	46.7 ± 9.45	35.3 ± 14.27
5. Non-Words	10	66.6 ± 12.55	NA

These results are qualitatively similar to empirical results with normal readers described in the literature. In research measuring the time taken for normal subjects to read words aloud (pronunciation latency), it has been found, in general, that words with regular pronunciations can be read faster than irregular words. Further, this effect of regularity on pronunciation latency is detectable only for words of low frequency. High-frequency words, whether regular or irregular, are pronounced uniformly quickly relative to low-frequency words. Thus, not only does this activation rule produce clear cut "winner-takes-all" behavior, but it also produces pronunciation latencies similar to those seen with adult readers [Reggia et al, 1988].

4. Diagnostic Hypothesis Generation

Several probabilistically-oriented causal models have been developed during the past few years for diagnostic problem-solving in situations where multiple disorders may occur simultaneously [Peng & Reggia, 1987; Peng & Reggia, 1989]. In these models disorders and manifestations are connected by causal links associated with probabilities representing the strengths of the causal associations. A hypothesis, consisting of one or more disorders with the highest posterior probability for the given set of manifestations (findings), is typically taken as the optimal problem solution. Conventional sequential search approaches in AI that solve diagnostic problems formulated in this fashion suffer from combinatorial explosion. We recently postulated that a globally optimal diagnostic explanation (set of disorders) could be approximated by a connectionist model using a causal network if a suitable competitive activation mechanism could be identified [Peng & Reggia, 1989].

The diagnostic inference process whose computation is carried out by the connectionist model is based on a formalization of the causal and probabilistic associative knowledge underlying diagnostic problem-solving. The particular formulation we use is called *parsimonious covering theory* [Reggia et al, 1985]. In parsimonious covering theory there is a set of disorders D, a set of manifestations M, and a relation C representing the causal associations between disorders and manifestations (see Figure 4). Saying that disorder d_i may cause manifestation m_j corresponds to a link in Figure 4. A subset of M, denoted M^+, represents the subset of all manifestations that are present, while $M^- = M - M^+$ represents the subset of all manifestations assumed to be absent. Based on the relation C, two sets, effects(d_i) and causes(m_j), are defined for each $d_i \in D$ and each $m_j \in M$, respectively: effects(d_i) = $\{m_j|\ d_i$ causes $m_j\}$ and causes(m_j) = $\{d_i|\ d_i$ causes $m_j\}$. Intuitively, effects(d_i) are all manifestations that d_i can cause, and causes(m_j) are all disorders that can cause m_j. A set of disorders D_I is called a *cover* of the given M^+ if it is a set of disorders which, when present, could cause or account for all of the manifestations in M^+. A set of disorders D_I is said to be a *hypothesis* (or *explanation*) if 1) D_I is a cover of M^+, and 2) D_I is "parsimonious". A number of criteria exist for characterizing a parsimonious set D_I [Peng & Reggia, 1987; Reggia et al, 1985]; we will not consider those criteria here.

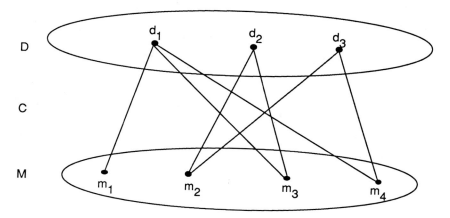

Figure 4. Two-layer diagnostic problem. The set D represents disorders, M represents manifestations, and C represents the causal associations between them.

The causal network in parsimonious covering theory can be augmented with relevant probabilities [Peng & Reggia, 1987]. Each $d_i \in D$ is associated with a number $p_i \in (0, 1)$, representing its prior probability. Each causal link, such as that between disorder d_i and manifestation m_j, is associated with a number c_{ij} ($0 < c_{ij} \leq 1$), the *causal strength* from d_i to m_j, representing how frequently d_i causes m_j. In other words, $c_{ij} = P(d_i$ causes $m_j \mid d_i)$. If there is no causal link between d_i and m_j, then c_{ij} is assumed to be zero. It is assumed that the disorders d_i are independent of each other, that whenever d_i occurs, it always causes m_j with the same probability c_{ij}, and that no manifestation can be present without being caused by some disorder. Based on these assumptions, a "relative likelihood measure" for a hypothesis D_I given M^+ can be derived according to Bayes' Theorem [Peng & Reggia, 1987]. This measure is

$$(7) \quad L(D_I, M^+) = \prod_{m_j \in M^+} \left[1 - \prod_{d_i \in D_I} (1 - c_{ij})\right] \cdot \prod_{m_j \in M^-} \prod_{d_i \in D_I} (1 - c_{il}) \cdot \prod_{d_i \in D_I} \frac{p_i}{1 - p_i}$$

The first product here, over all present manifestations M^+, can be thought of as a weight reflecting how likely D_I is to cause the manifestations given in M^+; the second product can be thought of as a weight based on expected but absent manifestations (M^-); and the third product represents a weight based on prior probabilities of disorders in D_I. The relative likelihood $L(D_I, M^+)$ calculated in equation (7) differs from the posterior probability $P(D_I| M^+)$ calculated with Bayes' Theorem only by a constant.

To solve a diagnostic problem means to identify one or more most probable diagnostic hypotheses with the highest relative likelihood (L value) among all possible hypotheses. Since disorders are assumed to occur independently of one another, any combination of disorders is possible. Provably-correct problem-solving methods have been developed for this task using search programs cast within the traditional symbol-processing framework of AI. However, the potential search space for a solution is generally extremely large (i.e., $2^{|D|}$) and thus, as noted earlier, diagnostic problem-solving in this formulation is combinatorially difficult.

A probabilistic causal network in parsimonious covering theory (e.g., Figure 4) can be used directly as a connectionist model network: disorders D and manifestations M are represented by two sets of nodes, and the causal relation C is represented by the set of weighted links connecting these nodes. There are no inhibitory or intra-set links. In formulating a diagnostic problem as a connectionist model, each disorder node d_i has an activation level at time t during the computation, denoted as $d_i(t) \in [0, 1]$, which serves as a measure of confirmation. Each manifestation node m_j has an activation level $m_j(t) \in [0,1]$. Initially, $d_i(0) = p_i$. When a simulation equilibrates with $d_i(t) \approx 1.0$ at time t, the disorder d_i is confirmed to be occurring (or is said to be a "winner") and thus becomes an element of the solution; when $d_i(t) \approx 0.0$ then d_i is disconfirmed or rejected. Each manifestation node m_j is marked as to whether it is present ($m_j \in M^+$) or absent ($m_j \in M^-$). This marking represents the external input to the connectionist network.

Each causal link (connection) is associated with a constant weight equal to the appropriate causal strength c_{ij} which, during a computation, can be accessed solely by the two nodes d_i and m_j. Note that all weights c_{ij} are positive or excitatory. For each $m_j \in M^+$, its neighboring nodes (nodes in causes(m_j)) can be viewed as competing with each other for activation. Processing continues until equilibrium is reached at time t_e. If

the model converges on a set of "winners", i.e., for each d_i, $d_i(t_e)$ approx-
imates either 1 or 0, then the set of disorders $D_S = \{d_i | d_i(t_e) \approx 1\}$ is taken
to be the connectionist model's problem solution. In other words, the
connectionist model derives D_S as its candidate for the most probable
cover D^+ of the given features M^+.

The crucial point here is that a set of disorders D_S is to be derived
through the concurrent *local* interactions occurring in the connectionist
model, where D_S represents a hypothesis about the identity of the *globally* optimal set of disorders D^+ as determined by the likelihood measure
(equation (7)). Since each node's processing is driven solely by local
information, it is not guaranteed *a priori* that the resultant locally optimal
solution will correspond to a globally optimal solution or even to a set of
multiple "winners". The specific competitive activation mechanism used
was derived by decomposing the formula for identifying a globally
Bayesian-optimal set of disorders (equation (7)) into local rules used by
each node to update its activation level [Peng & Reggia, 1989]. We
now briefly consider how this activation rule works.

At the beginning of a simulation, the manifestation nodes are
separated into two subsets referred to as M^+ and M^-, manifestations
which are present and those which are absent, respectively. The
influence of M^- nodes and prior probabilities on disorder activations is a
constant K_i, which is therefore computed once for each disorder node d_i
at the beginning of a simulation. The nodes which continuously partici-
pate in a simulation's computations consist of the manifestation nodes in
M^+ and all of the disorder nodes. Assuming a discrete representation of
time, let $d_i(t)$ be the activation level of node d_i at time t, and $m_j(t)$ be the
activation level of node m_j at time t. Both of these quantities lie between
0.0 and 1.0, inclusive. The manifestation nodes in M^+ are updated using
the activation rule

$$(8) \qquad m_j(t) = 1 - \prod_{d_i \in \text{causes}(m_j)} (1 - c_{ij}d_i(t-1))$$

(compare with equation (5)). At the start of a simulation, disorder node
activations are initialized to the values of their respective estimated prior
probablilities ($d_i(0) = p_i$ for all disorders). Activation values for manifestation nodes are computed at each iteration using equation (8), and for
disorder nodes using the sigmoid function

$$(9) \qquad d_i(t) = \frac{1}{1 + e^{-in_i(t)/T(t)}}$$

Here $T(t)$ is a control parameter analogous to an "annealing temperature" in simulated annealing systems; it is started at an initial value T_0 and progressively decreased. The variation of the control parameter $T(t)$ for the connectionist model is of the form $T(0)=T_0$ and $T(t)=\delta T(t-1)$, where $0 < \delta < 1$. The value $in_i(t)$ is determined by the rule

$$(10) \qquad in_i(t) = K_i \cdot \prod_{m_j \in M_i^+} \left[1 + c_{ij} \frac{1 - m_j(t)}{m_j(t) - c_{ij} d_i(t-1)} \right] - 1$$

where $M_i^+ = M^+ \cap$ effects (d_i). Note that equations (8-10) are all based on information locally available to the node doing the computation.

To see how competition plays a role in this computation, note that by equation (8) we can rewrite equation (10) as

$$in_i = \prod_{m_j \in M_i^+} \left[1 + \frac{c_{ij}}{\dfrac{1}{\displaystyle\prod_{\substack{d_k \in \text{ causes}(m_j) \\ d_k \neq d_i}} (1 - c_{kj} d_k)} - 1} \right] \cdot K_i - 1.$$

where the variable t has been omitted for brevity. This equation shows that the ith disorder's input, in_i, will tend to decrease if activation d_k ($k \neq i$) of some other disorder in causes(M_i^+) increases, and in_i will tend to increase if d_k decreases. In this sense, the ith disorder competes with all other disorders in causes(M_i^+), and whether d_i should increase or decrease depends on this competition as well as the constant K_i. For further analysis and discussion of this issue, see [Wald et al, 1989].

To show that the activation mechanism derived in the above fashion is effective, it was first studied using three small, abstract networks having randomly generated nodes and connections [Peng & Reggia, 1989]. Each network had 10 manifestations, 10 disorders, and a maximum of 40 connections (causal associations) between individual disorders and their manifestations. Each of the 2^{10} possible subsets of manifestations was used as M^+ in testing the resultant connectionist model. These simulations showed that 87% of the time the connectionist model successfully activated as D_s the globally most probable *set* of disorders D^+ when a set of manifestations M^+ was activated. Like with the print-to-sound model, clear-cut "winners" ($d_i = 1$) and losers ($d_i = 0$) occurred. If "partial resettling" was done (a few repeat simulations during which each initially activated disorder is "clamped" off in turn and the altered set of activated disorders examined), accuracy rose to 99%. While encouraging, these initial simulations were limited by the small size and the artificial nature of the networks used (i.e., randomly generated associations and weights).

To examine whether this specific formulation of a competitive activation mechanism for diagnostic problem-solving scales-up to larger and more realistic networks, a substantially larger network having 56 manifestations, 26 disorders, and 384 causal links in a medical domain was implemented [Wald et al, 1989]. On first thought, this network may not seem impressive, but it should be understood that the potential "hypothesis space" involved with such a network is enormous compared to that of the previous simulations. A network with 10 disorders represents $2^{10} = 1,024$ possible diagnostic hypotheses; in contrast a network with 26 disorders represents $2^{26} = 67,108,864$ possible hypotheses. In addition, this network is based on a "real" diagnostic application. The network structure (causal associations) and connection weights were provided by physicians and were not randomly generated. As a result, the connectionist model used in this experimental study was not only larger, but also more realistically structured than the previous ones.

In attempting to scale-up the diagnostic model, it was observed that frequently the system failed to converge on a problem-solution and instead began to oscillate. While some oscillations had occurred in the earlier study, this problem had been overcome by increasing the initial value of the control parameter T [Peng & Reggia, 1989]. Attempts to correct the undesirable oscillatory behavior in the larger network with a similar approach failed. An analysis was therefore undertaken to establish why oscillations occurred and, in particular, how the "annealing schedule" might be altered to improve performance. This analysis suggested two conclusions [Wald et al, 1989]. First, as long as T_0, the initial T value, is large enough so that simulations begin outside of a "critical period" when decisions are made, the value of T_0 should not matter, except in a random way. Second, by increasing δ, there should be a greater chance of disorders winning and suppressing other disorders during the critical period. Further, it is possible to estimate an expected T value for the critical period. Once one has an estimate for this critical value T_c, a value for T_0 can be calculated prior to starting a simulation by deciding how many ticks (iterations; time increments) to start before the critical point.

	Table 4: Simulations with Varying δ (T_0 = 1.0; 50 test cases)		
δ	Number (%) Reaching equilibrium	Number (%) Deriving Most Probable Hypothesis	Number (%) Deriving One of Top Three Hypotheses
.5	7 (14%)	7 (14%)	7 (14%)
.7	22 (44%)	17 (34%)	20 (40%)
.8	28 (56%)	24 (48%)	28 (56%)
.9	41 (82%)	33 (66%)	37 (74%)
.95	50 (100%)	37 (74%)	45 (90%)
.99	50 (100%)	38 (76%)	46 (92%)

Table 4 illustrates the kinds of results one obtains using the medical causal network and the above methodology. Each of 50 test cases was run with T_0 = 1.0, well above T_c, and with different δ values. Many simulations oscillated at $\delta = 0.5$ and almost none at $\delta = 0.99$ (Table 4). Once δ was increased to 0.95, every simulation reached a stable equilibrium. For all simulations that stabilized at any δ value, a clear cut set of "winners" was identified (i.e., all d_i values were 0.0 or 1.0 and not in between), and the set of disorders with $d_i \approx 1.0$ was always a cover for M^+. Without using resettling, roughly 90% of simulations produced one of the three globally optimal (most probable) diagnostic hypotheses (Table 4).

5. Minimum Vertex Covering Problems

Let G = <V,E> be an undirected graph where V = $\{v_1, v_2, \ldots, v_n\}$ is the set of *vertices* and E $\subseteq \{v_1, v_j\} \mid v_i, v_j \in$ V} is the set of undirected *edges*. A *minimum vertex cover* of G is a set of vertices V' $\subseteq$ V such that

(i) for each $\{v_i, v_j\} \in$ E, either v_i or v_j is in V', i.e., V' *covers* E; and

(ii) among all covers of E, V' has the smallest cardinality.

Finding a minimum vertex cover of an arbitrary graph is an NP-hard problem [Johnson, 1974].

A competitive activation mechanism has recently been developed for solving minimum vertex covering problems [Peng et al, 1990]. The graph G is used as the connectionist network directly, with each vertex (node) being a processing element and each edge (connection) being a communication channel between two nodes. Activation level $a_i(t)$ of node i is constrained to be between 0.0 and 1.0. Initially, $a_i(0) = 0$ for all nodes. As the model runs it settles into an equilibrium state at time T where all nodes are either fully activated ($a_i(T) \approx 1.0$) or fully deactivated ($a_i(T) \approx 0.0$). The fully active nodes represent the connectionist model's proposed minimum vertex cover.

The activation level of node i is governed by

(11)
$$\dot{a} = [in_i - A\, a_i](1 - a_i)$$

where $A > 0$ is constant and $in_i = \sum_j out_{ij}$. The output from node j to node i is

(12)
$$out_{ij} = (1 + A\, a_i)(1 - a_j)$$

equation (12) implies two things. First, the *total* output from node j decreases as a_j increases (because the factor $1 - a_j$ is common to all outputs from node j). This makes sense: when node j (vertex v_j) is fully active, it should cease trying to activate neighboring nodes because v_j covers all of its own edges. Second, the output from node j to node i increases as a_i increases. It can be shown that two nodes i and j are competitive in this model according to the definition associated with equation (1) whenever they are adjacent. Further, mathematical analysis shows that this model should converge on a multiple-winners-take-all state that approximates a minimum vertex cover [Peng et al, 1990].

This connectionist model was tested on a set of randomly-generated graphs. With 40 test graphs having 20 vertices, a minimum vertex cover was found 87.5% of the time and a cover one vertex larger was found the remaining 12.5% of the time. With 40 test graphs having 50 vertices, a minimum vertex cover was found 45% of the time. Covers one, two and three vertices larger were found 37.5%, 12.5% and 5% of the time, respectively. This performance was substantially better than that of a sequential "greedy algorithm" run on the same test networks.

6. Command, Communication, and Control

Command, communication and control problems are an area where connectionist models have the potential to be quite useful. Here we describe two applications where exploratory work has investigated this issue in the context of developing competitive activation mechanisms: communication scheduling and device control.

The satellite-antennas communication scheduling scenerio can be summarized as follows. Several low-level satellites gather information as they orbit the earth. During each revolution a satellite can broadcast its accumulated information to an antenna only during the short time period within which it is visible to that antenna. Since a satellite may gather information during a single revolution that exceeds the time within which that satellite is visible to a single antenna, its broadcasting might need to be split into messages to several antennas. It is assumed that two satellites cannot transmit to the same antenna at the same time, and that satellites have varying priorities according to the importance of their information.

A prototype connectionist model for solving satellite-antennas communication scheduling problems has been devised [Bourret et al, 1989]. The goal of this model is to generate communication schedules that maximize the priority-weighted transmission time. Nodes representing each satellite effectively compete for available time slices on appropriate antennas. Preliminary testing suggested that this approach may be used effectively, but some cases failed to converge on an appropriate solution. A revised model, in which competitive distribution of activation is generated by

$$(13) \qquad out_{ji} = \frac{a_j^3 w_{ji}}{\sum_k a_k^3 w_{ki}} \cdot a_i$$

rather than equation (2) resolved this problem [Bourret, 1990].

The final problem we consider is that of tracking and photographing designated targets with cameras on a spacecraft [Whitfield et al, 1989; Goodall & Reggia, 1990]. The scenario, simplified from real life, involves three mobile cameras that are available to photograph designated locations as the spacecraft passes over them. The problem to be solved is for the cameras to move so as to track incoming target locations; the cameras are to automatically position themselves to take a photograph just before the targets pass under the spacecraft. The cameras "compete" for targets to photograph, and a competitive activation mechanism is used to implement this competition. The competitive activation mechanism is driven by an output function similar to that in equation (2), although output from distant photographic targets is attenuated.

Two sets of experimental tests have been done [Whitfield et al, 1989; Goodall & Reggia, 1990]. Photographic targets were randomly generated at varying target densities. In simulations with target densities from 1% to 25% of possible locations, the percentage of targets photographed varied from 100% to roughly 50% (with higher target densities it is impossible for the cameras to photograph all targets). When the model was "damaged" by deleting a significant number of nodes, performance was mildly degraded but in general it showed remarkable fault tolerance. These results demonstrate that competitive activation mechanisms have potential applications to real-time control systems.

7. Discussion

While previous work with competitive activation mechanisms has suggested that the basic idea of using allocational competition is valid, the work described in this chapter is the first demonstration that this approach scales up to sizeable problems of interest in artificial intelligence and cognitive science. More importantly, the methods used to create the competitive activation mechanisms described here should be widely applicable to other areas where connectionist models might be developed. These results are very encouraging, and further study will no doubt uncover additional ways to derive competitive activation mechanisms for specific applications. Work on additional applications is already underway.

It was observed earlier in this paper that competitive activation mechanisms have a number of advantageous properties. They avoid the need for many inhibitory connections, and support multiple simultaneous "winners" of a competition. One important consequence of these properties has become evident from the applications described above: the graph structure describing the problem to be solved can often be used directly as the connectionist model network without modification. This was true for the associative network underlying print-to-sound transformation, the causal network describing diagnostic knowledge, and the graph representing a vertex covering problem. This is in contrast to many other approaches to connectionist modelling where a problem's graph structure must be substantially augmented or completely reformulated.

As noted in the *Introduction* to this chapter, a second barrier to more widespread use of competitive activation mechanisms is that no learning methods have been developed for them so far. This is an important issue since adaptability is one of the major strengths of connectionist modelling technology. For this reason, we have recently begun developing and studying learning methods for use with competitive activation mechanisms. One aspect of this work involves competitive learning [Sutton, Reggia & Maisog, 1989], an unsupervised learning rule which groups input patterns into classes based on the patterns' structure. A second aspect of this work involves recurrent error back-propagation [Cho & Reggia, 1990], a supervised learning rule. As these and other learning methods evolve the general usefulness and applicability of competitive activation mechanisms should improve substantially.

References

Amari, S., Arbib, M. (Eds.). "Competition and cooperation in neural nets", Springer-Verlag, 1982.

Benaim, M., Samuelides, M. "Inhibition virtuelle et prise de decision dans les reseaux multicouches de diffusion competitive", Proc. NeuroNimes '89 Conference, 1989.

Benaim, M. "A sufficient condition for convergence of competitive activation based feedforward neural networks, submitted, 1990.

Berndt, R., Reggia, J., Mitchum, C. "Empirically-derived probabilities for grapheme-to-phoneme correspondences in english", Beh. Res. Methods, Instruments and Computers, Vol. 19, 1-9, 1987.

Bourret, P., Goodall, S., Samuelides, M. "Optimal scheduling by competitive activation: application to the satellite antennae scheduling problem", Proc. Intl. Joint Conf. on Neural Networks, IEEE, Vol. I, 565-572, 1989.

Bourret, P. "A generalized competitive activation based neural network for solving the satellites to antennas broadcasting times scheduling problem", submitted, 1990.

Cho, S., Reggia, J. "Recurrent error back-propagation learning with competitive activation mechanisms", in preparation, 1990.

D'Autrechy, C.L., Reggia, J., Sutton, G., Goodall, S. "A general purpose simulation environment for developing connectionist models", Simulation, Vol. 51, 5-19, 1988.

Ellis, A. "Reading, Writing, and Dyslexia", Erlbaum, 1984.

Feldman, J., Ballard, D. "Connectionist models and their properties", Cog. Sci., Vol. 6, 205-254, 1982.

Findler, N. (Editor). "Associative Networks", Academic Press, New York, 1979.

Goodall, S., Reggia, J. "Competitive activation methods for dynamic control problems", Proc. Intl. Joint Conf. on Neural Networks, Washington, D.C., in press, Jan., 1990.

Grossberg, S. "Studies of Mind and Brain", Reidel, 1982.

Grossberg, S. "Competitive learning: from interactive activation to adaptive resonance", Cognitive Science, Vol. 11, 23-63, 1987.

Hirsch, M. "Convergence in neural networks", Proc. IEEE Intl. Conf. on Neural Networks, Vol II, 115-125, 1987.

Johnson, D. "Approximation algorithms for combinatorial problems", Journal of Computer and Systems Sciences, Vol. 9, 1974.

Pearl, J. "Distributed revision of composite beliefs, Artif. Intell., 33, 173-215, 1987.

Peng, Y., Reggia, J. "A probablistic causal model for diagnostic problem-solving", IEEE Trans. Systems, Man and Cybernetics, Vol. 17, 146-162 and 395-406, 1987.

Peng, Y., Reggia, J. "A connectionist model for diagnostic problem solving", IEEE Trans. on Systems, Man & Cybernetics, Vol. 19, 285-298, 1989.

Peng, Y., Reggia, J., Li, T. "A connectionist solution for vertex cover problems, in preparation, 1990.

Reggia, J. "Virtual lateral inhibition in parallel activation models of associative memory", Proceedings Ninth Intl. Joint Conference on Artificial Intelligence, 244-248, 1985.

Reggia, J., Nau, D., Wang, P., Peng, Y. "A formal model of diagnostic inference", Information Sciences, Vol. 37, 227-285, 1985.

Reggia, J. "Properties of a competition-based activation mechanism in neuromimetic network models", Proceedings of the First International Conference on Neural Networks, Vol. II, 131-138, 1987.

Reggia, J., Sutton, G. "Self-processing networks and their biomedical implications", IEEE Proc., Vol. 76, 680-692, 1988.

Reggia, J., Marsland, P., Berndt, R. "Competitive dynamics in a dual-route connectionist model of print-to-sound transformation", Complex

Systems, Vol. 2, 509-547, 1988.

Reggia, J., Edwards, M. "Phase transitions in connectionist models with rapidly varying connection strengths", in preparation, 1990.

Sutton, G., Reggia, J., Maisog, J. "Implementing competitive learning in connectionist models using competitive activation rules", submitted, 1989.

Wald, J., Farach, M., Tagamets, M., Reggia, J. "Generating plausible diagnostic hypotheses with self-processing causal networks", J. of Experimental & Theoretical Artificial Intelligence, Vol. 1, 91-112, 1989.

Wang, P., Seidman, S., Reggia, J. "Analysis of competition-based spreading activation in connectionist models", Int. J. Man-Machine Studies, Vol. 28, 77-97, 1988.

Whitfield, K., Goodall, S., Reggia, J. "A connectionist model for dynamic control", Telematics & Informatics, Vol. 6, 375-390, 1989.

NEURAL NETWORKS: Advances and Applications
E. Gelenbe (Editor)
© Elsevier Science Publishers B.V. (North-Holland), 1991

Improving the Learning Speed in Topological Maps of Patterns

Joaquim S. Rodrigues and Luis B. Almeida

INESC, Lisbon, Portugal

Abstract: Topological Maps of Patterns are a very powerful neural network paradigm. However, the learning method originally proposed by T. Kohonen for these maps, is very time-consuming. In this paper we propose a method for improving the learning speed, by starting the map with very few units and increasing that number progressively until the map reaches its final size. When the number of units increases, the locations of the new units are interpolated from the locations of the old units. The use of this method dramatically reduces the time needed for the "unfolding" phase and also yields some improvements in the asymptotic convergence phase. The improvements observed in this second phase can vary from marginal improvements for small sized networks, to very significant improvements for large networks.

1. Introduction

Topological Maps of Patterns were originally proposed by T. Kohonen as a means to represent complex empirical data by a self organizing network [1]. The data the network will represent can be expressed by multidimensional vectors, $x = (x_1 \; x_2 \; ... \; x_n)$, also called input patterns. The network is composed of units arranged in an N-dimensional lattice. Each unit is characterized by its internal state, $s_i = (s_{i1} \; s_{i2} \; ... \; s_{in})$, a vector of the same dimension as the input data, and by its output, $o_i = f(x, s_i)$, where $f(.)$ is a functional (usually a distance measure of some sort) of its arguments. In other words, the output of each unit is a measure of the similarity between the current input vector x, and the internal state s_i, of that unit.

The network is adaptive, i.e., the internal state of the units will change in response to an incoming input pattern. The process for adapting the network is the following:

- First, the input pattern is applied in parallel to all units, so that each unit can compute its output.

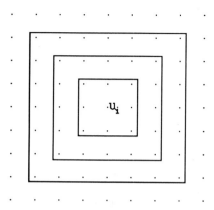

Figure 1. Bidimensional rectangular lattice showing possible topological neighbourhoods for unit u_i.

Finally, the selected unit, together with all the units that belong to its "topological neighbourhood" (units that are closer to the selected unit in the lattice sense, see Fig. 1), will change their internal states according to the rule:

$$s_i(t+1) = s_i(t) + \beta(t).[x(t)-s_i(t)] \qquad \text{for i belonging to the unit's neighbourhood}$$

(1)

$$s_i(t+1) = s_i(t) \qquad \text{for i outside the unit's neighbourhood}$$

where $\beta(t)$ is a positive parameter, $(0<\beta<1)$, called the adaptation step size. In other words, all the selected units will change their internal state in order to increase the similarity with the input pattern. The adaptation step size parameter β, must be decreased over time to ensure asymptotic stability. The overall result of the application of this adaptation rule is that the statistical distribution of the s_i vectors will tend to approximate the statistical distribution of the input vectors.

2. The Convergence Process

There are two phases in the formation of a map: one in which the map "unfolds" itself so as to situate the units in the correct order, and a second one in which the statistical distribution of the units in the map, will asymptotically approach the statistical distribution of the input vectors. To accelerate the "unfolding" phase it is convenient to start with a large neighbourhood that is then decreased over time. The second phase usually takes much more time than the first one.

The process of forming a map is a slow one, especially when the size of the map is not trivially small. There are two distinct factors that contribute to that slowness of convergence:

- The first one is the time required to perform each **step**, i.e., the processing of each input vector. The main part of this time is spent in the search for the unit that is closest to that vector. That search is performed once for every input vector and, to be optimal, it must be an exhaustive search among all the units of the map. A method that tries to improve that search in quasi-organized maps was recently proposed by Koikkalainen et al [2].

- The second one is the number of steps needed for a map to be formed. In this paper, we will present a method for improving the learning speed, by reducing both the number of steps needed to form a map and the average time required to process each input vector.

3. The Improved Learning Method

The new strategy consists in starting the map with very few units and increasing that number progressively until the map reaches its final size. When the number of units increases, the locations (i.e., the internal states, s_i) of the new units are interpolated from the locations of the old units, in such a way that, if the map were already quasi-organized (i.e., completely "unfolded", with the units near their final locations), it remains quasi-organized.

Fig. 2 illustrates the new convergence method for a bidimensional map. The input data are formed by bidimensional vectors representing points uniformly distributed inside a square. The map was started with 3x3 units with random locations (internal states), Fig. 2a. After 1000 steps (i.e., the processing of 1000 input vectors) the map was already well unfolded (Fig. 2b). At this point the number of units in the map was increased by interpolation. The locations of the new 6x6 units are shown in Fig. 2c. This process was then repeated: 1000 presentations of input vectors (Fig. 2d); interpolation to 12x12 units (Fig. 2e); presentation of 1000 input vectors (Fig. 2f).

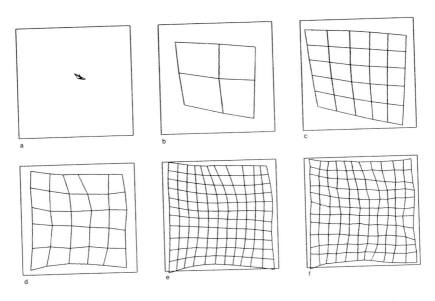

Figure 2. Example of the new map formation process (see text).

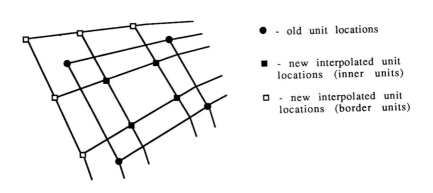

● - old unit locations

■ - new interpolated unit locations (inner units)

□ - new interpolated unit locations (border units)

Figure 3. Example of the interpolation procedure for bidimensional maps.

The interpolation procedure is illustrated in Fig. 3 for a bidimensional map. Consider that we wish to interpolate from an LxL map to a 2Lx2L one. Call s_{ij} the internal state of the unit located in the position ij of the lattice before interpolation, and s'_{ij} the internal state of the unit located in the position ij of the lattice after interpolation. We use for the inner units (i.e., units that are not on the border of the map):

(2a)
$$s'_{2i,2j} = \tfrac{1}{16} \cdot (9\,s_{i,j} + 3\,s_{i,j+1} + 3\,s_{i+1,j} + s_{i+1,j+1})$$
$$s'_{2i,2j+1} = \tfrac{1}{16} \cdot (3\,s_{i,j} + 9\,s_{i,j+1} + s_{i+1,j} + 3\,s_{i+1,j+1})$$
$$s'_{2i+1,2j} = \tfrac{1}{16} \cdot (3\,s_{i,j} + s_{i,j+1} + 9\,s_{i+1,j} + 3\,s_{i+1,j+1})$$
$$s'_{2i+1,2j+1} = \tfrac{1}{16} \cdot (s_{i,j} + 3\,s_{i,j+1} + 3\,s_{i+1,j} + 9\,s_{i+1,j+1})$$

$1 < i,j < L-1$

and for the border units:

first line:

(2b)
$$s'_{1,2j} = \tfrac{1}{16} \cdot (15\,s_{1,j} + 5\,s_{1,j+1} - 3\,s_{2,j} - s_{2,j+1})$$
$$s'_{1,2j+1} = \tfrac{1}{16} \cdot (5\,s_{1,j} + 15\,s_{1,j+1} - s_{2,j} - 3\,s_{2,j+1})$$

$1 < j < L-1$

first column:

(2c)
$$s'_{2i,1} = \tfrac{1}{16} \cdot (15\,s_{i,1} - 3\,s_{i,2} + 5\,s_{i+1,1} - s_{i+1,2})$$
$$s'_{2i+1,1} = \tfrac{1}{16} \cdot (5\,s_{i,1} - s_{i,2} + 15\,s_{i+1,1} - 3\,s_{i+1,2})$$

$1 < i < L-1$

last line:

(2d)
$$s'_{2L,2j} = \tfrac{1}{16} \cdot (5\,s_{L,j+1} + 15\,s_{L,j} - s_{L-1,j+1} - 3\,s_{L-1,j})$$
$$s'_{2L,2j+1} = \tfrac{1}{16} \cdot (15\,s_{L,j+1} + 5\,s_{L,j} - 3\,s_{L-1,j+1} - s_{L-1,j})$$

$1 < j < L-1$

last column:

(2e)
$$s'_{2i,2L} = \tfrac{1}{16} \cdot (15\,s_{i,L} + 5\,s_{i+1,L} - 3\,s_{i,L-1} - s_{i+1,L-1})$$
$$s'_{2i+1,2L} = \tfrac{1}{16} \cdot (5\,s_{i,L} + 15\,s_{i+1,L} - s_{i,L-1} - 3\,s_{i+1,L-1})$$

$1 < i < L-1$

vertex units:

(2f)
$$s'_{1,1} = \tfrac{1}{16} \cdot (25\,s_{1,1} - 5\,s_{1,2} - 5\,s_{2,1} + s_{2,2})$$
$$s'_{1,2L} = \tfrac{1}{16} \cdot (25\,s_{1,L} - 5\,s_{1,L-1} - 5\,s_{2,L} + s_{2,L-1})$$
$$s'_{2L,1} = \tfrac{1}{16} \cdot (25\,s_{L,1} - 5\,s_{L-1,1} - 5\,s_{L,2} + s_{L-1,2})$$
$$s'_{2L,2L} = \tfrac{1}{16} \cdot (25\,s_{L,L} - 5\,s_{L-1,L} - 5\,s_{L,L-1} + s_{L-1,L-1})$$

For N-dimensional maps, similar relations could be derived following the same idea.

Although, in the traditional method, the size of the map remains constant throughout the convergence process, in the new method, the size of the map is variable, starting with very few units, and increasing that number progressively. Another difference of the new paradigm concerns the size of the topological neighbourhoods. In the classical learning paradigm, the size of the topological neighbourhood is supposed to decrease according to some heuristic rule in order to facilitate the "unfolding" of the map. The choice of the heuristic, though not critical in general for the asymptotic convergence phase, is essential to allow the "unfolding" to be performed in useful time. In the new method, on the contrary, we use a fixed size topological neighbourhood (a square of 3x3 units centred on the selected unit). Only near the end of the convergence process, when the map has already reached its final size, the units can be freed if desired (the topological neighbourhood is then restricted to the selected unit itself). The rationale behind this is that for small sized networks the 3x3 neighbourhood is sufficiently large for unfolding it and, when the size of the map increases, as the units get closer to their final locations, the 3x3 neighbourhood becomes sufficiently small to allow the asymptotic convergence to approach the final state, ensuring at the same time the organization of the map.

In order for the improved method to achieve its best results, it is important to eliminate the border effects observed in the classical learning method. The border effect (i.e., the distortion observed near the borders of the map) is due to the fact that the border units do not belong to the same number of topological neighbourhoods in opposite directions: they belong to more topological neighbourhoods corresponding to selected units located towards the inner side of the lattice. This causes an asymmetry in what would be the correct movement of the border units: they are more often "pulled" towards the inner side. To solve that problem, in the new method, each unit belongs to the same number of topological neighbourhoods in opposite directions (Fig. 4). This implies, in particular, that the border units can only belong to the neighbourhood of other border units and, in rectangular lattices, the vertex units are free, and do not belong to the neighbourhood of any other unit. This introduces two new problems: the first is that in the new method, if the map is not completely unfolded before the first interpolation, it would never unfold itself. However, this is not a critical problem. If, as we suggest, we start the map with very few units, the map unfolds itself in a small number of steps (less than one hundred) avoiding the problem just mentioned. For the initial map to unfold itself efficiently we use the traditional definition of topological neighbourhood, so that there are no free units (units that just belong to their own topological neighbourhood). Only after the first interpolation, are the topological neighbourhoods used with the characteristics given above.

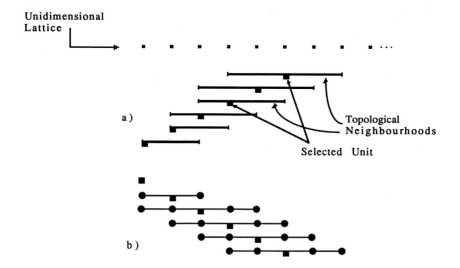

Figure 4. New Topological Neighbourhood definition.
a) Topological neighbourhoods. Each segment represents the topological neighbourhood of the unit represented by the square located on that segment.
b) Topological neighbourhoods to which each unit belongs. In each line, the square represents the unit under consideration, and the circles represent the other units to whose neighbourhood it belongs. Note that this agrees with the neighbourhoods in a), and that each unit belongs to the same number of neighbourhoods in both directions.

The second problem is related to the fact that if a certain unit belongs to a smaller number of topological neighbourhoods than another unit, the adaptation step size for the first one must be different from the adaptation step size for the second one. Consider a rectangular lattice in which the size of the topological neighbourhood is 3x3 units centred on the selected unit. Then each inner unit belongs to 9 different neighbourhoods, each border unit that is not a vertex unit belongs to 3 different neighbourhoods and the vertex units belong only to their own neighbourhood. Therefore, the adaptation step size for the vertex units must be 9 times larger than the adaptation step size for the inner units, and the adaptation step size for the other border units must be 3 times larger than the adaptation step size for the inner units, in order for all the units to be "pulled", in average, with the same strength.

4. Evaluation Tests

The evaluation of the improved learning method was performed with two distinct perspectives: finding how it behaved when exposed to input data with different statistical distributions, and comparing its performance with the traditional learning method.

A number of tests were performed with bidimensional nets and input data with different statistical distributions:

- Input data uniformly distributed inside a square.

- Input data uniformly distributed inside a triangle.

- Input data with a gaussian distribution.

- Input data with a distribution obtained by the superposition of 10 different gaussian distributions (Fig. 5).

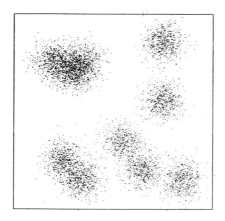

Figure 5. Input data distribution obtained from the superposition of 10 different gaussian distributions.

The size of the nets used in the tests was 48x48 units. For comparable situations, the tests were performed with the same training set, and the same test set, distinct from the training set but with the same statistical distribution. The size of both the training and the test sets was 10.000 input patterns. The degree of organization of the net was measured by averaging, for all the patterns in the test set, the distance to the closest unit in the learned map.

In both methods, the adaptation step size, ß, was decreased according to the rule:

$$\begin{array}{ll} ß(t) = ß_{init} & 0 < t < N/3 \\ ß(t) = ß_{init} \cdot \emptyset & N/3 < t < 2N/3 \\ ß(t) = ß_{init} \cdot \emptyset^2 & 2N/3 < t < N \end{array}$$

(3)

where, $ß_{init}$ is the initial adaptation step size, N is the total number of steps and $0 < \emptyset < 1$ is the decreasing factor.

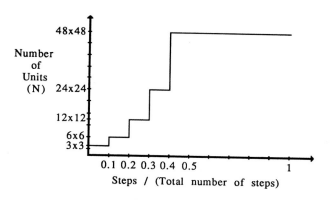

Figure 6. New Method - Evolution of the size of the map.

In the tests performed with the new method, the maps were started with 3x3 units. After some preliminary tests we decided to increase the number of units when 1/10, 2/10, 3/10 and 4/10 of the total number of input patterns had been processed, until the map reached its final size of 48x48 units (Fig. 6). After that, when half (5/10) of the input patterns had been processed, the topological neighbourhood, which had been kept constant until then (3x3 units centred in the selected unit), was reduced to the selected unit itself.

In the tests performed with the traditional method, the net always kept the size 48x48, and the topological neighbourhood was started with 31x31 units centred in the selected unit. The size of that neighbourhood was reduced to 13x13, 7x7, 5x5, 3x3 and 1x1 when respectively 1/4, 1/3, 1/2, 2/3 and 4/5 of the total number of input patterns had been processed (Fig. 7).

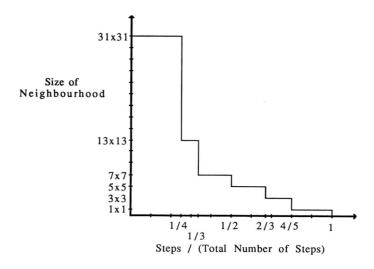

Figure 7. Evolution law for the Topological Neighbourhood size for the traditional method.

The convergence time (i.e., the CPU time in one processor of an Alliant FX/8 computer) was measured for each test. Tables 1, 2 and 3 and Figs. 8, 9 and 10 show the results of the tests, with the new and the traditional method, for input data with three different statistical distributions. The values of the parameters β_{init} and ϕ used in the tests, were chosen after some preliminary tests, among the ones that yielded the best results. As can be seen from these results, the new method always achieved better results, in less time, than the traditional method.

Number of Steps - N	CPU time New Method	CPU time Traditional Method	Average Dist. New Method	Average Dist. Traditional Method
5000	82	130	4,8539	11,2046
10000	165	262	4,7781	7,5769
20000	328	526	4,7113	6,0481
50000	822	1319	4,6184	5,1781
100000	1642	2611	4,3456	4,7302
200000	3288	5218	4,4665	4,4363
400000	6721	10407	3,9525	4,1274

Table 1. Results of evaluation tests for the case of input data uniformly distributed inside a triangle. The parameters used were: $\beta_{init}=0.05$ and $\phi=0.7$.

Number of Steps - N	CPU time New Method	CPU time Traditional Method	Average Dist. New Method	Average Dist. Traditional Method
5000	83	131	8,4804	20,8533
10000	165	261	8,1823	13,9322
20000	331	524	8,0099	10,701
50000	826	1315	7,7985	9,0113
100000	1667	2632	7,5259	8,2459
200000	3324	5321	7,1682	7,5789
400000	6643	10483	6,7188	6,9517

Table 2. Results of evaluation tests for the case of input data uniformly distributed inside a square. The parameters used were: $\beta_{init}=0.05$ and $\phi=0.7$.

Number of Steps - N	CPU time New Method	CPU time Traditional Method	Average Dist. New Method	Average Dist. Traditional Method
5000	82	131	4,2574	10,3796
10000	164	262	4,2628	7,3221
20000	333	524	3,9354	5,7
50000	821	1323	3,7633	4,6095
100000	1654	2640	3,5489	4,2014
200000	3322	5141	3,4448	3,8122
400000	6610	10278	3,3093	3,4913

Table 3. Results of evaluation tests for the case of input data with a gaussian distribution. The parameters used were: $\beta_{init}=0.05$ and $\phi=0.7$.

Uniform inside a Triangle

New Method ◆

Traditional Method ◇

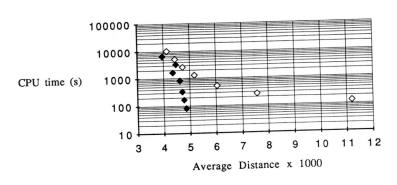

Figure 8. Results of evaluation tests for the case of input data uniformly distributed inside a triangle. The parameters used were: $\beta_{init}=0.05$ and $\phi=0.7$.

Uniform inside a Square

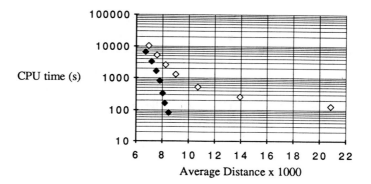

Figure 9. Results of evaluation tests for the case of input data uniformly distributed inside a square. The parameters used were: $\beta_{init}=0.05$ and $\phi=0.7$.

Gaussian Distribution

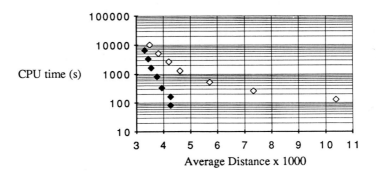

Figure 10. Results of evaluation tests for the case of input data with a gaussian distribution. The parameters used were: $\beta_{init}=0.05$ and $\phi=0.7$.

To thoroughly evaluate the gain in convergence time, a number of extra tests were performed for the case of input data with the distribution shown in Fig.5, varying the values of β_{init} and ϕ. Tables 4 and 5 show results of these tests performed with both the new method (Table 4) and the traditional method (Table 5). The best results for each method are plotted against each other in Fig. 11, where we can see that the new method shows an improvement in learning speed of about one order of magnitude for well organized maps (average distance around 6.0). For less well organized maps, the improvements are even bigger.

In a few tests made to evaluate the improvements in larger networks, with sizes 192x192 and 384x384, the gain in learning speed was, as expected, even bigger. For smaller networks, where this gain was not so big, the map still attained a quasi-organized form much earlier, compared to the time it would take with the traditional training method.

Number of Steps - N	Average Dist. $\beta_{init}=0,04$	CPU time $\phi=0,7$	Average Dist. $\beta_{init}=0,02$	CPU time $\phi=0,7$	Average Dist. $\beta_{init}=0,08$	CPU time $\phi=0,7$
5000	6,0472	83	6,1226	81	5,9335	83
10000	5,6952	164	5,8787	164	5,7736	165
20000	5,4495	329	5,597	324	5,4072	331
50000	5,2217	816	5,3094	806	5,0662	831
100000	5,015	1622	5,0807	1612	4,9347	1654
200000	4,9506	3267	5,1321	3222	4,6986	3285

Table 4. Results of evaluation tests, performed with the new method, for the case of input data with a distribution shown in Fig. 5.

Number of Steps - N	Average Dist. ßinit=0.05	CPU time ø=0.5	Average Dist. ßinit=0.05	CPU time ø=0.7	Average Dist. ßinit=0.1	CPU time ø=0.7
5000	15,1163	128	12,7679	130	9,7893	130
10000	10,6669	268	9,3197	259	7,7523	274
20000	8,0865	515	7,5195	533	6,7883	522
50000	6,697	1288	6,2265	1321	5,7573	1367
100000	6,2394	2579	5,6782	2607	5,2815	2602
200000	5,6011	5260	5,1592	5234	4,7771	5263

Table 5. Results of evaluation tests, performed with the traditional method, for the case of input data with a distribution shown in Fig. 5.

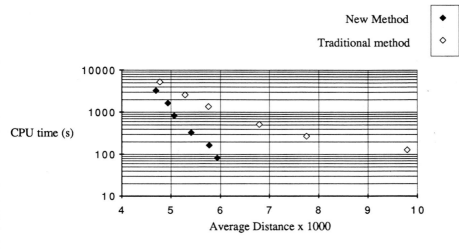

Superposition of 10 Gaussian Distributions

New Method   ◆

Traditional method   ◇

CPU time (s)

Average Distance x 1000

Figure 11. Comparison of the best results obtained with the new and the traditional methods, for the case of input data with a distribution shown in Fig. 5.

The fact that the map attains a quasi-organized form much sooner has significant advantages allowing, for instance, the use of the acceleration technique proposed by Koikkalainen et al [2], very early in the convergence process. The combined use of that technique with the learning method proposed here, should provide further improvements in learning speed.

5. Conclusions

We have proposed a new version of the learning method for Topological Maps of Patterns, which improves the learning speed by about one order of magnitude, for the examples presented. This new method consists in starting the map with very few units and progressively increasing that number by interpolation. This technique is very efficient in the map unfolding phase, and also yields significant improvements in the asymptotic convergence phase. It can be advantageously combined with the acceleration technique proposed by Koikkalainen et al [2].

References

[1] Kohonen, T. "Clustering, Taxonomy, and Topological Maps of Patterns", Proc. 6th Annual Conf. on Pattern Recognition, pp 114-128, Los Angeles, 1982.

[2] Koikkalainen, P., Lampinen, J., and Oja, E. "Fast Implementations for the Kohonen Self-Organizing Learning Algorithm", Neuro-Computing: Algorithms, Architectures and Applications, F. Fogelman-Soulié (ed.), Springer-Verlag, Berlin, 1989.

[3] Rodrigues, J.S. and Almeida. L.B. "Improving the Learning Speed in Topological Maps of Patterns", INESC Technical Report, Jan. 1990.

NEURAL NETWORKS: Advances and Applications
E. Gelenbe (Editor)
© Elsevier Science Publishers B.V. (North-Holland), 1991

Performance of Higher Order Neural Networks in Invariant Recognition

Stefanos Kollias, Andreas Stafylopatis and Andreas Tirakis *
National Technical University of Athens
Computer Science Division
157 73, Zographou, Athens, Greece

Abstract

The use of higher-order neurons for invariant recognition of patterns and images is examined in this paper. Appropriate forms of such networks are proposed, which can provide invariance with respect to transformations, such as scale, translation and rotation, as well as other types of distortions. Various techniques for efficiently training and designing such networks are presented and their performance is illustrated using the problem of digit recognition.

1 Invariant Pattern Recognition

A great part of the information processed in real life is in the form of complex patterns. Consequently, the capability of automatic pattern recognition is indispensable to modern systems dealing with advanced information processing. It would be desirable that such systems had the additional property of recognizing patterns, without being influenced by distortions or transformations. For example, in image processing, we might want to recognize the presence of a pattern in the field of view independent of the position or orientation of the pattern or its size. Similarly, in the recognition of handwritten letters, our interest is the

---

*This work has been partly supported by ESPRIT Project No. 2092 (ANNIE)

structure within the letter rather than the size or location or orientation of that letter.

Invariant pattern recognition is one of the hardest families of problems in the theory of perception and in computer vision. The problem of invariant recognition is to understand how our perception of an object remains unaffected in spite of the considerable changes that the retinal image of the object may undergo [9]. Thus, for the practical application of neural networks, there is a need for models that are capable of object recognition, invariant under certain transformations [30]. Among the most important of these transformations are translation, scale, rotation and distortion (usualy perspective distortion).

One approach to the problem of invariant pattern recognition consists in deriving the functional characteristics of appropriate image representations. The internal structure of these representations can be used to provide invariant recognition when presented to a suitable system. The problem is in finding appropriate transformations of the original input space, such that the resulting representations have the desired properties. Neural network techniques based upon this principle are usually adaptations of existing conventional techniques, in the sense that invariance is obtained by preprocessing of the input and then the transformed input is presented to the network, which performs a classical recognition job [22, 35, 36]. These techniques involve, in general, two components : a transformation or preprocessing part providing invariant representation and a neural network yielding the final recognition. Common transformation techniques include the method of moments, Fourier and related mappings.

Other approaches are derived from biological concepts and attempt to implement physiological mechanisms in artificial neural systems. One approach, which has raised significant interest in the last years, is the 'Labelled Graph Matching' technique. Under this general title we refer to the work done by C. Von der Malsburg and E. Bienenstock in the direction of invariant pattern recognition [4, 5, 6, 26]. The basic idea is biologically plausible and is based upon the belief that the incapability of conventional neural networks to face the problem of invariance is linked to the format of knowledge representation. The key issue is the notion of dynamical connectionism, which consists in manipulating states of connectivity rather than states of activity. From a theoretical point of view, this model is capable of full invariant recognition, but its complexity and time requirements do not permit its implementation. However it suggests a strategy for designing systems capable of limited pattern recognition.

The work of K. Fukushima has been for many years in the main line of researh focusing on the problem of invariant pattern recognition. The models developed by Fukushima are based on the principle of receptive fields and are deduced from physiological evidence. His main model is the Neocognitron [10, 12, 13, 14], which extends the Cognitron originally developed in the 70s. His latest work copes with the problems of associative recall, selective attention and segmentation [11]. Although Fukushima's models appear to have many desirable properties and abilities, the main theoretical issues involved in their construction and manipulation seem rather intractable.

Other techniques are based on the exhaustive training of neural networks over a set of input patterns containing all possible transformed versions of the patterns. It has, however, been argued that a drawback of multilayered feedforward networks, which are generally used for this purpose, is the fact that they take no advantage of any inherent relationships between the input nodes of the network. As a consequence, they require a great deal of training and they produce solutions that are specific to particular training sets. Moreover, it has not been evident, whether hidden units can represent feature sets, which are efficient, or even sufficient for classification, in invariant pattern recognition applications [33]. For this reason, it has been proposed to use higher order networks [27, 15, 16].

The increased complexity of such networks can be overcome, by building invariance into them, using information about the expected relationships between pairs of input values [31]. Consequently, higher order neural networks provide a promising solution to invariant pattern recognition, because feature extraction is functionally built into the network architecture. Apart from invariant recognition, the use of higher order networks has been addressed in several contexts, including implementations which intend to increase the storage capacity of Hopfield type associative memories [17].

2   Theoretical Background

Neural networks with high order interactions have been explored in several contexts, in an attempt to overcome the limitations of typical first order neural models. Higher order units have been shown to have important computational capabilities and to be appropriate for the encoding of a priori knowledge. We are going to discuss, here, several issues concerning the theoretical justification of approaches involving higher order invariant representation.

Our presentation will focus mainly on the work by Maxwell et al. [27, 15, 16], which contains important results for certain types of invariance. The idea is that, if it is known in advance that a problem possesses a certain set of invariances, it is possible to solve it, by constructing a network which already incorporates these invariances, requiring therefore a rather small learning phase.

One approach for implementing transformation invariances in neural networks is based on averaging the input of each unit over an appropriate transformation group [27], so that all features that are equivalent under the transformation group are treated equivalently by the invariant units. This invariance constraint restricts the possible responses of the system to a given set of inputs, and, in many cases, leads to a reduction of the correlation matrix order, thus reducing the number of high order terms required to implement the desired function. In this sense, learning can be represented as a process of imposing a set of correlations, that express the invariance structure of the problem, into the structure of the network. The method of averaging over transformation groups was first presented by McCulloch and Pitts [28], who considered the hypothesis that some form of this averaging process is also the method by which the brain learns invariant properties. Later Minsky and Papert [29] used similar methods in a group-invariance theorem to demonstrate the limitations of perceptrons.

A slightly different formulation of the same approach is developed in [16] without making any appeal to group theoretical concepts. Consider a transformation on the input space and suppose that the output of a unit is required to be invariant with respect to this tranformation. Application of this requirement provides a set of equations, which yield constraints on the interconection weights and thus imply a particular structure for the network.

Let us consider the output y_i of the i-th unit in a network of order M, as shown in Figure 1, which is computed as follows

$$
\begin{aligned}
y_i(\mathbf{x}) \;=\; & f(w_i^0 + \sum_j w_i^1(j)x_j + \\
& \sum_j \sum_k w_i^2(j,k)x_j x_k + \cdots \\
& \sum_{j_1} \cdots \sum_{j_M} w_i^M(j_1,\ldots,j_M)x_{j_1}\cdots x_{j_M})
\end{aligned}
\tag{1}
$$

where $\mathbf{x}$ is the input pattern applied at unit positions, $w_i^m(j_1,\ldots,j_m)$ is the weight connecting the product of m input units, i.e. $j_1,\ldots,j_m$, to the i-th output unit and $f(u)$ is some threshold or sigmoid function. The summations extend over the input space and thus the limits are defined by the problem.

In terms of the notation of Eq. (1), the output of a unit is invariant with respect to the transformation g on the input pattern if

$$y_i(g[\mathbf{x}]) = y_i(\mathbf{x}) \tag{2}$$

2.1 Translation Invariance

To illustrate the method, we first consider the derivation of weight constraints for the case of translation invariance. If g is a translation of the input pattern x_j by m positions, we have

$$g[x_j] = x_{j+m} \tag{3}$$

Since $\mathbf{x}$ can be any pattern, an application of Eq. (2) imposes term-by-term equality in the argument of the threshold function f. Hence, we have from Eq. (1) for the first and second order terms:

$$\sum w_i^1(j)x_j = \sum w_i^1(j)x_{j+m} \tag{4}$$

$$\sum\sum w_i^2(j,k)x_jx_k = \sum\sum w_i^2(j,k)x_{j+m}x_{k+m} \tag{5}$$

If we make the substitutions $j \to j - m$, $k \to k - m$, etc., we obtain

$$\sum w_i^1(j)x_j = \sum w_i^1(j-m)x_j \tag{6}$$

$$\sum\sum w_i^2(j,k)x_jx_k = \sum\sum w_i^2(j-m,k-m)x_jx_k \tag{7}$$

The limits of the summations on the right-hand side must be adjusted according to the change of variables. It can be easily verified that, if the limits are infinite or if a grid with periodic boundary conditions is considered, then the limits can be set equal on both sides. (Simulation results reported in [16] indicate that the method works satisfactorily even when the ranges of summation are not identical.) It follows that the weight functions must be equal and their form implies that

$$w_i^1(j) \quad = \quad w_i^1(j - m) \tag{8}$$

$$w_i^2(j, k) \quad = \quad w_i^2(j - m, k - m) \tag{9}$$

These equations imply that the first order weight is independent of the input position, and depends only upon the output position i, whereas the second order weight is a function of vector differences only, i.e. the weights for equally spaced input position pairs are set equal:

$$w_i^1(j) \quad = \quad w_i^1 \tag{10}$$

$$w_i^2(j, k) \quad = \quad w_i^2(j - k) \tag{11}$$

If N input units are fully connected to an output unit, the above requirement reduces the number of second order weights from order N^2 to order N, since weights correspond only to differences of indeces (or distances of positions) and not to every pair of combinations. This advantage gets more important, as the number of fully-connected output units increases. In most cases, the second order terms are sufficient to implement translation invariance.

2.2   Scale Invariance

For the case of transformation of scale consider a scale operator g such that:

$$g[x_j] = x_{aj} \tag{12}$$

where a is the scale factor. Application of the same procedure to this transformation leads to the following constraints on the weights:

$$w_i^1(j) \quad = \quad w_i^1(j/a) \tag{13}$$

$$w_i^2(j,k) = w_i^2(j/a, k/a) \qquad (14)$$

$$(15)$$

In order to determine the functional form of the weights, any solution that satisfies the constraint may be used. (This freedom increases with the order of the weights.) Consider a scale transformation for a two-dimensional system in rectangular coordinates (u,v), so that position j is expressed as the vector $j = [u_j, v_j]$. A set of solutions to the second order weight constraint is:

$$w_i^2(u_j, v_j, u_k, v_k) = w_i^2(u_j/v_j, u_k/v_k) \qquad (16)$$

$$w_i^2(u_j, v_j, u_k, v_k) = w_i^2(u_j/u_k, v_j/v_k) \qquad (17)$$

$$w_i^2(u_j, v_j, u_k, v_k) = w_i^2((u_j - u_k)/(v_j - v_k)) \qquad (18)$$

2.3 Rotation Invariance

A third example of geometric transformation is the case of rotation about the origin considering a two-dimensional space in polar coordinates (r, θ). One can readily show that the weight constraints are satisfied if

$$w_i^1(r_j, \theta_j) = w_i^1(r_j) \qquad (19)$$

$$w_i^2(r_j, r_k, \theta_j, \theta_k) = w_i^2(r_j, r_k, \theta_j - \theta_k) \qquad (20)$$

The form of the results reminds of the results for translation invariance, which is not uncommon, since seemingly different problems often have similar constraint requirements.

2.4 Combination of Transformations

An interesting issue concerns combinations of invariances, e.g. scale and translation. In this case, one should investigate the effect of the order in which the transformations are applied. Consider first the case of translation by m positions, followed by a change of scale by a factor a; the constraints on the weights of first and second order are:

$$w_i^1(j) \;=\; w_i^1((j-m)/a) \tag{21}$$

$$w_i^2(j,k) \;=\; w_i^2((j-m)/a,(k-m)/a) \tag{22}$$

while for scale followed by translation the constraints are:

$$w_i^1(j) \;=\; w_i^1((j/a)-m) \tag{23}$$

$$w_i^2(j,k) \;=\; w_i^2((j/a)-m,(k/a)-m) \tag{24}$$

If we consider the two-dimensional case in rectangular coordinates (u,v), we can see that the solution

$$w_i^2(u_j,v_j,u_k,v_k) = w_i^2((u_j-u_k)/(v_j-v_k)) \tag{25}$$

satisfies both cases, i.e. is invariant to scale and translation, being independent of the order. In the general case, however, the order is significant. The above equation implies that $w_i^2(j,k)$ is set equal to $w_i^2(j',k')$, if the slope of the line connecting node positions j and k is equal to the slope of the line drawn between j' and k'. An object represented on a two-dimensional space contains lines of different slopes. These slopes do not change when the object is translated in position or scaled in size, as long as it is not rotated.

Let us next consider the case of a change of scale by a factor a and rotation about the origin by an amount φ for a two-dimensional system in polar coordinates (r,θ). In this case, the order of transformation makes no difference. The weight constraints up to second order are:

$$w_i^1(r_j,\theta_j) \;=\; w_i^1(r_j/a,\theta_j-\varphi) \tag{26}$$

$$w_i^2(r_j,\theta_j,r_k,\theta_k) \;=\; w_i^2(r_j/a,\theta_j-\varphi,r_k/a,\theta_k-\varphi) \tag{27}$$

We observe that the first order weight is independent of the input, whereas a convenient solution to the second order onstraint will be:

$$w_i^2(r_j, \theta_j, r_k, \theta_k) = w_i^2(r_j/r_k, \theta_j - \theta_k) \qquad (28)$$

This implies that with second order weights, one can construct a unit that is insensitive to changes is scale and rotation of the input space. This constraint can be interpreted by noting that $w_i^2(j, k)$ is set equal to $w_i^2(j', k')$, if the triangles $0, j, k)$ and $(0, j', k')$ are similar, where 0 denotes the origin.

Simultaneous invariance with respect to translation, scale and rotation can be achieved using third order connections. Combining the above described cases leads to the following straightforward formulation of the constraint: the weights $w_i^3(j, k, l)$ and $w_i^3(j', k', l')$ are set equal if the corresponding triangles (j, k, l) and (j', k', l') are similar as shown in Figure 2. Any three points within an object represented in two dimensions define a triangle with included angles (a, b, c). When the object is translated, scaled and rotated the three points at the same relative positions within the object still form a triangle with the same angles. We should note that the order of the angles matters for rotation invariance, whereas, if the order is not taken into account, reflection invariance is also obtained.

3   Higher-Order Neural Network Architectures and Implementations

Implementations of higher order networks, which are reported in the litterature concern Hopfield type associative networks [27] and feedforward error correction networks [16, 31, 32]. In general, building invariances into the network architecture helps to overcome the problem of combinatorial explosion of higher order terms. The combinatorial explosion of higher order terms is a major drawback in the calculation of weights, which rapidly becomes impractical as the order M of units increases. Several methods can be applied to keep the calculation at an acceptable level. Such methods either truncate the order, i.e. use a small value of M, or restrict the higher order connections to a window around each neuron than to the whole pattern, or reduce the summations to a sparse set of terms, usually generated randomly. In general, experimental results suggest that keeping only second or third order is sufficient for many applications.

As has already been explained, higher order networks can be used for invariant, with respect to scale, translation and rotation, recognition of patterns or images. Simple experiments, applying such networks for the solution of the T-C problem, have been reported in the litterature [31, 32]. However, the ability of higher order netorks to provide solutions to more complex real-life problems, especially in cases where invariance with respect to other types of distortion, such as random or systematic noise, is required, is still an open problem. The investigation of the capabilities of these networks in such cases is the main purpose of the rest of the paper. It should be mentioned that the capabilities of higher order networks are closely related to their specific architecture, as well as to the learning algorithm used for their training. A third order network, which can ensure invariance with respect to scale, translation and rotation, is considered in the rest of the paper.

3.1 A Higher Order Multilayered Architecture

In the simplest case, a single layer higher order network is used to perform non-linear separation of a set of input images or patterns. In many applications the inputs take only binary values. By setting the network weights initially to zero, a simple perceptron learning rule can be then used, where each weight is updated as follows

$$\Delta w_{ijkl} = (d_i - y_i)x_jx_kx_l \tag{29}$$

where w_{ijkl} denotes here the weight of the third order connection from units j, k, l to output unit i, d_i is the desired output, y_i the actual output and x denotes the input image. Based on the binary nature of the data, the above perceptron rule is efficient and can lead to rapid convergence. The use of backpropagation has also been proposed, as an alternative to perceptron learning [16], for the training of such networks.

A scheme, that can be very powerful for recognizing patterns, shapes, or images, being invariant to transformations, such as scale, translation and rotation, or other types of distortions, is described next. It is based on a combination of first and higher order networks, as is, for example, shown in Figure 3. A multilayered network is shown in this Figure, the first hidden layer of which is connected to the input layer by third order connections, sharing therefore the invariant properties of higher order networks. On the other hand, the output and the other, if any, hidden layers use only first order connections. This scheme has, therefore, the form of a general feedforward network that achieves invariance through an input space transformation, using higher order networks. Based on results concerning the capabilities of multilayered networks [2], [24], it is expected that the number of distorted versions of the same pattern, which can be loaded to such a network (i.e. the number of different patterns, or images, which the network is able to distinguish), will be larger than in the case of a single-layer higher order network. This is investigated further, in the examples given in the following Section. It is shown next that the weights of the interconnections in the higher order part of the resulting network, can be updated during its training, using an extension of the normal backpropagation equations.

Let us assume that the input to the network is in the form of a two-dimensional image, raster-scanned line by line. Let us also assume that backpropagation is used to train the network shown in Figure 3, by minimizing the sum of squared errors between the desired and actual outputs of neurons in the output layer. The outputs y_i of the higher order neurons belonging to the first hidden layer are computed as follows

$$y_i = f(\sum_j \sum_k \sum_l w_{ijkl} x_j x_k x_l) \tag{30}$$

Following the discussion of the previous Section, the updating of the weights w_{ijkl}, connecting the input products to the higher order neurons, should be performed under the following constraint

$$w_{ijkl} = w_{iabc} = w_{icab} = w_{ibca} \tag{31}$$

This constraint refers to all triplets of points within the image, which define a triangle with included angles (a, b, c), as shown in Figure 2. Introducing the above constraint in the computation of y_i, we get the following expression

$$y_i = f\left[\sum_{j,k,l/(j,k,l)\in A} w_{ijkl} \sum_{j',k',l'} x_{j'} x_{k'} x_{l'} \right] \tag{32}$$

where variables j', k', l' refer to all input triplets, forming similar triangles with the triplet indexed by j, k, l and the model region A contains only input triplets j, k, l which do not form similar triangles with each other. The above operation of each neuron is the same as in first order networks, the only difference being that it contains products of input values in place of single input values. This operation can be implemented by first searching for all similar triangles in the input image, forming at the same time model region A and computing the required sums of input products. Following this input space transformation, the general form of backpropagation learning algorithm [33] can be used to train both the higher and the first order part of the proposed network architecture. Two topics, which are still under investigation, are the convergence properties of backpropagation, as well as its generalization abilities, when training multilayered networks. These topics are examined in the next Subsection, applied to higher order networks.

3.2 Learning and Generalization in Higher Order Networks

The two most important features of supervised learning algorithms in training feedforward networks are the amount of required learning time and the generalization performance. As far learning speed is concerned, we propose next a version of backpropagation, which can train multilayered higher order networks efficiently. Furthermore, it is usually accepted that good generalization performance on real-world problems cannot be achieved, unless some a-priori knowledge about the task is built into the system. The building of knowledge, related to usage of higher order networks, is also examined in the following.

3.2.1 The Learning Algorithm

Backpropagation converges slowly, even for medium sized network problems. This fact results from the usually large dimension of the weight space and from the particular shape of the error surface. Oscillation between the sides of deep and narrow valleys, for example, is a well known case where gradient descent provides poor convergence rates. The search for faster and more robust training methods must meet two requirements: simplicity, in order to reduce the total computational load, and locality, in order to maintain compatibility with distributed hardware architectures.

A technique that is currently used for speeding up the learning rate lets each synapse have its own learning rate parameter, increasing or decreasing its value according to the number of sign changes observed in the partial derivative of the error function with respect to the corresponding weight [21]. The basic idea of this technique is that if the sign of a certain component of the gradient remains constant for several iterations, it corresponds to a smooth variation of the error surface; the learning rate for this component should, therefore, be increased. On the other hand, if the sign of some component changes in several consecutive iterations, the learning rate parameter should be decreased to avoid oscillation.

A simple and effective way of implementing this idea, in the case of higher order neurons, is to adapt the learning rate parameter μ_{ijkl} in the weight update equation

$$w_{ijkl}(n) = w_{ijkl}(n - 1) + \mu_{ijkl}(n)\partial_{ijkl}E(n) \tag{33}$$

where $\mu_{ijkl}(n)$ is the specific learning rate parameter of the $ijkl$-th synapse at iteration n, according to the following rule

$$\mu_{ijkl}(n) = d_m \, \mu_{ijkl}(n - 1) \tag{34}$$

for $m = 1, 2$, with $m = 1$ corresponding to the case where the derivative of the minimized error function E has the same sign in the $(n - 1)$ and n iterations and with $m = 2$ implying the contrary. In general d_1 is slightly greater than unity (between 1.1 and 1.3) and d_2 slightly below $1/d_1$. The above equations imply an exponential increase and decrease of the learning rate parameter [1].

An interesting feature of the method, proposed in this paper, is its combination with higher order variants of backpropagation that use an approximation of the Hessian matrix of the error function in the minimization procedure [25]. These variants are not believed to bring a tremendous increase in learning speed, but converge reliably, without requiring extensive adjustments of the learning parameter. In this paper, we investigate the improvement in learning speed produced by the combination of the above-mentioned acceleration technique with a second order least squares backpropagation variant, which is based on the Marquardt-Levenberg optimization technique, described in [23]. This variant has several interesting advantages over standard non-linear optimization techniques, such as the method of conjugate gradient, since on the one hand scales quite well and on the other hand makes use of the analytical expression, and not of an estimate, of the diagonal Hessian matrix. As will be shown in the next Section, the results obtained, indicate that the combined approach converges much faster than either the original backpropagation scheme or its variant.

3.2.2 Generalization Issues

Generalization may be viewed as the main property that should be sought when designing a network, since it determines the amount of data needed to train the network, so that it provides a correct response when a pattern outside of the training set is presented at its input. In the early advent of neural networks, it was assumed that there was not much need for modelling the underlying problem and that an artificial neural network solution could be obtained instead, by training from empirical data, with little or no a-priori information about the application. Recent studies, however, indicate that the right network architecture is fundamental for a good solution to exist. Nevertheless, this is in general a difficult task. Other results, [19],[34], indicate that the likelihood of correct generalization depends on the size of the hypothesis space, i.e. the total number of networks being considered, the size of the solution space (the set of networks which give good generalization) and the number of training examples. If good generalization is required, when the generality of the network is increased, the number of training examples should also be increased [3] .

Since overfitting effects are due to oversized networks, an increase in the likelihood of correct generalization can be obtained, by minimizing the number of free parameters, thus reducing the size of the network. Some techniques, such as 'weight decay', dynamically delete 'useless' connections 'on line', during training, penalizing big networks with many parameters [7],[18],[20]. A drawback of such techniques is that they generally slow down the convergence of the method. Another technique is *weight sharing*. This technique imposes equality constraints among the connection strengths, in the sense that several interconnections in the network are controlled by a single weight. Weight sharing can be used for shift-invariant feature extraction. It should be mentioned that in this paper we have used the principle of weight sharing to obtain rotational invariance, through third order networks. We achieved this, by letting all input nodes that form similar triangles be controlled by the same weight.

In the previous Subsection we considered a fully connected higher-order network, where the input to each neuron was the whole image or pattern. Recent results [24], [8] however, indicate that any a-priori knowledge about the task should be built into the network, in order to achieve better generalization. In such a case, a network could be designed, which would extract local features in the first hidden layer and would combine them in the following layers to form more complex features. Higher order neurons could also be used in such a network, so that the extracted features at each level be invariant with respect to scale, translation, or rotation. These aspects are discussed in the example presented in the next Section.

4 An Example: Digit Recognition

The following experimental results are presented to illustrate the performance of higher-order network architectures in the invariant recognition of handdrawn numerals. The problem described is not a real world application, but is sufficient for our purpose, since it allows extensive tests of learning speed and generalization performance.

The set of data, that has been considered, was composed of examples of numerals represented as binary images of different sizes, starting from 5 pixels by 5 pixels, up to 10 pixels by 10 pixels. The training set was formed by choosing half of the examples at random. The remaining ones, as well as transformed, i.e. translated, scaled and rotated versions of the training examples, were used in the test set. Figure 4 shows some of the training examples, while Figure 5 shows some examples from the test set. It can be easily seen that both sets contain a number of distorted patterns of each numeral. Thus they permit an investigation of the performance of the networks in the recognition of generally distorted versions of the training patterns. For reasons that will be explained later, a standard window size of six pixels by six pixels was used in both the training and test data sets.

A single layer fully connected network, with 10 output units, was used first to learn the training set of numerals. The standard form of backpropagation has been initially used for this purpose. The network has succesfully learned the set, which implies that the problem is linearly separable. However, its generalization performance was only 73 per cent, in the test set consisting of distorted versions of the numerals. Moreover, its performance became worse, when transformed versions of the training data were used in the test set, especially when the results of the transformation (e.g. rotation) were more evident. Similar results, concerning generalization, were obtained when using the perceptron learning algorithm instead of backpropagation. For this reason we inserted a hidden layer, consisting of 12 hidden units, fully connected to the input and output layers. By using standard backpropagation (a value of $\mu = 0.3$ and a momentum term 0.9 were chosen as more appropriate), the network was able to learn all training data, i.e. provide an output error of less than 10 per cent, in 120 iterations (i.e. passes through its data set). We then used the proposed second order variant of backpropagation to train this network. Convergence was much faster, as is shown in Figure 6, where the learning speed of both algorithms, measured as the logarithm of the minimized error function, is examined with respect to the number of iterations. What is also important is that the generalization performance of the network was, in this case, increased to 86 per cent over the test set. However, generalization continued to be poor in the case of transformed versions of the training data.

We then used the multilayerd network, shown in Figure 3, to handle the problem of invariant recognition of the handdrawn numerals. In this network, the output layer also consisted of 10 units, while the hidden layer consisted of 12 higher-order units, each of which was fully connected to the input layer. As has been explained in Section 3, standard backpropagation can be used for training the network, if each hidden unit is viewed as being connected to every group of input pixel triplets, forming similar triangles, by a single weight. Implementing this technique, we observed that the generalization performance of the network remained constant over distorted versions of the training data, but became very good in recognizing transformed versions of the training data, where it reached 100 per cent. In this case the training using standard backpropagation (a value of $\mu = 0.1$ and the same momentum term were chosen as more appropriate) was slower, being able to learn all data after 1400 iterations. However, the second-order variant of it managed to learn the training set in 40 iterations. A comparison of the learning speed of both versions of backpropagation is shown in Figure 7.

It should be mentioned that as the size of the input image is augmented, the number of groups of similar to each other triangles is increased as well. Moreover, the number of weights w_{ijkl}, connecting the sums of input triplet products to the hidden units, equals the above-mentioned number of groups; thus, the number of weights is also increased. Table 1 shows the number of groups which are computed in the case of images with sizes from 3 pixels by 3 pixels, up to 8 pixels by 8 pixels. It can be seen, that the number of weights, as well as the number of computations for selecting similar triangles, will become excessive for large input image sizes. In case of large sizes, it is, therefore, better to use higher-order neurons with small-sized receptive fields, so as to reduce the number of connection weights. This usage is consistent with recent results on the design of multilayered networks using constraints for reducing the number of weights.

A constrained shift-invariant network, designed for recognizing handwritten numerals has been recently proposed in [25]. To achieve shift-invariance, this network uses hidden layers composed of several planes (feature maps). All units in a plane are designed so as to perform two-dimensional convolutions over their input image and share the same set of weights, thereby detecting the same feature at different locations. Following this approach, the network shown in Figure 8 was designed, having ten outputs and being fed by an 8 pixel by 8 pixel input image. The network has two hidden layers, labeled H_1, H_2 respectively. H_1 is composed of two 4 by 4 feature maps. Each unit in the feature map receives its input from a 3 by 3 neighborhood on the input plane. Moreover, for units in the feature map that are one unit apart, their receptive fields in the input layer are two pixels apart (undersampling), to ensure that some location information is discarded during the feature extraction. H_2 consists of four feature maps, each of which is a 2 by 2 plane. Units in these feature maps have a 5 pixel by 5 pixel receptive field in the first hidden layer, also sharing the same set of weights (with an independent, for each unit, bias) and using the same undersampling strategy. After training, the generalization ability of this network, has been measured to be over 96 per cent, which shows that it can solve the problem quite adequately. We have replaced each neuron in the feature maps by a higher-order one, providing not only translational, but also rotational and scale invariance within its receptive field. With this technique we managed to achieve the same generalization performance, but also invariance with respect to all the above-mentioned transformations.

5   Conclusions

The use of higher-order neurons for invariant recognition of patterns and images has been examined in this paper. Appropriate forms of such networks have been proposed, which can provide invariance with respect to transformations, such as scale, translation and rotation, as well as other types of distortions. Various techniques for efficiently training and designing such networks have been presented and their performance has been illustrated using the problem of handwritten digit recognition. The results indicate that higher-order networks can be very useful, especially in cases where it is possible to reduce the number of 'free' parameters to rather small sizes.

References

[1] Almeida L. and Silva F, *Acceleration Techniques for the Backpropagation*

Algorithm, Lecture Notes in Computer Science, Springer Verlag, vol.412, pp. 110-119, 1990.

[2] Baum E. and Haussler D., *What Size Net Gives Valid Generalization?*, Neural Computation 1, pp. 151-160, 1989.

[3] Baum, *When Are n-Nearest Neighbor and Backpropagation Accurate for Feasible Sized Sets of Examples?*, Lecture Notes in Computer Science, Springer Verlang, vol.412, pp. 2-27, 1990.

[4] Bienenstock, E. and Von der Malsburg, C., *A neural network for the retrieval of superimposed connection patterns*, Europhysics Letters, Vol. 3, 1243-1249, 1987.

[5] Bienenstock, E. and Von der Malsburg, C., *A neural network for invariant pattern recognition*, Europhysics Letters, Vol. 4, 121-126, 1987.

[6] Bienenstock, E., *Connectionist approaches to vision*, Models of Visual Perception: from Natural to Artificial, M. Imbert (editor), Oxford University Press, 1987.

[7] Chauvin Y., *A backpropagation Algorithm with Optimal Use of Hidden Units*, in D. Tourketzy (Ed.), Advances in Neural Information Processing Systems 1, Palo Alto, CA, Morgan, Kaufman, 1989.

[8] Denker J, et al, *Handwritten Digit Recognition: Applications of Neural Network Chips and Automatic Learning*, IEEE Communications Magazine, November 1989.

[9] Duda R. and Hart P., *Pattern Classification and Scene Analysis*, John Wiley and Sons, New York, 1973.

[10] Fukushima, K., Miyake, S. and Ito, T., *Neocognitron: A Neural Network Model for a Mechanism of Visual Pattern Recognition*, IEEE Trans. on Sys. Man and Cyb., 13, 5, 826-834, 1983

[11] Fukushima, K., *A Neural Network Model for Selective Attention in Visual Pattern Recognition and Associative Recall*, Applied Optics, 26, 23, 4985-4992, 1987.

[12] Fukushima, K., *Neocognitron: A Hierarchical Neural Network capable of Visual Pattern Recognition*, Neural Networks, 1, pp. 119-130, 1988.

[13] Fukushima, K., *A Neural Network for Visual Pattern Recognition*, IEEE Computer, 21(3), pp. 65-75, 1988.

[14] Fukushima, K., *Analysis of the Process of Visual Pattern Recognition by the Neocognitron*, Neural Networks, Vol 2, pp. 413-420, 1989.

[15] Giles, G.L. and Maxwell, T., *Learning, Invariance and Generalization in High-Order Neural Networks*, Applied Optics, 26, 1987.

[16] Giles, G.L., Griffin, R.D. and Maxwell, T., *Encoding Geometric Invariances in Higher-Order Neural Networks*, Neural Information Processing Systems, American Institute of Physics Conference Proceedings, 1988.

[17] Guyon, I., Personnaz, L., Nadal, J.P and Dreyfus, G., *High Order Neural networks for Efficient Associative Memory Design*, Neural Information Processing Systems, American Institute of Physics Conference Proceedings, 1988.

[18] Hanson S., *Comparing Biases for Minimal Network Construction with Back-propagation*, in D. Tourketzy (Ed.), Advances in Neural Information Processing Systems 1, Palo Alto, CA, Morgan, Kaufman, 1989.

[19] Haussler D., *Generalizing the PAC Model for Neural Nets and Other Learning Applications*, Techn. Report, UCSC-CRL-89-30, 1989.

[20] Ishikawa M., *A structural Learning Algorithm with forgetting of Weight Link Weights*, Proceedings of the IJCNN vol.2, Washington D.C, June, 1989.

[21] Jacobs R., *Increased Rates of Convergence Through Learning Rate Adaptation*, Neural Networks, vol.1, no.4, 1988.

[22] Khotanzad, A. and Lu, J.H., *Distortion Invariant Character Recognition by a multilayer Perceptron and Backpropagation Learning*, IEEE International Conference on Neural Networks, Vol.1, 1988.

[23] Kollias S. and Anastassiou D., *An Adaptive Least Squares Algorithm for the Efficient Training of Artificial Neural Networks*, IEEE Transactions on Circuits and Systems, vol.36, pp. 1092-1101, August 1989.

[24] LeCun, Y., *Generalization and Network Design Strategies*, Connectionism in Perspective, North Holland, Switzerland, pp. 143-155, 1989.

[25] LeCun Y., *A Theoretical Framework for Backpropagation*, in Tourketzy D, Hinton G., and Sejnowski T., eds., Proceedings of the 1988 Connectionist Models Summer School, CMU, Pittsburgh, Morgan Kaufman, 1989.

[26] Von der Malsburg, C., *Pattern Recognition by Labelled Graph Matching*, Neural Networks, Vol. 1, 141-148, 1988.

[27] Maxwell, T., Giles, C.L., Lee, Y.C. and Chen, H.H., *Transformation Invariance Using High Order Correlations in Neural Net architectures*, Proc. IEEE Int. Conf. on Systems, Man and Cybernetics, Atlanta, Georgia, Oct. 1986.

[28] McCulloch, W. and Pitts, W., *A Logical Calculus of the Ideas Immanent in Nervous Activity*, Bull. of Math. Biophysics, 7, 115-133, 1943.

[29] Minsky, M. and Papert, S., *Perceptrons*, MIT Press, Cambridge, 1969.

[30] Pao, Y.H., *Adaptive Pattern Recognition and Neural Networks*, Addison-Wesley, 1989.

[31] Reid, M.B., Spirkovska, L. and Ochoa, E., *Rapid Training of Higher-Order Neural Networks for Invariant Pattern Recognition*, Proc. Joint Int. Conf. on Neural Networks, Washington, D.C., June 1989.

[32] Reid, M.B., Spirkovska, L. and Ochoa, E., *Simultaneous Position, Scale, and Rotation Invariant Pattern Classification Using Third-Order Neural Networks*, Neural Networks, Vol. 1, No. 3, July 1989.

[33] Rumelhart, D. and McClelland, J., (eds), *Parallel Distributed Processing : Explorations in the Microstructure of Cognition*, Vol. 1, MIT Press, 1986.

[34] Valiant L., *A Theory of the Learnable*, Communications of ACM, vol. 27, pp. 1134-1142, 1984.

[35] Wechsler, H. and Zimmerman, G. L., *Invariant Object Recognition Using a Distributed Associative Memory*, Proc. IEEE Conference on NIPS, American Institute of Physics, 1988.

[36] Widrow, B. and Winter, R., *Neural Nets for adaptive filtering and adaptive pattern recognition*, IEEE Computer, 21, 3, 1988.

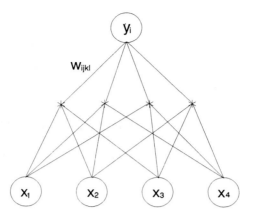

FIGURE 1

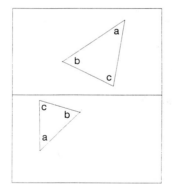

FIGURE 2

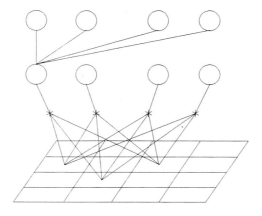

FIGURE 3

FIGURE 4

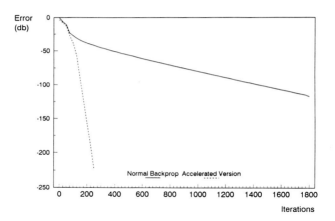

FIGURE 5

FIGURE 6

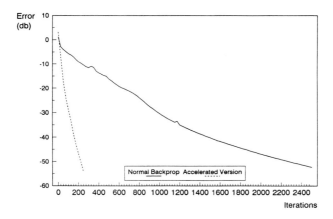

FIGURE 7

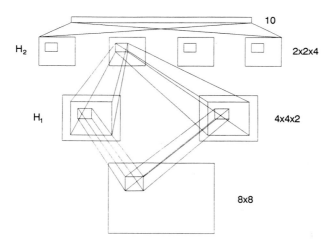

FIGURE 8

ORDER	No OF GROUPS
2	1
3	7
4	21
5	56
6	120
7	230
8	403
9	668
10	1020

TABLE 1

NEURAL NETWORKS: Advances and Applications
E. Gelenbe (Editor)
© Elsevier Science Publishers B.V. (North-Holland), 1991

Visual Recognition of Script Characters and Neural Network Architectures

Josef Skrzypek
Jeffrey Hoffman
Machine Perception Laboratory
Computer Science Department
University of California
Los Angeles, CA 90024

Abstract

Visual recognition of script characters is introduced in the context of the neural network paradigm and the results of applying one specific neural architecture are analyzed. First, computer classification of script characters is partitioned into preprocessing, recognition and postprocessing techniques which are briefly reviewed in terms of suitability for implementation as neural net architectures. The second part of the paper introduces one example of neural net solution to script recognition. Handwriting is assumed to be defined as concatenation of ballistic hand movements where characters can be represented as functions of position and velocity. We adapt a hypothesized model of human script generation where characters can be composed from a limited number of basic strokes which are learned using visual and positional feedback. The neural representation of these characters is used for assembling motor program during writing and it can be used for their visual recognition during reading. A modified, three-layer "backpropagation" algorithm is used to learn features of each single character that are independent of writing style. Preliminary results suggest 80% recognition rate.

1   Introduction

1.1   Scope of the paper

Practical benefits of automating the character recognition process in application to man-computer interactions are well understood and a number of algorithms exist to verify signatures [1], identify writers, recognize printed characters [2,3], numerals [4, 5,6], hand-printed characters [3], cursive script [7], English and Kanji characters, etc. However, a system that could input hand written documents for further processing including understanding of its content, has not been realized as yet and engineering attempts based on integration of available techniques seem to result in solutions that cannot operate in real time. In this paper we are only interested in visual recognition of the handwritten text regardless of writing style, for the purpose of further cognitive analysis of its content. This differs from such problems as verification of signature or identification of a writer (see [1]) where special purpose devices can be instrumented to extract such attributes of handwriting as pressure and acceleration. Because of the wide variety of fonts and hand written styles and because of the noise inherent in any electronic system, the simplest solution of directly matching data against a stored template becomes a difficult problem and is perhaps analytically intractable.

The purpose of this paper is to introduce the problem of visual recognition of script in the context of the neural network paradigm. We first introduce background material by reviewing some existing techniques and assumptions underlying character recognition. These are analyzed in terms of applicability to script recognition and the potential advantages of implementing them in "neural" architectures. Most of the existing algorithms for recognition can be classified into distinct methodologies by identifying them with three separate functions; *preprocessing, recognition, and postprocessing*. Within each function we try to identify fundamentally different methodologies and we relate them to the possible neural network solutions. In our view many preprocessing techniques need not be specific to character recognition, therefore it is not clear that specialized "neural" architectures for preprocessing script will be of interest to the vision community. In fact, it is conceivable that "neural" nets developed for "general" vision might make it unnecessary to, for example, skeletonize the original character image.

Next, we review algorithms for recognition. It is our belief that some specific solutions must emerge which are not general to vision but only apply to character recognition. This is also the area where we introduce our "neural" architecture for script recognition. Our solution is based on assumptions depicted in Figure 1. and discussed in detail in the second part of the paper. Briefly, each script character is composed of a few basic strokes of ballistic hand movements that can be modeled as an oscillation of a two-spring system [8]. During the first attempts to write characters, style-invariant features are extracted by learning, under both visual and positional/tactile feedback. These features are components of a neural representation that allows to express characters in their minimal configuration of basic strokes. This representation is accessible during the visual recognition and it is also used when generating a motor program for execution of handwriting. The adult script characters might appear to differ from this representation because of changes in hand mechanics and other psychological variants of a writer at the given time. To simplify the problem we focus on recognition only, which presupposes the existence of apriori acquired "templates" or memories of each character; we are not attempting to optimize or model the human learning process. Consistent with this model, we decompose script characters into horizontal and vertical frequency waveforms, from which the style-invariant features are extracted and fed to the neural network.

In this paper we are focusing only on the recognition of single characters, but it should be clear that when information about them is only partially available higher level cognitive processes might be invoked to infer missing data before recognition can take place. These problems are partially addressed by the postprocessing functions which are briefly reviewed in the first part of the paper for completeness.

1.2 Neural net algorithms for character recognition

Serial techniques require autonomous functions that rely only on input from previous stages of computation. For perceptual tasks, a serial approach does not seem adequate to explain the levels of performance seen in human subjects. It has been suggested [9,10,11] that a parallel set of interacting processes is necessary to achieve high rates of recognition over different styles of input (i.e. accents and speed of spoken language, varied writing styles and sizes).

There are many reasons why "neural" networks could be useful in perceptual tasks as well as other problems where input data is naturally organized in massively parallel representations [11,12,13]. "Neural" architectures have a potential to speed up computation while assuring fault tolerant performance. Usually a correct decision made at the output of a neural net depends on pattern of activity in a subset of all neurons. Thus, the representation does not have to consist of the exact connectivity between neurons but only an approximate pattern of activity related to the topology of the network. Neural systems exhibit inordinate amount of plasticity. This guarantees graceful degradation in case of erroneous decisions or novel stimuli. Consequently the network is always capable of some response that can often be made to converge on the desired output. For many real-world problems such as script recognition, it is extremely difficult to enumerate *a priori* all possible rules that apply to each specific case. Equally impossible is the task of completely specifying all contextual conditions that might affect such rules. Hence, the precise analysis of all numerical decisions that might have to be made is not feasible and an approximate response of a neural net is better than no response at all.

Neural networks appear to be better suited for realization of very complex systems. For example, information in "analog" neurons expressed as a temporal variation of signal amplitude makes interfaces between modules easier than multidimensional symbols such as words. Thus the "connectionist" paradigm allows integration to be based physically on signals going through the links between nodes, while in symbol processing systems complex communication interfaces are needed. Nevertheless, there is no clear formal way at the present time to develop separate modules and have *a priori* specification of link weights in order to connect the modules into a complex system. In other words, a nontrivial problem which has not been addressed satisfactorily in traditional AI, is the question of programming systems to perform perceptual or cognitive tasks. Here, the neural net paradigm offers interactive solutions that are based on primitive forms of supervised learning or some form of self-organization of a neural network in the process of learning. All of these advantages make "neural" net techniques ideally suited for pattern classification, a key component of any recognition system [11,14].

1.3   Performance criteria

In order to propose improvements in character recognition techniques one must be able to evaluate the performance of existing algorithms. Since, we lack standards in this area, individual investigators are not always consistent in the evaluation of their own algorithms. Below we attempt to summarize several criteria which could be used to this purpose.

RECOGNITION RATE criteria may include correct or incorrect recognition rate, and rejection rate. A rejected character can be better than an incorrectly recognized character since it can be flagged by the system for further review by the user. *CONSTANCY* under rotation, translation and scaling can be considered as another criterion of performance. Systems that are not invariant to these conditions must constrain their input to only certain formats. Interestingly, the human perceptual system is not rotationally invariant at the preattentive level, and therefore, humans must consciously rotate the image in order to achieve recognition [15,16]. Constancy problems are of general interest to vision and are not specific to recognition of script. Some neural net solutions to these problems are discussed in the later sections. The system must display sufficient *NOISE IMMUNITY* so that noisy images of characters are recognizable. This parameter can be implicitly expressed in the recognition rate of an algorithm that has been tested on noisy character images. Humans excel in this parameter, and no recognition algorithm has been devised that comes close to human capabilities unless character shape is severely constrained. Some algorithms are only usable for Chinese characters, some for numerals and some only for machine printed characters. Therefore, the *GENERALITY* of an algorithm is a very important parameter. There are certain format "characters" which should be handled in a recognition algorithm. They include, an underline, a dash across 't', dot over 'i' and 'j', and other special emphasis characters. Current algorithms do not take these into account, because it would involve integrating higher level information (e.g. recognizing the underline in the whole word) with lower level algorithms.

1.4 Parameters versus functions

Handwritten characters can be represented in terms of parameters or functions or both. Since in our approach we are interested only in visual input, a limited number of parameters and functions of handwritten text will apply. Basic function is a position of a character trace in x and y at different points in time. However, since the time information underlying character generation is lost in a static image this function is difficult to compute. The data are successive points expressed in x,y coordinates, obtained from sampling script characters at some regular intervals. Form this data we can build higher level features that represent strokes. At the higher level of processing, recognition may be aided by symmetry or other characteristic points that remain invariant regardless of the writing style. Handwriting velocity, computed as a first derivative of position can add new information about the dynamics of the hand in the process of writing. Additional information can be obtained from acceleration which can be computed from the second derivative of position. Other functions such as pressure and force can not be extracted from the visual input and are not considered here (but see [17]). In continuous writing, additional information can be obtained from considering spaces between characters when the hand is in motion but the pen is in the air. It is conceivable that in human perception these invisible "traces" are processed by the so called "illusory contour" neurons [18] as an additional aid in script recognition.

The parameters that can be extracted directly from the script by visual means include local curvature, starting direction and peaks with respect to some local reference. Some of the more global parameters that apply more to text than to characters are number of breaks when the pen is lifted, maximal and minimal excursions for each continuous segment of characters and perhaps proportions. An interesting feature set has been proposed by Sabourin and Plamondon [19], where they computed an angular orientation of the signature intensity gradient. This was assumed to reflect the stroke orientation. Another approach to features extraction, derived from traditional techniques used in graphoanalyzis is to divide the text into upper, middle and lower zones and to performed analysis of subimages referenced on initial and end strokes [20]. A variation on this approach is to divide the image into vertical and horizontal segments and then analyze their content [21].

The approaches to handwriting recognition based on extraction of parameters versus computing functions cannot be qualitatively compared at the present time. Clearly it seems that parametric description would offer advantages in storage requirement, but this may be offset by increased computational expense in composing and recognizing characters. Many of these problems are basic to pattern recognition in general and it is not clear that their solution will emerge from analysis of handwritten text. These problems include: questions as to which feature set is best and offers most discriminant power, how to determine and control thresholds for binary images and for making decision based on processed data, how to best combine parametric and functional approaches to recognition and many others. Our approach to character recognition as detailed in later sections combines both parametric and function based techniques. We use a position function to represent the character in the form of X and Y oscillation waveforms from which we extract parameters related to basic strokes.

2　Preprocessing Stages

Most character recognition algorithms use many discrete preprocessing stages which prepare, enhance and extract relevant information. These include correction for nonuniformity of acquisition devices, localization of a character in the image, character - background segmentation, filtering, thresholding and perhaps data reduction by signal to noise enhancement, etc. Preprocessing operations can be classified according to at least three objectives all of which have the common goal of converting the data into a form useful for the final recognition stage. One objective is to enhance and/or blurr certain parameters. For instance, noise might be removed while character borders might be enhanced by using thresholding and filtering. Another objective is to translate the low-level spatial data into a higher level symbolic notation; for example, extracting lines, curves, loops, and strokes [22,7] from the original image and linking them into outlines of characters. Examples of these operations include feature extractions and segmentation. Finally, an objective might be to add a performance criteria that is missing from the recognition algorithm. For instance, a particular algorithm might not be rotationally invariant, but this invariancy can be established by rotating the character to a standard orientation in the preprocessing stage.

Many problems addressed by preprocessing stages remain only partially solved. For example, in case of a very simple script, the localization problem can be solved by using a variable size window operator [21] but it is in general a difficult problem for connected text. Thresholding techniques for enhancing characters are in general insufficient for noisy background images with partially missing traces, uneven trace width etc. Intensity discontinuity operators such as Sobel or Difference of Gaussian can be applied to a binary version of the original image to extract characters. However, setting of binary threshold remains in general an unsolved problem [21].

2.1 Input image

Acquisition of script characters from static, grey-level images is a more desirable method because of the need to process previously written documents. Here, documents are read by scanning them optically. In general, the output of this device is a number recording light reflected from the paper at each point. This "grey level image" is usually processed to yield a "binary image" by thresholding as described in the next section. Visual means of acquiring data implies problems not present in the graphics tablet. First of all, some spatial information may be degraded during transformation from a gray level image to a binary image. Secondly, algorithms for segmenting the input into separate characters must be used since sloppy written characters might be overlapping or touching; a pressure-based system can segment the characters by noting the temporal sequence of the character strokes [23]. With visual acquisition, the user doesn't have control of the format of the input. Finally, although it is not too difficult to acquire an image of a character optically, most of the information about the dynamic process of script generation is degraded or missing. It is conceivable that humans can recover some of this information from the saccadic eye movements during scanning [24], but these ideas have not been incorporated into machine recognition as yet.

2.2 Noise reduction by thresholding and filtering

An example of a preprocessing algorithm is a simple thresholding which converts a grey level image into binary values. The intensity of each pixel in the grey level image is compared to a threshold value. If the intensity is larger than the threshold then a zero is substituted for the intensity (denoting no image point), otherwise a one is substituted for the intensity. This results in a binary image. Most of the noise is filtered out by this process since noise usually yields intensity values small in comparison to the actual image intensity. Moreover, the amount of information in the stored image is reduced, yielding a saving in storage space and a simpler recognition algorithm. The disadvantage of the thresholding algorithm is that it marks many valid points as noise points and vice versa. One simple solution is to vary the threshold of a point depending on its neighboring pixels. For example, if all the neighboring points are part of the character (or are likely to be part of the character), the threshold can be lowered. Since noise tends to come in single pixel spurts while the character is many pixels wide, this will reduce the likelihood of a bad decision. Other possible solutions include averaging over a neighborhood of points and varying the threshold depending on local measures of busy-ness [25].

Thresholding operations in general have been of considerable interest within the "neural" net paradigm. One generalization is that lateral interactions within neural layers are amenable to various space and temporal adaptive threshold algorithms as for example automatic gain control in early stages of visual processing [26]. The basic principle here is that the threshold can be automatically adjusted depending on the value of neighboring units. The adjustment can be a function of multiple spatial scales. The complete process can be viewed as automatic shifting of the operating characteristic for a "neuron" along the domain of the feature. Basic to this operation is concentric organization of the center surround receptive fields. In some sense this can also be viewed as predictive coding where the surround predicts what the center should be and the difference between center and surround encodes the error in prediction. "Neural" networks are very appealing for thresholding based on the above principles, because it is very easy to implement a concurrent filtering operation using the same "neurons".

A filtering step is usually added to the algorithm to reduce the noise. The type of filter used ultimately depends on the noise statistics of an image and of the system. Undesired result of low-pass filtering is blurring effect on character boundary (this is critical in some algorithms). In addition, filters implemented as a convolution, are computationally expensive on sequential machines. There are many solutions to these problems in the neural net paradigm. Analog neural nets with built-in lateral inhibition can perform convolution-like operation as a relaxation with convergence being practically instantaneous, while at the same time enhancing any discontinuities [26,27]. Many other filtering operation can be performed in this mode. In general, interactions between layers of neurons can be considered as two-dimensional mappings between arrays of instantaneous values. These can include space invariant image processing that allows restoration of motion-blurred images or removal of other translational and rotational distortion [28].

2.3 Trace detection: region growing and border following

Region growing is the process of defining a small region and then expanding it (i.e. making it grow) by adding as many neighboring pixels as possible such that they satisfy a certain criteria. For instance, the algorithm might search for four pixels in a square which are larger than a certain threshold, thereby finding a region. Then, pixels are added to the region by comparing each pixel that is adjacent to the region to a second threshold. The output of this algorithm is an image which is decomposed into many different regions. In general, the algorithm tries to find two regions: the character region and background region. The location of the character region can then be fed to a recognition algorithm. This might replace the thresholding stage when thresholding isn't robust enough against noise. Boundary detection by region growing seem naturally suited for neural implementation. Lateral comparison of neighboring "neuron" activities can spread rapidly to determine the uniformity of a region [29].

The dual to region growing is border following. There are many different algorithms to find and follow a border (see [30,31]). The simplest is the turtle algorithm which operates on a binary image. The border is found by locating a transition from white to dark at which point a 'turtle' follows the border and marks it. This algorithm usually creates closed borders which can be a very useful property in some recognition schemes. More sophisticated algorithms operating on a grey level image use filters (usually directional) to follow the boundary of a character. For example the Sobel operator sums up pixels in a window (using weights) to determine if there is an edge in a certain direction [32]. One disadvantage of this method is that it requires at least two passes–one with a filter sensitive in the x direction and the other sensitive to the y direction. This of course suggests the use of the Laplacian of the Gaussian which can be implemented as a resistive neural network [27]. Another approach to determining discontinuities has been recently developed by Gleeson and Skrzypek [33] which differs from all other edge detection algorithms based on local differentiation. Here, we make no assumptions about the location or the type of discontinuities but we take advantage of the fact that away from discontinuities, pixel values are highly correlated. Image approximation with a nearly second order function fails at the contrast boundaries. Statistics generated in the process of improving approximation can be used to predict the occurrence of a boundary. A higher level approach for organizing neural nets is to infer curves from images as introduced by Zucker [34]. The tangent field is first computed by labeling relaxation from discrete tangent measurements at each contrast discontinuity. This is followed by dynamically fitting splines to the tangent field. Since the curves can be recovered to subpixel accuracy, skeletonization is unnecessary. This method is motivated by end-stopped receptive fields and neural structures at the infero-temporal cortex level.

2.4 Performance improvement by normalization and skeletonization

Because size invariance is desirable, the character height and width must be normalized if the length of line segments is used in the recognition algorithm. This can be done by finding the character height and width using either the border following or region growing algorithms and then normalizing to a chosen height and/or width. Some recognition algorithms require the character to be oriented correctly. Current approaches make a character positioning dependent on the needs of the recognition algorithm. There are already some neural network based algorithms that give rotationally invariant recognition of simple objects [35]. Neural net solutions to size invariancy are based on findings that early visual processing in biological systems, follows space-invariant mapping from the retina to the cortex which can be captured by a log-polar function [36]. Combination of this mapping with a saccadic response directed by the focus of attention results in size and translation invariant mappings. The foveation response recenters the target while the log-polar function gives size invariance. A combination of an "adaptive resonance network" [29] with a neural net that mimicks the log-polar function and foveal response was recently tested on noisy objects [66]. The system gave rotation, position and scale invariant recognition by classifying correctly all objects which were partially obscured and embedded in a 50% noisy background.

A character image is sometimes skeletonized. This is a process in which the character is thinned to its basic shape [30,31]. It is important in this process to preserve the shape and connectivity of the character. A typical thinning algorithm, the medial axis transformation has the properties that the connectivity of the skeleton is preserved, the original image can be exactly reconstructed, and the geometry of the skeleton is invariant under rotation [30]. The ('minor') problem with this algorithm is that it is theoretically impossible to implement it exactly on a digital computer [37]. Another skeletonization technique is Hilditche's algorithm [38] which involves many passes over the image. Each pass deletes image points that have neighboring image points. The skeleton resulting from this algorithm however, depends on the orientation of the character. Finally another variation is line thinning by line following [39,31].

In essence, skeletonization algorithms examine and manipulate pixels within some local (3x3) window. With larger windows, (5x5) it is possible to reduce the noise sensitivity and to better preserve straight edges. Since, larger kernels require more computing, they are good candidates for implementations in neural architectures as some forms of convolutions [4,40].

2.5 Data abstraction by segmentation and feature extraction

Some aspects of segmentation, the dividing of the image into separate characters, may be performed in the preprocessing stage. This is easily done with machine printed characters and sometimes with hand printed characters. However, segmentation of joined script characters requires interaction between the character recognition scheme and the feature extraction scheme. In general, the representation of the context as available from the recognition level is a very difficult problem in vision. Various forms of relaxation labeling schemes have been used to iteratively remove labels that are not congruent with other local labels and with global (context) labels. Unfortunately there are no general methods to decide what contextual labels are. One possibility is that a backpropagation neural net could encode and learn global descriptors of the context without recourse to relaxation [41].

Feature extraction is the most critical issue in character recognition. Some recognition algorithms try to match the different lines and curves of a character against a template. In that case, the preprocessing stage segments the character into a set of features (e.g. a set of lines and curves). Most of the previous algorithms use features selected subjectively by the designer according to intuitive hints about significance of topology and geometry in shape perception. Neural network techniques show promise in their ability to independently extract important features of the input data, useful in classifying object types. This approach has the advantage of adaptively choosing the appropriate discriminatory features depending on writing style. A disadvantage is the inability to perform this function in real time because current neural nets can require long training periods.

3 Recognition Algorithms

In order to achieve recognition some comparison must be performed between functions or parameters extracted from the trace of a character and the previously stored memory. This comparison preceeds a decision about identification of a character. It is difficult if not impossible to apply a simple correlation procedure based on a fixed number of temporal samples because with constant sampling the same characters can be stretched out or compressed. Additional random variations can take place due to the biomechanical problems or even due to the mood or hesitation of a writer. Some of these problem can be in part compensated for by using adaptive sampling techniques [42]. All other problems caused by translation, rotation and scaling have been traditionally dealt with by using some normalization procedure [2,19,23,43].

3.1 Algorithm classifications

In general, most recognition algorithms involve comparison of a character to a template followed by a decision reflecting quality of the match. Characters consist of features that are useful in distinguishing between classes of characters. Input patterns of features represent points in some multidimensional space. A pattern classifier, partitions the multidimensional input space into some decision regions that could be used to classify the input. We can categorize all algorithms depending on whether the template is a direct replica of the input data or some transform of it.

Direct recognition algorithms recognize characters by comparing their topological features with templates where the comparison can be based on geometrical, structural or statistical aspects of a character. For example, a statistical approach may use a number of horizontal and vertical intensity changes [44]. Geometrical aspects may be based on shape parameters such as the minima and maxima of character segments [45]. Finally, character structures such as loops can be used to describe and recognize script letters as a concatenation of loops and arcs with a relatively high degree of accuracy [22,7]. In general, direct recognition methods are computationally and algorithmically simpler than the transform based techniques.

Certain aspects of direct recognition techniques map naturally to neural nets and are consistent with general ideas about the structure and function of the perceptual system. Feature detectors [46,47] and their aggregation according to Gestalt laws are such examples [48]. A more difficult problem for neural nets is rapid development of a template. One solution to this problem is the ART network developed by Carpenter and Grossberg [29]. Another possible model for rapid learning has been recently introduced by Lynch et.al. [49]. The problems of making a comparison and reaching a decision about the match has been also addressed within a neural network paradigm but not specifically in application to cursive script recognition [50,35,51,4,52]

Transform methods re-represent the character image in a separate domain (e.g. the Fourier domain) and compare the character to its template in that domain. Fourier shape descriptors could be designed as a function of the first few Fourier coefficients of the character boundary [44]. Template matching in the frequency domain seem consistent with the idea that neural structures of the perceptual system could process spatial frequencies [53] instead of features. However, neural net architecture for transforming spatial data from characters into the frequency domain have not been developed as yet.

A further classification of algorithms can be made based on the kind of characters they are designed to read. For instance, there are special algorithms for machine printed characters and numerals, for handprinted characters, and for script. Also, the language and therefore the alphabet, is an important consideration when designing an algorithm. This can be seen from the many algorithms designed specifically for the Chinese alphabet (which consists of thousands of characters). However, there are more distinct feature groups and context may not play as large a role as in roman script recognition. These algorithms are very different from their Roman-Script counterparts in that they employ very sophisticated data structures and tree algorithms in order to effect the recognition [54].

3.2 General techniques

Many algorithms employ a unique method to perform the recognition. However, some general techniques are used in various forms by most of the algorithms. The most general group of classifiers which incorporate recent advances in neural networks is based on building decision regions bounded by hyperplanes computed from the input space. These include, perceptrons [55], multilayer - backpropagation nets [56], Boltzman machines [57] and decision tree classifiers [58]. A different category of classifiers which are most plausible from a biological perspective build decision regions bounded by the properties of neural functions determined by the overlapping receptive fields. Examples of such classifiers are the Cerebellar Model Articulation Controller (CMAC) [59,60] and a multi-map classifier [61,62]. A subgroup of classifiers within this category performs classification by identifying exemplars that are nearest to the input. These include, k-nearest neighbor classifier [63], learning vector classifier [62] and adaptive resonance theory classifier (ART) [29]. The differences between various classifiers are in training time and memory requirements. For example, Boltzman machine and back-propagation classifiers require very long training sessions, while the ART and k-nearest neighbor classifiers require a lot of memory for classification. In this respect, decision trees seem to be optimal.

Decision tree classifiers, used by many of the newer algorithms, allow complex decisions to be made by a number of simple and local decisions. In a decision tree, a classifier is used to decide which group of characters the image belongs to. That group is then further subdivided by a different classifier. This process continues indefinitely until the group is composed of a single character. For example, Gu et. al. [54] use Walsh coefficients as the classifiers to a decision tree in order to recognize 3000 noisy Chinese characters with a 99.5% recognition rate. The computational demand of a decision tree is low and they can be implemented using fine grain parallelism. They can use signal or symbols as an input. However their training is not biologically motivated, and requires access to all training examples simultaneously.

There are a number of different problems that must be dealt with when designing the decision rules for trees. For instance, a tree might contain overlapping decision rules [64], for example, an initial grouping might be performed at the main node by dividing the input space according to characters that contain horizontal lines and characters that contain vertical lines. In that case, 'H' would belong to both groups. In the Chinese character set, which is very large, this can result in dramatic increases in tree size. This problem can be avoided by redesigning the classifier so that there are no overlapping regions; this is a very difficult task to perform with a large character set.

Another tree design question is whether to make the decisions completely binding. For instance, a decision might be made for a membership in a certain character group. However, other classifiers might disagree with this classification and determine that the character belongs to a different group. Certain tree structures allow a branching back to the group whereas others do not. A difficult problem with this approach concerns who makes the final decision. This might be an interesting application area for the neural net paradigm.

Concatenated Classifiers are often used in conjunction with decision trees in an attempt to increase accuracy by using more than one type of classifier. Some classifiers are good at differentiating certain characters but not others. In that case, one type of a classifier can be used to divide the characters into groups and individual characters. Then, another type of classifier is used to make the final decision. For example, Fourier descriptors used for the first grouping couldn't differentiate between rotationally symmetric numerals (for instance: '2' and '5') [44]. Therefore, a second descriptor- average number of intensity crossings in x and y directions, was used to differentiate those numerals. Similarly, Shridhar and Badreldin [65] were able to recognize handwritten numerals with a 98.8% accuracy with a first subdivision using the number of horizontal and vertical intensity crossings and a second subdivision using the approximate location of the peak of the character contour. Considering that recognition of numerals involves only 10 characters, as opposed to 26 characters in the alphabet, the problem is not as complex.

Learning techniques are used in many algorithms designed to recognize hand written characters. Typically, a user will input many examples of a character. Using these examples, the algorithm can "learn" what a character looks like. Usually this means that the algorithm is able to learn how much the data differs from the template and this information can subsequently be used during the matching process. This technique, which is usually used during an initial "learning" stage, creates a system that is efficient for a single user or a small group of users. An alternate approach to learning used by [66], allows the algorithm to learn while performing the recognition. This is done by assuming that the algorithm makes a correct decision and then updating the stored statistics of the character with the statistics of the character just recognized. In order to de-emphasize wrong decisions, the algorithm can reduce allowed variance bounds as well as increase them.

Shape and Size Constraint based techniques are usually not acceptable from the users' point of view. However, it is sometimes the only way to create an algorithm which has very high accuracy. Shingal and Suen [67] describe results from research they performed into the effect of different handwriting styles on recognition rates. One of their conclusions is that recognition rates depend significantly on writing styles and therefore, certain styles should be taught in order to increase accuracy of recognition.

Most of the traditional techniques are linear techniques. There is good reason to assume however, that the optimum technique is non-linear. This can be seen by noting that a perturbation of a character form will almost always involve a large number of pixels. Therefore, the location of the next pixel to be matched depends on the location of the pixel appearing before it. Using this logic, it might be possible to find some type of matching algorithm that would use the information from local pixels to modulate the matching process [68]. Other heuristics are possible; for instance, a pattern match in one part of the character is more important than no match in a different part of the character (since noise or perturbations could have caused the no match condition).

Neural Network Classifiers are the most recent developments in the field of handwritten character recognition. Neural network based feature extraction can select the most discriminating points among a set of characters. This information can be used by a second network to classify the characters, taking other factors (such as letter and word context) into account. This approach requires a large amount of training time; however after that initial investment future adaptation would be minimal, and operation could be real-time.

All neural net classifiers applied to character recognition are based on learning, and the multilayer architectures appear to concatenate different functions. The best known neural-net classifiers that are trained under supervision using gradient-descent training methods are backpropagation algorithms [56,14,69]. In general the properties of a three-layer backprop can be described in term of the operations that various layers can perform on an n-feature space. The first layer partitions the input space into hyperplanes. The hidden layer nodes combine the hyperplanes of the first layer into a product that represents a convex region of the feature space. Nodes could typically have a sigmoidal nonlinearity as a transfer function. Iterative training, allows to backpropagate the error between the desired and computed output and this is used to modify the weights. Training is considered completed when the error value reaches some predetermined level (for review see [13,14,56,70]). Despite the initial hope and the resounding popularity, there is no evidence that backpropagation resembles biological processes [71]. Backpropagation has been used successfully in many application and all attempts to use neural nets in character recognition are based on this technique. A disadvantage of backpropagation is the long training period, which can be reduced and performance improved if the size of the net is tailored to the problem [69].

A simple neural net classifier based on back-propagation [50] uses grey level image where learning features are vectors of stroke's lengths. Piecewise linear, neurons organized in multiple layers of full connectivity after being trained on the representative sample of inputs can achieve recognition rates that are not as good as standard nearest neighbor classifiers. Another example of neural networks applied to recognition of handprinted, block characters, was shown to achieve recognition rates comparable to a conventional nearest neighbor classifier [70]. The peak rates reached 94% with a network of 20 hidden units that learned graded-value activities in a specialized 13-segment, bar-mask, character sensor. This is comparable to Bayes [63] classifier which is theoretically the best performance one can expect. Unfortunately the input sample in [70] was limited to one writer.

Le Cun et. al. [4,51] developed a hardware/software, neural-net system for recognition of handwritten isolated numerals obtained from postal zip codes. The system combines skeletonization, feature extraction and classification as one huge feedforward network. The architecture consists of three hidden layers, besides the input and the output layers. Grey level images are used at the input and the system can correctly classify 94% of test examples after only 15 training sessions. The maximum rate of classification was 10 digits per second which could be improved to 30 digits per second after normalization of input images. The most interesting feature of this neural network is breaking hidden units into separate maps that combine only local sources of information. This is similar to our approach of clustering hidden nodes, which we found to improve performance by constraining learning to local features [69].

An example of a different approach to modelling handwritten character recognition is provided in a recent paper by Morasso [7]. This work investigates the use of self-organizing maps to model cursive script handwriting. Written words are broken down into strokes bounded by points of zero vertical velocity. Each stroke was then represented by a five point polygonal curve which was used as input to a so-called graphotopic map, similar in design to Kohonen's phonetic typewriter [62]. Through training (with 200 words or about 1600 characters), an organized map of curved segments was formed on a 15x15 matrix. The segments on the resulting map were organized by pen direction, pen pressure (up or down), stroke length and amount of curvature.

4 Postprocessing

The preprocessing and recognition stages output a string of characters in binary format. In general, this string will contain errors. Errors can be classified as substitution errors, deletion errors, and addition errors depending on whether a character was substituted, added, or deleted. In most character recognition systems, substitution errors are the most common, and therefore, much of the literature attempts to solve that problem. In the script recognition systems, all three types of errors are possible due to the connectivity of the letters. The Viterbi algorithm is applicable to correction of substitution errors. Additions and deletions have been dealt with specialized dictionaries to search for such errors [72].

In a typical error correction scheme, the recognition algorithm outputs error probabilities along with the character. If the probability of error is very large, then the error correction routine will try to find the most likely substitute for the character. There are at least two general approaches to the correction problem [73]. In *STATISTICAL ERROR CORRECTION*, letter transition properties for the English language are used. For example, the probability that 'a' follows 'b' is computed from English text beforehand. These probabilities are usually computed with a depth of two; i.e. the probability that this character is an 'a' given that the last *two* characters were 'b' and 'c'. Using the Viterbi algorithm, the word with the minimum distance can be computed by searching the trellis using the transitional probabilities as the distance measure. The major disadvantage to this algorithm is that it doesn't guarantee that the resulting string is a valid or correct word. In a *CONCEPT DRIVEN CORRECTION* scheme, special properties such as syntax, semantics, or valid words are used to guess the word. For instance, an inputted word can be compared to a dictionary of legal words. If the word is not valid then the most likely word is computed and the word is replaced. Although this dictionary can be large the search can be narrowed down if certain assumptions are made about the errors (for instance, only letter substitutions need to be considered in most cases).

Both of these methods assume that the text will follow certain patterns. This assumption is repeatedly violated with proper nouns and other special text. However, it should be noted that human capabilities are also severely tested when trying to recognize unfamiliar names and the words which are not legible. In addition, these methods do not take the context of a word into account. Statistical recognition favors high incidence words which may or may not fit a given context.

Although the computation involved in the transitional probability algorithm is minimal, it does very poorly at replacing the word with a valid word. Conversely, the dictionary algorithm is very slow (due to the large number of legal words), but it always replaces the incorrect word with a valid word - which because of the large constraint inherent in the dictionary, has a higher probability of being the correct word. It is therefore obvious that some type of hybrid approach to the problem would be expedient. There are two ways to combine algorithms, by cascading and by integrating [73].

In a cascaded approach, a word can be obtained by computing the letter transitional probabilities. The resulting word can be checked with the dictionary to determine whether it is a legal word. If the word is illegal, then a new word can be tried. Although this further constrains the dictionary, it still results in a large number of comparisons.

The second hybrid approach, integration, involves searching both the Viterbi trellis (for the transitional probabilities) and the dictionary simultaneously. The dictionary is stored as a linked list of characters (called tries). Each node has a successor and a brother. The successor is the next letter in the word whereas the brother is another possible word with the same prefix. For example, 'S' can appear with two possible continuations (S)mooth and (S)krzypek. With this dictionary, the set of possible letters after a given prefix can be computed. This set is used to constrain the trellis to search only the valid combinations thereby greatly constraining the search. The problem becomes difficult when there are many possible continuation of words which do not exist in the dictionary. Comparison between these algorithms shows that for a given sample, a better translation algorithm recognized 30% words correctly [73]. This rate increased to 83% and 86% for the Dictionary algorithm and Integrated algorithm respectively.

This integration could be carried one step further by combining it with the character recognition algorithm. Here, the trellis and dictionary can be used to constrain the set of possible characters. Although this might not increase efficiency for machine or even hand printed characters, it could benefit the recognition of script characters by improving their segmentation. A typical algorithm might feed the recognition routine a list of expected characters and the algorithm would search only for those expected characters. A number of problems associated with this method can be addressed. For instance, although in general, proper nouns won't be included in the dictionary, they can be flagged by the recognition of a capital letter at the beginning of the word. Moreover, AI techniques can be used to 'understand' the sentence and predict the part of speech of the word and perhaps even the word itself!

One approach to using AI techniques in recognition of recursive script was introduced by Bozinovic and Srihari [45]. They presegmented script characters by finding the minima then used topological features to hypothesize the character and attach probabilities to each possibility. Then they used a simple dictionary look up to compute the correct string. They found (with a small character subset) that although in may cases the algorithm converged to the correct word quite quickly, there were some cases where the algorithm spent a lot of time searching the dictionary for possible words. Nevertheless, they did demonstrate the need and the possibility of combining lexical analysis (string correcting techniques) with the recognition algorithm.

At the present time there are no examples where neural networks were used to perform postprocessing in script recognition. Perhaps one reason is that computing contextual information is a difficult problem in itself. In addition it seems that segmentation of a connected, cursive script is a difficult problem. Furthermore, symbolic processing as known in traditional AI, at the level of words or meaning behind a sentence, cannot be easily mapped onto neural nets. It is intuitively clear that context information would be very important in segmentation. Perceptual completion of familiar patterns was modeled as an interactive activation of context effects in letter perception [74]. The study illustrated how "neural" net models can resolve multiple, parallel constraints to recognize familiar patterns and fill in missing portions. Unfortunately, the study was limited to recognition of four letter words and the method of computing context information in general was not elucidated.

5 Script Generating Process–Assumptions

One of the key problems in character recognition is selection of features that could be independent of style or font. It is hoped that combinations of such features can uniquely differentiate various characters. The examples of such features, selected in past rather intuitively, include lines, cusps, holes and loops. Our approach is also feature based, but the motivation for feature selection derives from a model of handwriting.

The functional block diagram on which we based our approach is shown in Figure 1. In this diagram we make many assumptions which are reasonable in view of our belief that preprocessing stages are not specific to character recognition but subserve the vision process in general. The three, thick-line boxes within the shaded box called **High Level Cognitive Areas** are the focus of our interest and below we try to justify some of the connectivity between them.

Neurophysiological as well as psychophysical (for review see [75]) evidence suggests that extensive local connectivity, cortical magnification factor [76,61] and asynchronous simultaneous processing [77] in the layer of cells allow to synthesize a data driven architecture that achieves location, size and orientation invariance. Gaps in traces or boundaries such as when the pen is lifted although the hand is following a

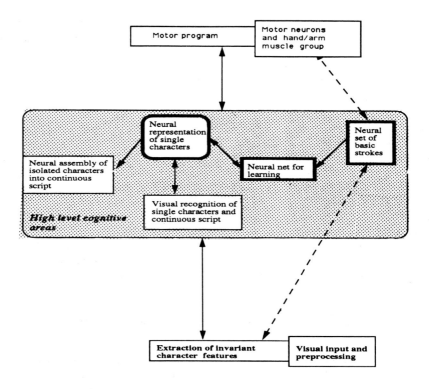

Figure 1: Functional block diagram showing organization of the proposed neural representation of characters.

trace, can be completed or filled in by combining lateral agonistic and antagonistic interactions between neuronal feature detectors of various modalities. This is similar to the combination of spreading activation [52] with local feedback [26]. It is conceivable that "illusory contour" neurons [18] also play some role in this process. Features can be extracted at multiple spatial scales [48,26] and they can be clustered in a scale space. Segmentation is possible by localizing and integrating regions of the image by "saccading" through locally enhanced features that attract foveal attention as compared to surrounding regions where activities are low. Finally, it is conceivable to have recognition and a primitive form of visual learning in such simple structures provided some mechanism of short-term memory is available [78]. Most of these functions are localized to boxes that deal with visual input in Figure 1.

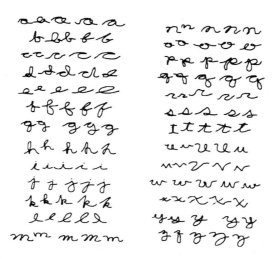

Figure 2: Example characters from 'a' to 'z' used in training and testing the clustered neural network for script recognition.

The motivation of our approach to the problem of recognizing cursive script is based on the assumption that handwritten characters are formed from a limited number of primitive hand motions [22,8,7]. The strokes resulting from these primitive hand motions have a separate neural representation as indicated by the right-most box in the middle of Figure 1. This differs from traditional approaches in that our selection of recognizable features which define characters are constrained by the accepted model of handwriting. Hence the dashed arrow from the motor neurons and/or motor program area to the box called "Neural set of basic strokes". The characteristic features are invariant under rotation, translation, changes in size and/or style. These features can be used for categorizing visually sensed characters and for controlling motor activities during writing. We assume that after the initial learning period, motor programs underlying handwriting result in ballistic hand movements, where there is no instantaneous positional feedback. Higher levels of the central nervous system issue appropriate commands which through some intermediate neural structure control the fine behaviour of the motor neurons and hand muscles in a feedforward manner. This simplifies the question as to at which point positional and visual feedback become important in this process. The representation which we used is derived from the Oscillation Theory of cursive script [8]. It can be learned by a modified "backpropagation" neural network, thus overcoming many image preprocessing problems.

Another assumption that we make is that characters are not stored in iconic form, to be recognized later by matching with specific templates each time the character is presented. Simply there are too many variations due to fonts and writer styles. A more effective way is to encode patterns according to a set of invariant properties. For example, the spatial relationships between parts of a character are invariant. These relationships have iconic coordinate representation in the visual domain that is perhaps localized within parietal lobe. At a higher level the same coordinate information is translated into the symbolic domain, resulting in categorical representation, where parts are related to each other with verbal symbols such as "above", "below", "adjacent", etc. This is consistent with neurophysiological results [79], which suggest two separate visual pathways. One path, including parietal lobe is concerned with spatial vision where the main function is description of location and spatial relationships between object/parts. The other, pathway, concerned with shape analysis, revolves around the question "what?" and includes the inferior temporal lobe. Both of the systems might have their own memory and the recognition of the object may involve sequential tasks of combining parts of object according to separately stored description of organization of the object. In other words, parts of a shape are stored separately from the description of spatial relations among parts and only one reference point at a time specifies the location of one part with respect to other parts [80]. In this context we assume that a few basic strokes, out of which each script character is composed, are stored in one location and the font and writing-style independent description of how strokes should be organized into characters are perhaps stored separately (Figure 1.).

6 Procedure

Each hand written character is first generated as a binary image. Sample characters were created via three procedures which have been used in previous studies (see [81,22]). Figure 2 shows examples of characters between "a" and "z" used for the training and testing sets. First, data was mapped onto bitmaps (approximately 60x60 pixels) using a mouse and a graphical interface. Second, similar bitmaps were created with a digitizing board. Third, some sample bitmaps (approximately 150x200) were generated by a simulation of Hollerbach's Oscillation Theory [8]. These bitmaps are used to create the training and testing sets for a backward error propagation network according to the procedure described below. In total, 364 characters bitmaps were generated, half reserved for the training set, and the other half for the testing set.

A sequence of points is extracted from the bitmap representation of the character using a modification of the line following technique described in [31]. This procedure, which we have labeled dynamic feature extraction (see Figure 3), attempts to recreate the method of producing the character by traversing the points in their

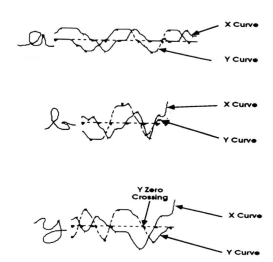

Figure 3: Sample X and Y waveforms derived from characters in the testing and training sets.

original order, while thinning the line to a nominal width. The resulting values can be used to create two separate graphs of horizontal (X) and vertical (Y) oscillations that are principal to localization of the modulation points in both dimensions. To overcome the differences in size we normalize both X and Y graphs to values between zero and one. The structure inherent in the learning network is used to accommodate any shifts in the modulation points. In the end the modulation points from both X and Y graphs are used as a minimal representation of characters that are fed to the neural network (see Figure 3).

These graphs were analyzed to detect and localize the major positive and negative peaks, as well as zero vertical velocity crossings. Each peak is listed by its relative position on the time axis, along with an indicator whether it occurred on the X or Y velocity graph, and its relative magnitude (-1 to +1). The zero crossings are recorded with a relative position on the time axis (for the Y graph only), and a relative magnitude of 1.0. This list of peaks is preceded by the number of points scanned in the image (this value is used to normalize the peak positions), and the letter that is represented (for the net "supervisor"). Supplemental data can then be added to the input representation. In our experiments, the only information added was the indication of the presence or absence of a cross-stroke on the letter. This improved performance by helping to differentiate among letter pairs such as 'l' and 't' and 'c' and 'x'.

Our approach is based only on the relative velocity profile derived from the curvature of the input script. This differs from Morasso's [7] approach where he segments the written word at the Y zero crossing points of the velocity profile while using the curved segments from the input. Also, the graphotopic map cannot directly recognize a given character, but may provide a compact representation based on the temporal sequence of activated map cells.

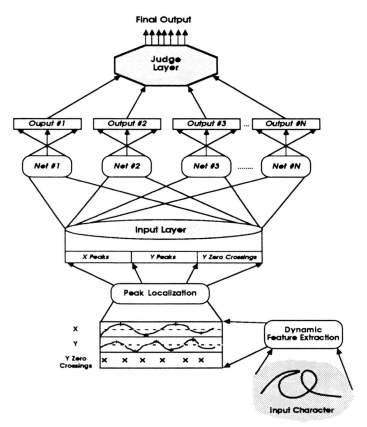

Figure 4: Overall diagram of the cluster network structure and dynamic feature extraction.

The formatted character data is presented to a modified three-layer backward error propagation network [69]. The net is actually composed of several small networks, of the same size, that share a common set of input nodes. Each small network has independent hidden and output layers, and the output of the whole "cluster" of networks is the average of the corresponding output node values. The averaging function is performed by a selection or "judge" layer. An example of the structure of a cluster is shown in Figure 4; it consists of ten separate backpropagation networks each constructed with six hidden nodes and twenty-six output nodes. One possible refinement to increase recognition accuracy using the cluster architecture would be to implement a more sophisticated judge layer. Better solutions would include a judge with weighted links and memory in order to select a sub-network's output depending on its strength.

The activation function performed by each node is the familiar sigmoid $(1/1+exp(-a))$, where a is the sum of all the weighted inputs to the node. Output strength is measured in the range 0, +1. When presented with novel data, the network tends to activate several output nodes (three to four) with varying strengths. These strength values indicate the closeness of the match between the input data and the character representation learned from the training set data.

7 Results

Dynamic feature extraction essentially localizes the character in the bitmap and normalizes its size. Additionally, the output produced by the line-following method of extracting points is not affected by character slant or orientation, as long as the system can locate the beginning stroke. The preprocessed character features are stored as a sequence of peak values, and the average number of features for all examples in both the training and testing set is about sixteen. The order of examples in the testing set is also irrelevant, as the network is newly activated at each presentation.

The sequence of peak points chosen by the preprocessing step are identified only by their occurence on the X or Y waveforms. There is no explicit coupling of X or Y peaks with non-peak values on the other waveform. The use of Y zero crossings gives the network some reference to the shape of the Y graph, but there is no information concerning the slope of the crossing. This problem is addressed in [82]. Note that the coupling of X and Y values does not directly follow from Hollerbach's Oscillation Theory [8].

Clusters networks converge in approximately one half the number of epochs as single networks. An epoch is a period in which all examples are presented to the network exactly once. Convergence occurs when the network has learned to correctly classify the training examples within a specified tolerance for error. In our trials, the cluster networks converged in approximately 1000 to 1200 epochs with a mean squared

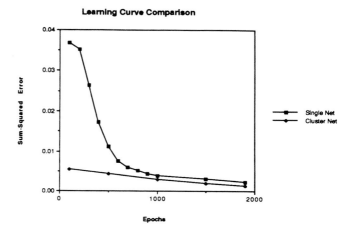

Figure 5: Learning curves for Cluster and single Backward Error Propagation networks.

error of 0.001 (about three percent) as compared to single networks which require an average of 2000 epochs to reach this error value. The learning curves for a cluster and a single network are compared in Figure 5.

Cluster networks easily recognize the characters in the training set (100 percent), however, with novel data, the correct character is contained in the output group about eighty percent of the time. This is a significant (ten to fifteen percent) improvement over the performance of single backward error propagation networks. The errors are generally of substitution character (about twenty percent), with a less than one percent omission rate. Recognition has been improved further by the use of supplemental information involving the cross-stroke needed to complete the t and the x. The study by Corrieu and DeFalco [83] has shown that children can classify about eighty percent of printed script characters presented to them.

As in other backward error propagation networks [69,70], there is an optimal number of hidden units necessary to maximize generalization when the network is presented with novel examples. This character recognition task performs optimally with fifty to sixty hidden nodes, divided among seven to ten sub-networks. Generalization tends to decline for over one hundred hidden nodes, and similarly training becomes poor for fewer than thirty hidden nodes.

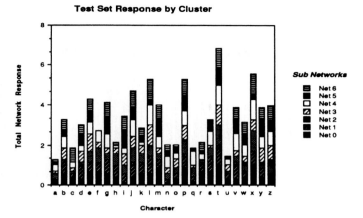

Figure 6: Activities within each sub-network of a cluster during test on each character in the alphabet.

The cluster networks tend to confuse such letter groups as (b,f,h,k), (e,i,r,l), (g,p,-q,y,z) and (m,n,u,w). This agrees with data from Bouma [84], who defined seven major confusion classes: (a,s,z,x), (e,o,c), (n,m,u), (r,v,w), (d,h,k,b), (t,i,l,f), and (g,p,j,y,q). The letters most easily recognized by the network are in the group (e,g,j,l,m,p,t,x) and those most difficult are (a,b,c,h,n,o,q,r,u). The Corrieu and DeFalco study found that the group of characters (c,e,i,j,m,w,x,y) were most easily recognized by the children. On the other hand, the group (b,h,k,n,p,q,r,s,u) included the most difficult characters. While the data sets compared above are similar, their disagreement can be accounted for in the difference between cursive and printed script.

Figures 6 and 7 show activities in each subnet of a cluster during training and during the test of the net. At the present time we have no explanation why some of the subnets would display similar activities during learning letters, as for example "j, k, l", nor can we hypothesize uneven activities by the same subnets during the testing phase with "j, k, l". These analysis will be addressed in our future work [82].

A system of this nature is designed to work interactively with other (possibly network-based) higher-level classifiers. These would include links to systems that recognize different word shapes, linguistic properties and semantic information.

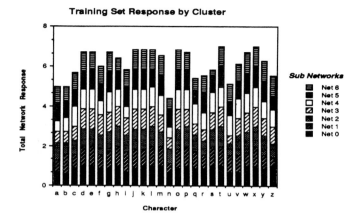

Figure 7: Activities within each sub-network of a cluster during training with each character in the alphabet.

Word shapes are useful indicators to frequently used words (the, it, a). Linguistic properties include the part of speech as well as the orthographic rules governing letter juxtaposition. Semantic information can narrow down the choice of candidate words, and hence impact letter identification. Taken together, these various classification systems could be used to identify handwritten word patterns, and hence, the constituent letters.

8   Conclusion

In the future we would like to extend the script recognition problem in the following way; instead of deciding which features are important to learn, we want to set up a stochastic relaxation network that could differentiate the strokes by learning the correspondence between strokes within the internal model of a character. In other words given that we know the model, i.e. script characters of various styles, the network must first develop its own representation for basic components that are constrained by visual feature detectors. The recognition of any character would then become a very fast neural learning implemented as a relaxation, constrained by the existing models. A further extension would be to develop an interactive activation model that could select features through competitive learning, by satisfying multiple constraints of letter-feature detectors, motorprograms for character generation and contextual information at the word or sentence level.

Many algorithms for character recognition have very limited applicability. Some algorithms apply to the characteristics of Chinese characters while others to the characteristics of English script. It seems however, that humans have no structural preference, that could be detected in all alphabets. There is a wide variety of alphabets and of structural differences in individual letters within those alphabets. Moreover, the evidence that humans "turn" objects over in their minds in order to match rotated objects [15] implies that the object representation is a spatial one. It is also interesting to note that when reading words that are upside down, there is an initial period when the reading is very slow. After this initial "training" period people adapt and are able to read at a normal pace. This fact can be explained by assuming that during the initial training period, the letters are rotated mentally and then recognized. Afterwards, a representation of the inverted character is stored for immediate recognition. Finally, it is also interesting that objects that complicate the character structure for instance, serifs, do not impede recognition. Some recognition algorithms need a special preprocessing step to eliminate the serifs. Humans however, seem to have a preference for serifs. This would seem to rule out statistical methods for the human recognition system since serifs can easily change any statistical properties for the character.

In conclusion, to approach human recognition capabilities some radically different approach is needed. This should involve a spatial representation of the character that can be manipulated and deformed easily. Moreover, this method should be integrated with lexical analysis and other high level routines (such as underline recognizers). Obviously, this algorithm must be highly parallel and have a large memory cache at its disposal.

Acknowledgements

Support for the UCLA Machine Perception Laboratory environment is provided in part by generous grants from IBM and Hewlett Packard. We sincerely acknowledge support by ARCO-UCLA Grant #1, MICRO-Hughes grant #541122-57442, ONR grant #N00014-86-K-0395, ARO grant DAAL03-88-K-0052 and PMTC-ATI grant #N00123-87-D-0364. Special thanks to the students of the MPL for critical comments of previous versions of this manuscript.

References

[1] R. Plamondon and G. Lorette. Automatic signature verification and writer identification–the state of the art. *Pattern Recognition*, 22(2):107–131, 1989.

[2] S.T. Kahan, T. Pavlidis, and W. Baird. On recognition of printed characters of any font and size. *IEEE Pattern Analysis and Machine Intelligence*, 9:274–285, 1987.

[3] A. Rajavelu, M.T. Musavi, and M.V. Shrivaikar. A neural network approach to character recognition. *Neural Networks*, 2:387–393, 1989.

[4] Y. Le Cun, L.D. Jackel, B. Boser, J.S. Denker, H.P. Graf, I. Guyon, D. Henderson, R.E. Howard, and W. Hubbard. Handwritten digit recognition: applications of neural network chips and automatic learning. *IEEE Communications Magazine*, 27(11):41–46, 1989.

[5] L. Lam and C.Y. Suen. Structural classification and relaxation matching of totally unconstrained handwritten zip-code numbers. *Pattern Recognition*, 21:19–32, 1988.

[6] I. Guyon, I. Poujand, I. Personnaz, G. Dreyfus, J. Denker, and Y. Le Cun. Comparing different neural network architectures for classifying handwritten digits. In *Proceedings of the International Joint Conference on Neural Networks, Washington, DC*, pages 127–132, June 1989.

[7] P. Morasso. Neural models of cursive script handwriting. In *Proceedings of the International Joint Conference on Neural Networks, Washington, DC*, pages 539–542, June 1989.

[8] J. Hollerbach. An oscillation theory of handwriting. *Biological Cybernetics*, 39:139–156, 1981.

[9] W. Marslen-Wilson and L.K. Tyler. The temporal structure of spoken language understanding. *Cognition*, 8(1):1–71, 1980.

[10] V.W. Berninger, A.C.N. Chen, and R.D. Abbott. A test of the multiple connections model of reading acquisition. *Internationall Journal of Neuroscience*, 42:283–295, 1988.

[11] J.L. McClelland, D.E. Rumelhart, and G.E. Hinton. The appeal of pdp. In *Parallel Distributed Processing: Explorations in the Microstructure of Cognition*, pages 3–44, MIT Press, 1986.

[12] E. Mesrobian, M. Stiber, and J. Skrzypek. *SFINX - structure and function in neural connections*. Technical Report UCLA-MPL-TR-89-8, Machine Perception Laboratory, University of California, Los Angeles, November 1989.

[13] R.P. Lippman. An introduction to computing with neural nets. *IEEE ASSP Magazine*, 4–22, 1987.

[14] R.P. Lippman. Pattern classification using neural networks. *IEEE Communications Magazine*, 27:47–64, 1989.

[15] L.A. Cooper and R.N. Shepard. Turning something over in the mind. *Scientific American*, 251(6):106–115, December 1984.

[16] S.C. Fischer and J.W. Pellegrino. Hemisphere differences for components of mental rotation. *Brain and Cognition*, 7:1–15, 1988.

[17] M. Ammar, Y. Yoshida, and T. Fukumara. A new effective approach for off-line verification of signatures by using pressure features. In *8th International Conference on Pattern Recognition*, pages 566–569, Paris, 1986.

[18] R.E. von der Heydt, Peterhans, and G. Baumgartner. Illusory contours and cortical neuron responses. *Science*, 224:1260–1262, 1984.

[19] R. Sabourin and R. Plamondon. Preprocessing of handwritten signatures from image gradient analysis. In *8th International Conference on Pattern Recognition*, pages 576–579, Paris, 1986.

[20] P.C. Chuang. Machine verification of handwritten signature image. In J.S. Jackson and R.W. De Vore, editors, *1977 International Conference on Crime Countermeasures,*, pages 105–109, University of Kentucky, 1977.

[21] R.N. Nagel and A. Rosenfeld. Computer detection of freehand forgeries. *IEEE Transactions on Computers*, 26:895–905, 1977.

[22] S. Edelman and T. Flash. A model of handwriting. *Biological Cybernetics*, 57:25–36, 1987.

[23] W. W. Loy and I. E. Landau. An on-line procedure for recognition of hand-printed alphanumeric characters. *IEEE Transactions on Pattern Analysis and Machine Intelligence*, PAMI-4(4):422–427, July 1982.

[24] M.K. Babcock and J.J. Freyd. Perception of dynamic information in static handwritten forms. *American Journal of Psychology*, 101(1):111–130, 1988.

[25] P.A. Dondes and A. Rosenfeld. Pixel classification based on gray level and local business. *IEEE Transactions on Pattern Analysis and Machine Intelligence*, PAMI-4(4):79–84, January 1982.

[26] J. Skrzypek. A unified computational architecture for preprocessing visual information in space and time. In *Proceedings of SPIE Conference on Computer Vision*, pages 258–263, 1985.

[27] C. Koch, J. Marroquin, and A. Yuille. Analog neuronal networks in early vision. In *Proceedings National Academy of Science USA*, 1986.

[28] H.A. Mallot and W. von Seelen. Neural mappings and space invariant image processing. In *Abstracts, 1st Annual INNS Conference*, page 514, Boston, 1988.

[29] G.A. Carpenter and S. Grossberg. The art of adaptive pattern recognition by self-organizing neural network. *IEEE Computer*, 21:77–88, March 1988.

[30] D.H. Ballard and C.M. Brown. *Computer Vision*. Prentice-Hall, New Jersey, 1982.

[31] O. Baruch. Line thinning by line following. *Pattern Recognition Letters*, 8(4):271–276, November 1988.

[32] A. Iannino and S.D. Shapiro. An iterative generalization of the sobel edge operator. In *International Conference on Pattern Recognition and Image Processing*, pages 130–137, 1979.

[33] R.J. Gleeson and J. Skrzypek. Boundaries as unpredictable discontinuities. In *SPIE Image Understanding and the Man-Machine Interface II*, Los Angeles, 1989.

[34] S.W. Zucker. The organization of curve detection: coarse tangent fields and fine spline coverings. In *Abstracts, 1st Annual INNS Conference*, page 534, Boston, 1988.

[35] S. Busenberg and L. Rossi. Optimization of rotationally invariant object recognition in neural network. In *Abstracts, 1st Annual INNS Conference*, page 483, Boston, 1988.

[36] E.L. Schwartz. On mathematical structure of retinotopic mapping of primate striate cortex. *Science*, 227:1066, 1985.

[37] T. Wakayama. A core line tracing algorithm based on maximal square moving. *IEEE Transactions on Pattern Analysis and Machine Intelligence*, PAMI-4(1):68–74, January 1982.

[38] N.J. Naccache and R. Shinghal. An investigation into the skeletonization approach of hilditch. *Pattern Recognition*, 17(3):279–283, 1984.

[39] F. Banch. Correspondence. *Pattern Recognition Letters*, 8:271–276, November 1988.

[40] I. Heisey and J. Skrzypek. Color constancy and early vision: connectionist model. In *IEEE First International Conference on Neural Networks*, San Diego, CA, 1987.

[41] W.A. Wright. Contextual image segmentation with a neural network. In *Abstracts, 1st Annual INNS Conference*, page 531, Boston, 1988.

[42] M Yasuhara and M. Oka. Signature verification experiment based on nonlinear time alignment: a feasibility study. *IEEE Trans Systems, Man and Cybernetics*, 17:212–216, 1977.

[43] Y. Sato and K. Kogura. On-line signature verification based on shape, motion and handwriting pressure. In *6th International Conference on Pattern Recognition*, pages 823–826, 1982.

[44] A. Badreldin and M. Shridhar. High accuracy character recognition algorithm using form and topological descriptors. *Pattern Recognition*, 17:515–524, 1984.

[45] R. Bozinovic and S.N. Srihari. Knowledge based cursive script interpretation. In *International Conference on Pattern Recognition*, pages 774–776, 1984.

[46] H.B. Barlow. General principles: the senses considered as physical instruments. In H.B. Barlow and J.D. Mollon, editors, *The Senses*, Cambridge University Press, 1982.

[47] O.G Selfridge and U. Neisser. Pattern recognition by machine. *Scientific American*, 203:60–68, 1960.

[48] J. Skrzypek and E. Mesrobian. Textural segmentation: gestalt heuristics as a connectionist hierarchy of feature detectors. In *IEEE Conference of the Engineering in Medicine and Biology*, Boston, 1987.

[49] G. Lynch, R. Grangner, M. Baudry, and J. Larson. Cortical encoding of memory: hypotheses derived from analysis and simulation of physiological learning rules and anatomical structures. In L. Nadel, L. Cooper, P. Culicover, and R.M. Harnish, editors, *Neural Connections and Mental Computation*, pages 247–289, MIT Press, Cambridge, MA, 1988.

[50] M.V. Shirvaikar and M.T. Musavi. A neural network classifier for character recognition. In *Abstracts, 1st Annual INNS Conference*, page 524, Boston, 1988.

[51] J.S. Denker, W.R. Gardner, H.P. Graf, D. Henderson, R.E. Howard, W. Hubbard, L.D. Jackel, H.S. Baird, and I. Guyon. Neural network recognizer for handwritten zip code digits. In D. S. Touretzky, editor, *Advances in Neural Information Processing Systems 1*, Morgan Kaufman Publishers, San Mateo, CA, 1989.

[52] S. Grossberg. Competitive learning: from interactive activation to adaptive resonance. *Cognitive Science*, 11:23–63, 1987.

[53] Campbell and Robson. Application of fourier analysis to the visibility of gratings. *Journal of Physiology*, 197:551–556, 1968.

[54] Y.X. Gu, Q.R. Wang, and C.Y. Suen. Application of a multilayer decision tree in computer recognition of chinese characters. *IEEE Transactions on Pattern Analysis and Machine Intelligence*, PAMI-5(1):83–89, January 1983.

[55] F. Rosenblatt. *Principles of Neurodynamics*. Spartan, New York, 1962.

[56] D.E. Rumelhart, G.E. Hinton, and R.J. Williams. Learning internal representations by error propagation. In *Parallel Distributed Processing: Explorations in the Microstructure of Cognition*, MIT Press, 1986.

[57] D.H. Ackley, G.E. Hinton, and T.J. Sejnowski. A learning algorithm for boltzman machines. *Cognitive Science*, 9:147–160, 1985.

[58] J.R. Quinlan. Simplifying decision trees. *International Journal of Man-Machine Studies*, 27:221–234, 1987.

[59] J.S. Albus. *Brains, behavior and robotics*. Byte Books, New Hampshire, 1981.

[60] F.H. Glanz and W.T. Miller. Shape recognition using a cmac-based learning system. In *Intelligent Robots and Computer Vision*, SPIE, Cambridge, MA, 1987.

[61] A. Rojer and E. Schwartz. A multiple-map model for pattern classification. *Neural Computation*, 1(1):104–115, 1989.

[62] T. Kohonen. An introduction to neural computing. *Neural Networks*, 1:3–16, 1988.

[63] R.O. Duda and P.E. Hart. *Pattern classification and scene analysis*. J. Wiley and Sons, New York, 1973.

[64] C.Y. Suen and Q.R. Wang. Analysis and description of a decision tree based on entropy and its application to large character set recognition. *IEEE Transactions on Pattern Analysis and Machine Intelligence*, PAMI-6(4):406–417, July 1984.

[65] A. Badreldin and M. Shridhar. A true classification algorithm for handwritten character recognition. In *International Conference on Pattern Recognition*, pages 615–618, 1984.

[66] T. Sagawa, E. Tanaka, M. Suzuki, and M. Fajita. An unsupervised learning of handprinted character with linguistic information. In *International Conference on Pattern Recognition*, pages 766–769, 1984.

[67] R. Shingal and C.Y. Suen. A method for selecting constrained hand-printed character shapes for machine recognition. *IEEE Transactions on Pattern Analysis and Machine Intelligence*, PAMI-4(1):74–78, January 1982.

[68] K. Asai and J. Tsukumo. Non linear method for handprinted character recognition. In *International Conference on Pattern Recognition*, pages 770–773, 1984.

[69] W. Lincoln and J. Skrzypek. Synergy of clustering multiple back-propagation networks. 1989. To appear in NIPS Proceedings, Denver, CO.

[70] D.J. Burr. Experiments on neural net for recognition of spoken and written text. *IEEE Transactions on Acoustics, Speech And Signal Processing*, 36(7):1162–1168, 1988.

[71] R. Crick. The recent excitment about neural nets. *Nature*, 337:129–132, 1989.

[72] R. Bozinovic and S.N. Srihari. A string correction algorithm for cursive script recognition. *IEEE Transactions on Pattern Analysis and Machine Intelligence*, PAMI-4(6):655–663, 1982.

[73] J.J. Hull, S.N. Srihari, and R. Choudhari. An integrated algorithm for text recognition: comparison with a cascaded algorithm. *IEEE Transactions on Pattern Analysis and Machine Intelligence*, PAMI-5(4):384–395, July 1983.

[74] J.L. McClelland and D.E. Rumelhart. An interactive activation model of context effects in letter perception: part 1 an account of main findings. *Psychological Review*, 88:375–407, 1981.

[75] E.R. Kandel and J.H. Schwartz. *Principles of Neural Science*. Elsevier, New York, 1985.

[76] E.L. Schwartz. Computational anatomy and functional architecture of striate cortex: a spatial mapping approach to perceptual coding. *Vision Research*, 20:645–669, 1980.

[77] J.L. Adams. *Principles of Complementarity, Cooperativity, and Adaptive Error Control in Pattern Learning and Recognition: A Physiological Neural Network Model Tested by Computer Simulation*. Technical Report, University of California, Los Angeles, 1989. Department of Neuroscience.

[78] M. Seibert and A.M. Waxman. Early vision applications of feature-map diffusion-enhancement nets. In *Abstracts, 1st Annual INNS Conference*, page 523, Boston, 1988.

[79] L.G. Ungerlaider and M. Mishkin. *Analysis of visual behavior,*. MIT Press, 1982.

[80] S.M. Kosslyn. Aspects of cognitive neuroscience of mental imagery. *Science*, 240:1621–1626, 1988.

[81] R.M. Bozinovic and S.N. Srihari. Off-line cursive script recognition. *IEEE Transactions on Pattern Analysis and Machine Intelligence*, 11(1):68–83, January 1989.

[82] J. Hoffman, J. Skrzypek, and J.J. Vidal. Cluster network for recognition of handwritten script characters. In preparation.

[83] P. Corrieu and S. De Falco. Segmental vs. dynamic analysis of letter shape by preschool children. *European Bulletin of Cognitive Psychology*, 9(2):189–198, 1989.

[84] H. Bouma. Visual recognition of isolated lower-case letters. *Vision Research*, 11:459–474, 1971.

NEURAL NETWORKS: Advances and Applications
E. Gelenbe (Editor)
© Elsevier Science Publishers B.V. (North-Holland), 1991

A Distributed Decorrelation Algorithm

Fernando M. Silva   Luís B. Almeida
INESC - Instituto de Engenharia de Sistemas e Computadores
IST - Instituto Superior Tecnico
R. Alves Redol, 1000 Lisboa, Portugal

Abstract Given a set of correlated random variables, it is often of practical interest to find a linear transformation of this set such that the transformed random variables are uncorrelated. In this study we present a simple, recursive algorithm that converges to a linear transformation with this property, directly from the observation of the transformed set of random variables. As the algorithm is adaptive by nature, it can be extended to situations where the input correlation matrix is slowly varying with time. Moreover, it is shown that the algorithm has "distributed" properties, and that it can be implemented using a fully parallel network structure. Conditions for the convergence of the algorithm are also presented.

1. Introduction

Given a set of correlated random variables, it is often of practical interest to find a linear transformation of this set such that the transformed random variables are orthogonal. Such transformation, while keeping all information available in the input data, is able to produce a set of uncorrelated random variables, which can be more convenient for statistical reasons.

A simple solution to the orthogonalization problem is to estimate the correlation matrix of the input random variables, and then use a conventional orthogonalization technique, such as the Gram-Schmidt procedure. However, if the input correlation matrix is slowly varying with time, this procedure must be repeated periodically, in order to keep the output random variables uncorrelated.

In this work, we present a simple, recursive algorithm that produces one estimate of a linear transformation that is able to produce a set of uncorrelated and normalized random variables. As the algorithm is adaptive by nature, it can be extended to situations where the input correlation matrix is slowly varying with time. Moreover, it is shown that the algorithm has distributed properties, and that it can be implemented using a network structure.

This work is structured as follows. In section 2, the orthonormalization problem is stated, and subsequent notation is introduced. In section 3, the orthonormalization algorithm is presented using an intuitive approach and a simple bi-dimensional example. In section 4, the procedure is generalized for the N variable case. In section 5, we prove that, if certain conditions are met, the algorithm converges to the desired solution. In section 6, we show that this algorithm minimizes a simple cost functional. In section 7, we present the stochastic version of the algorithm, and we discuss conditions of convergence in this case. In section 8, we show that the algorithm can be implemented using a distributed network architecture. Finally, in section 9, conclusions of this work are reported.

2. Formulation

Consider one set $X = \{X_i, i = 1, \cdots, N\}$ of observable random variables. Denote by $\mathbf{X}$ the vector

$$(1) \qquad \mathbf{X} = \left[\begin{array}{cccc} X_1 & X_2 & \cdots & X_N \end{array}\right]^T$$

Let $Y = \{Y_i, i = 1, \cdots, N\}$ be a second set of random variables obtained from X by the linear transformation

$$(2) \qquad \mathbf{Y} = \mathbf{AX}$$

where $\mathbf{A}$ is a $N \times N$ matrix and $\mathbf{Y}$ is the vector

$$(3) \qquad \mathbf{Y} = \left[\begin{array}{cccc} Y_1 & Y_2 & \cdots & Y_N \end{array}\right]^T$$

Denoting by $E[]$ the expected value operator, the correlation matrix $\mathbf{R}_{yy}$ of Y is given by

$$(4) \qquad \mathbf{R}_{yy} = E[\mathbf{Y}\mathbf{Y}^T] = E[\mathbf{A}\mathbf{X}\mathbf{X}^T\mathbf{A}^T] = \mathbf{A}E[\mathbf{X}\mathbf{X}^T]\mathbf{A}^T$$

or

$$(5) \qquad \mathbf{R}_{yy} = \mathbf{A}\mathbf{R}_{zz}\mathbf{A}^T$$

where $\mathbf{R}_{zz} = E[\mathbf{X}\mathbf{X}^T]$ is the correlation matrix of X.

The orthonormalization problem can now be stated as follows: for a given set X of random variables, find a linear transformation $\mathbf{A}$ of X such that

$$(6) \qquad \mathbf{R}_{yy} = \mathbf{A}\mathbf{R}_{zz}\mathbf{A}^T = \mathbf{I}$$

where $\mathbf{I}$ denotes the identity matrix, i.e., a matrix $\mathbf{A}$ such that the components of $\mathbf{Y}$, as given by (2), are uncorrelated and normalized.

Since $\mathbf{R}_{zz}$ is a symmetric matrix, it can be decomposed as

$$(7) \qquad \mathbf{R}_{zz} = \mathbf{U}\mathbf{D}\mathbf{U}^T$$

where $\mathbf{D}$ is the diagonal matrix of eigenvalues of $\mathbf{R}_{zz}$ and $\mathbf{U}$ is the $N \times N$ matrix whose columns are the orthonormal eigenvectors of $\mathbf{R}_{zz}$. Setting

$$(8) \qquad \mathbf{A} = \mathbf{U}^T$$

and by direct substitution of (8) and (7) in (6), is possible to verify that (8) is a possible solution to the orthogonalization problem alone. In this case, the linear transformation $\mathbf{A}$ performs a principal component decomposition of the input data and, in this sense, it has several optimal properties (note, however, that (8) does not normalize the output variables). A stochastic estimation procedure to find this optimal solution was presented by Sanger in [1].

However, it is possible to find situations where the main requirement is the orthonormalization of the input data, and where principal component decomposition is not necessary. For theses cases, a simpler algorithm, as described below, can be used.

3. Basic Concept

To understand the basic concept underlying this new algorithm, we consider first the two variable case. Assume that at step n we have an estimate $\hat{\mathbf{A}}(n)$ of $\mathbf{A}$, and denote by $\hat{\mathbf{a}}_j(n)$ the vector formed by the elements of the j-th line of matrix $\hat{\mathbf{A}}(n)$, such that $Y_j = \hat{\mathbf{a}}_j^T(n)\mathbf{X}$. In this case, the cross-correlation $r_{12}(n)$ between Y_1 and Y_2 at time n is given by

$$(9) \qquad r_{12}(n) = E[Y_1 Y_2] = E[\hat{a}_1^T(n)\mathbf{X}\mathbf{X}^T \hat{a}_2(n)] = \hat{a}_1^T(n)\mathbf{R}_{xx}\hat{a}_2(n)$$

Note that $\mathbf{R}_{xx}$, being a correlation matrix, is symmetric non-negative. Since our goal is the orthonormalization of the input data, a fundamental assumption of this work is that the random variables X_i are linearly independent. In this case, the matrix $\mathbf{R}_{xx}$ is also positive definite and it can be interpreted as a metric matrix. With this hypothesis, (9) shows that the cross-correlation between Y_1 and Y_2 can be seen as the dot product of $\hat{a}_1(n)$ and $\hat{a}_2(n)$ with metric $\mathbf{R}_{xx}$. To make $r_{12} = 0$, we must orthogonalize $\hat{a}_1(n)$ and $\hat{a}_2(n)$, with respect to the metric $\mathbf{R}_{xx}$.

If $\mathbf{R}_{xx}$ was exactly known, we could simply perform the Gram-Schmidt orthonormalization procedure [2] to get the desired solution in a single iteration. In the N variable case, the Gram-Schmidt procedure can be performed by taking the following consecutive steps:

- Normalize the first vector with respect to metric $\mathbf{R}_{xx}$, by making

$$(10) \qquad a_1 = \frac{\hat{a}_1(n)}{\sqrt{\hat{a}_1^T(n)\mathbf{R}_{xx}\hat{a}_1(n)}}$$

- For $j = 2, ..., N$ repeat the following steps:

1. Find a vector a_j^u orthogonal to the hyperplane defined by the $j - 1$ vectors already orthonormalized. This can be accomplished by making

$$(11) \qquad a_j^u = \hat{a}_j(n) - \sum_{k<j}[\hat{a}_j^T(n)\mathbf{R}_{xx}a_k]a_k$$

2. Normalize a_j^u with respect to metric $\mathbf{R}_{xx}$:

$$(12) \qquad a_j = \frac{a_j^u}{\sqrt{(a_1^u)^T\mathbf{R}_{xx}a_1^u}}$$

The Gram-Schmidt orthogonalization procedure has a simple geometric interpretation if one considers the case $\mathbf{R}_{xx} = \mathbf{I}$. Fig. 1 shows an example of this procedure for the two variable case.

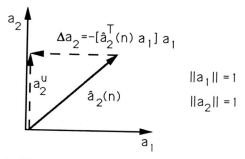

Figure 1: Illustration of the Gram-Schmidt orthogonalization procedure, for $N = 2$ and $\mathbf{R}_{zz} = \mathbf{I}$.

Unfortunately, in the more general case, $\mathbf{R}_{yy}(n)$ and $\mathbf{R}_{zz}$ are not known, and provision must be made to estimate correlation values from observations of X or Y. Moreover, if $\mathbf{R}_{zz}$ is slowly varying with time, one would like to have an adaptive algorithm to automatically correct small changes in the input correlation matrix. To introduce this algorithm, let us consider again the bi-dimensional case and assume that at step n $\mathbf{R}_{yy}(n)$ is exactly known[1] and that we have an estimate, say $\hat{\mathbf{A}}(n)$, of $\mathbf{A}$. A new estimate of $\mathbf{A}$ can be obtained by updating the lines of $\hat{\mathbf{A}}(n)$ according to the rule

(13)
$$\begin{aligned}
\hat{a}_1(n+1) &= \hat{a}_1(n) - \alpha \hat{a}_1^T(n)\mathbf{R}_{zz}\hat{a}_2^T(n)\hat{a}_2(n) \\
\hat{a}_2(n+1) &= \hat{a}_2(n) - \alpha \hat{a}_2^T(n)\mathbf{R}_{zz}\hat{a}_1^T(n)\hat{a}_1(n)
\end{aligned}$$

or

(14)
$$\begin{aligned}
\hat{a}_1(n+1) &= \hat{a}_1(n) - \alpha r_{12}(n)\hat{a}_2(n) \\
\hat{a}_2(n+1) &= \hat{a}_2(n) - \alpha r_{21}(n)\hat{a}_1(n)
\end{aligned}$$

where α is a small positive number. In order to suggest the way by which (14) contributes to the desired orthogonalization, Fig. 2 depicts the basic idea underlying this adaptation law, assuming that $\mathbf{R}_{zz} = \mathbf{I}$.

---

[1]Note that all the analysis carried out in this work can be extended to finite training sets, by substitution of the correlation on that set for the statistical correlation. In this case, $\mathbf{R}_{yy}(n)$ can be, in fact, exactly known, and the weight update procedure given below corresponds to what is generally called the batch, offline or deterministic training mode.

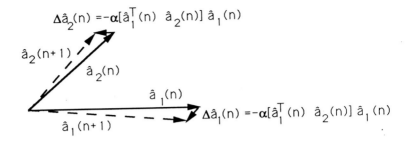

Figure 2: Illustration of the proposed adaptation procedure for $N = 2$ and $\mathbf{R}_{zz} = \mathbf{I}$.

Until now we were only concerned with orthogonalization, and we have not yet considered the normalization problem. However, equations (14) can be modified to include a small positive or negative contribution of the adapted vector itself depending on whether the variance r_{jj} of the output variable is larger or smaller than 1. With this modification, equations (14) become

(15)
$$\begin{aligned}
\hat{a}_1(n+1) &= \hat{a}_1(n) - \alpha r_{12}(n)\hat{a}_2(n) + \alpha(1 - r_{11})\hat{a}_1(n) \\
\hat{a}_2(n+1) &= \hat{a}_2(n) - \alpha r_{21}(n)\hat{a}_1(n) + \alpha(1 - r_{22})\hat{a}_2(n)
\end{aligned}$$

4. Generalization to N variables

An intuitive generalization of equations (15) to the N variable case is straightforward, and it results from the extension of the single cross-correlation term to all possible combinations of Y variables. The proposed algorithm can now be stated as follows: for each line of matrix $\hat{\mathbf{A}}(n)$, adapt $\hat{a}_j(n)$ as

(16)
$$\hat{a}_j(n+1) = \hat{a}_j(n) - \alpha \sum_{\substack{k=1 \\ k \neq j}}^{N} r_{jk}(n)\hat{a}_k(n) + \alpha(1 - r_{jj}(n))\hat{a}_j(n)$$

or, bringing the normalization term into the sum,

$$(17) \qquad \hat{a}_j(n+1) = (1+\alpha)\hat{a}_j(n) - \alpha \sum_{k=1}^{N} r_{jk}(n)\hat{a}_k(n)$$

Equation (17) can be written in matrix notation as

$$(18) \qquad \hat{\mathbf{A}}(n+1) = (1+\alpha)\hat{\mathbf{A}}(n) - \alpha\mathbf{R}_{yy}(n)\hat{\mathbf{A}}(n)$$

or

$$(19) \qquad \hat{\mathbf{A}}(n+1) = [(1+\alpha)\mathbf{I} - \alpha\mathbf{R}_{yy}(n)]\hat{\mathbf{A}}(n)$$

which represents a recursive equation for $\hat{\mathbf{A}}(n)$.

Until now, we have used an intuitive approach to suggest the update rule described by (19). In the next section, we will show that this algorithm converges, in fact, to a solution of (6).

5. Proof of convergence for the stationary case

To show that (19) converges to the desired solution, it is convenient to express the algorithm as a recursion in $\mathbf{R}_{yy}(n)$. The correlation matrix of Y at step $n+1$ is given by

$$(20) \qquad \mathbf{R}_{yy}(n+1) = \hat{\mathbf{A}}(n+1)\mathbf{R}_{zz}\hat{\mathbf{A}}^T(n+1)$$

Considering the recursion defined by (19), we can also write

$$(21)\ \mathbf{R}_{yy}(n+1) = [(1+\alpha)\mathbf{I} - \alpha\mathbf{R}_{yy}(n)]\hat{\mathbf{A}}(n)\mathbf{R}_{zz}\hat{\mathbf{A}}^T(n)[(1+\alpha)\mathbf{I} - \alpha\mathbf{R}_{yy}(n)]^T$$

Since we have $\hat{\mathbf{A}}(n)\mathbf{R}_{zz}\hat{\mathbf{A}}^T(n) = \mathbf{R}_{yy}(n)$, and since the last factor in square brackets is a symmetric matrix, we can drop the transposition operator and then develop the product to obtain

$$(22) \qquad \mathbf{R}_{yy}(n+1) = (1+\alpha)^2\mathbf{R}_{yy}(n) - 2\alpha(1+\alpha)\mathbf{R}_{yy}^2(n) + \alpha^2\mathbf{R}_{yy}^3(n)$$

Assuming that $\mathbf{R}_{yy}(n)$ is a positive definite matrix (we will discuss this hypothesis in appendix A), it can be decomposed as in (7), hence we can write

(23)
$$\mathbf{R}_{yy}(n) = \mathbf{V}(n)\mathbf{\Lambda}(n)\mathbf{V}^T(n)$$

where $\mathbf{\Lambda}(n)$ is the diagonal matrix of eigenvalues of $\mathbf{R}_{yy}(n)$ and $\mathbf{V}(n)$ is the $N \times N$ matrix whose columns are the orthonormal eigenvectors of $\mathbf{R}_{yy}(n)$. Since we have $\mathbf{V}(n)\mathbf{V}^T(n) = \mathbf{I}$, we can see that

(24)
$$\mathbf{R}_{yy}^s(n) = \mathbf{V}(n)\mathbf{\Lambda}^s(n)\mathbf{V}^T(n)$$

and (22) can be written as

(25)
$$\begin{aligned}\mathbf{R}_{yy}(n+1) = {} & (1+\alpha)^2\mathbf{V}(n)\mathbf{\Lambda}(n)\mathbf{V}^T(n) - \\ & 2\alpha(1+\alpha)\mathbf{V}(n)\mathbf{\Lambda}^2(n)\mathbf{V}^T(n) + \alpha^2\mathbf{V}(n)\mathbf{\Lambda}^3(n)\mathbf{V}^T(n)\end{aligned}$$

or, putting in evidence the eigenvector matrices,

(26)
$$\mathbf{R}_{yy}(n+1) = \mathbf{V}(n)[(1+\alpha)^2\mathbf{\Lambda}(n) - 2\alpha(1+\alpha)\mathbf{\Lambda}^2(n) + \alpha^2\mathbf{\Lambda}^3(n)]\mathbf{V}^T(n)$$

Now we note that the middle factor in square brackets is still a diagonal matrix which, as in (23), is multiplied by $V(n)$ and $V^T(n)$. This means that the proposed algorithm does not change the eigenvectors of the output correlation matrix, performing only a recursive update of the eigenvalues of $\mathbf{R}_{yy}$. In fact, (26) can also be written as

(27)
$$\mathbf{R}_{yy}(n+1) = \mathbf{V}(n)\mathbf{\Lambda}(n+1)\mathbf{V}^T(n)$$

with

(28)
$$\mathbf{\Lambda}(n+1) = (1+\alpha)^2\mathbf{\Lambda}(n) - 2\alpha(1+\alpha)\mathbf{\Lambda}^2(n) + \alpha^2\mathbf{\Lambda}^3(n)$$

Since all matrices in (28) are now diagonal, the analysis of this procedure can be reduced to the study of a scalar recursion in the eigenvalues of $\mathbf{R}_{yy}$. Call $\lambda(n)$ a generic eigenvalue of $\mathbf{R}_{yy}(n)$. In this case, $\lambda(n+1)$ is given by

(29)
$$\lambda(n+1) = (1+\alpha)^2\lambda(n) - 2\alpha(1+\alpha)\lambda^2(n) + \alpha^2\lambda^3(n)$$

To show that (21) converges to the identity matrix, one has only to show that all eigenvalues of $\mathbf{R}_{yy}(n)$ converge to 1, at least for some values of α. It is possible to show that convergence can be ensured by taking the following steps[2]:

---

[2] See appendix A for a detailed discussion

1. Initially set $\hat{\mathbf{A}}$ to the identity matrix, i.e., make

(30)
$$\mathbf{A}(0) = \mathbf{I}$$

2. Denote by λ_{max}^X the largest eigenvalue of $\mathbf{R}_{xx}$. Set $\alpha < 1/2$. In addition, if $\lambda_{max}^X > 1$, set

(31)
$$\alpha < \frac{1}{3\lambda_{max}^X - 1}$$

As noted in appendix A, it is in practice possible to increase the value of α during the training procedure. In fact, as the eigenvalues of $\mathbf{R}_{yy}(n)$ approach 1, the theoretical maximum of α increases. This fact is of practical usefulness to increase the rate of convergence of the algorithm.

6. Gradient Interpretation

In this section we will show that the proposed algorithm can be seen as a modified gradient procedure.

Consider again an arbitrary estimate $\hat{\mathbf{A}}$ of a linear transformation $\mathbf{A}$ that orthonormalizes the random variables X (for the sake of simplicity, we will drop the dependence on n in the following discussion). As was shown before, the cross-correlation between the output variables Y_k and Y_l is given by

(32)
$$r_{kl} = \hat{\mathbf{a}}_k^T \mathbf{R}_{xx} \hat{\mathbf{a}}_l$$

$\hat{\mathbf{a}}_i$ being the vector formed by the elements of the i–th line of the matrix $\hat{\mathbf{A}}$. This shows that, for a given statistical distribution of the input variables, the output correlation matrix $\mathbf{R}_{yy}$ is a simple quadratic function of the linear transformation $\hat{\mathbf{A}}$. Hence, to study the evolution of the algorithm, it would be desirable to define a cost functional of $\hat{\mathbf{A}}$ that were able to measure the "distance" between the actual $\mathbf{R}_{yy}$ and its target value, $\mathbf{I}$. One of the simplest cost functionals that one can imagine is the quadratic function

(33)
$$C(\hat{\mathbf{A}}) = \sum_{k=1}^{N} \sum_{\substack{l=1 \\ l \neq k}}^{N} r_{kl}^2 + \sum_{k=1}^{N} (1 - r_{kk})^2$$

where r_{kl} is defined by (32). The absolute minimum of this cost functional is, clearly, $C(\mathbf{A}) = 0$, which is satisfied by any matrix $\mathbf{A}$ such that $\mathbf{A}^T \mathbf{R}_{zz} \mathbf{A} = I$.

Let us now consider the gradient of $C(\hat{\mathbf{A}})$ relative to an arbitrary line of $\hat{\mathbf{A}}$, say, $\hat{\mathbf{a}}_j$. After some algebra (see appendix B), we obtain

$$(34) \qquad \frac{\partial C}{\partial \hat{\mathbf{a}}_j} = 4\mathbf{R}_{xx}[\sum_{k=1}^{N} r_{jk}\hat{\mathbf{a}}_k - \hat{\mathbf{a}}_j]$$

Note that $\frac{\partial C}{\partial \hat{\mathbf{a}}_j}$ is the gradient of $C(\hat{\mathbf{A}})$ relative only to $\hat{\mathbf{a}}_j$. The "complete" gradient of $C(\hat{\mathbf{A}})$ includes the N^2 partial derivatives of $C(\hat{\mathbf{A}})$ relative to all elements of matrix $\hat{\mathbf{A}}$. In view of this fact we will introduce the following notation to denote the "vectorization" of a given matrix:

$$(35) \qquad \mathbf{B}^v = [b_{11}, ..., b_{1N}, b_{21}, ..., b_{2N}, ..., b_{j1}, ..., b_{jN}, ..., b_{N1}, ..., b_{NN}]^T$$

where b_{ij} is the ij-th element of matrix $\mathbf{B}$, and we will denote by C^v the cost function C using the "vectorized" argument, i. e., $C^v(\mathbf{A}^v) = C(\mathbf{A})$. With this notation, the complete gradient of $C(\hat{\mathbf{A}}) = C^v(\hat{\mathbf{A}}^v)$ is given by $\frac{\partial C^v}{\partial \hat{\mathbf{A}}^v}$, and results from the concatenation of the "partial gradients" $\frac{\partial C}{\partial \hat{\mathbf{a}}_j}$ for $j = 1, ..., N$.

Now, consider again the proposed adaptation procedure described by equation (17). It can be written as

$$(36) \qquad \hat{\mathbf{a}}_j(n+1) = \hat{\mathbf{a}}_j(n) + \alpha \Delta \hat{\mathbf{a}}_j(n)$$

with $\Delta \hat{\mathbf{a}}_j(n)$ defined as

$$(37) \qquad \Delta \hat{\mathbf{a}}_j(n) = \hat{\mathbf{a}}_j(n) - \sum_{k=1}^{N} r_{jk}(n)\hat{\mathbf{a}}_j(n)$$

Comparing (34) and (37), it is clear that this adaptation procedure can be written as

$$(38) \qquad \hat{\mathbf{a}}_j(n+1) = \hat{\mathbf{a}}_j(n) - \frac{\alpha}{4}\mathbf{R}_{xx}^{-1}\frac{\partial C}{\partial \hat{\mathbf{a}}_j(n)}$$

While (38) does not yield a steepest descent procedure, one can show that this algorithm still performs a descent in $C(\hat{\mathbf{A}})$. In fact, if $\mathbf{R}_{zz}$ is a symmetric positive definite matrix, $\mathbf{R}_{zz}^{-1}$ is also symmetric positive definite, hence

$$(39) \qquad \frac{\partial C}{\partial \hat{a}_j}^T \Delta \hat{a}_j = -\frac{\alpha}{4} \frac{\partial C}{\partial \hat{a}_j}^T \mathbf{R}_{zz}^{-1} \frac{\partial C}{\partial \hat{a}_j} < 0, \qquad \text{if } \frac{\partial C}{\partial \hat{a}_j} \neq 0$$

Note that the introduction of $\mathbf{R}_{zz}^{-1}$ in the gradient update introduces a distortion factor which amplifies the gradient components disposed along the eigendirections of $\mathbf{R}_{zz}^{-1}$ with the largest eigenvalues. However, the dot product of the gradient and the adaptation vector is still negative, hence, choosing a small enough value for α, we will still obtain a descent procedure.

The extension of this result to the complete gradient of $C(\hat{\mathbf{a}})$ is straightforward. Write the recursive procedure as

$$(40) \qquad \hat{\mathbf{A}}^v(n+1) = \hat{\mathbf{A}}^v(n) + \alpha \Delta \hat{\mathbf{A}}^v(n)$$

where we have defined

$$(41) \qquad \Delta \hat{\mathbf{A}}(n) = \hat{\mathbf{A}}(n) - \mathbf{R}_{yy} \hat{\mathbf{A}}(n)$$

With the above definitions, one can easily see that

$$(42) \qquad \frac{\partial C^v}{\partial \hat{\mathbf{A}}^v}^T \Delta \hat{\mathbf{A}}^v(n) = -\frac{\alpha}{4} \sum_{k=1}^{N} \frac{\partial C}{\partial \hat{a}_k}^T \mathbf{R}_{zz}^{-1} \frac{\partial C}{\partial \hat{a}_k} < 0,$$

$$\text{if } \frac{\partial C}{\partial \hat{a}_j} \neq 0 \text{ for any } j = 1, \cdots, N$$

because all terms within the sum are non-negative.

Hence, we can conclude that $C(\hat{\mathbf{A}})$ is a Lyapunov function relative to the adaptation vector $\Delta \hat{\mathbf{A}}^v(n)$, since the dot product of $\Delta \hat{\mathbf{A}}^v(n)$ and the "complete" gradient $C(\hat{\mathbf{A}})$ is negative for any $\hat{\mathbf{A}}$ such that $\frac{\partial C^v}{\partial \hat{\mathbf{A}}^v} \neq 0$. Note again that this conclusion is only valid if $\mathbf{R}_{zz}$ is positive definite, in order to ensure that $\mathbf{R}_{zz}^{-1}$ is also positive definite.

7. Stochastic Approximation

Consider again the proposed algorithm, expressed as

(43)
$$\hat{\mathbf{A}}(n+1) = \hat{\mathbf{A}}(n) + \alpha[\hat{\mathbf{A}}(n) - \mathbf{R}_{yy}(n)\hat{\mathbf{A}}(n)]$$

Until now we have assumed that $\mathbf{R}_{yy}(n)$ is known. If we want to use a stochastic or real-time learning mode, the best we can do, is to estimate the elements of $\mathbf{R}_{yy}(n)$ from observations of Y. In this section we study the effect of a stochastic approximation of (43) which results from the substitution of the product $y_j(n)y_k(n)$ for $r_{jk}(n)$, where $y_i(n)$ is an observation of Y_i at time n. Defining the vector $\mathbf{y}(n) = [y_1(n), ..., y_N(n)]^T$, this approximation is given by

(44)
$$\hat{\mathbf{A}}(n+1) = \hat{\mathbf{A}}(n) + \alpha(n)[\hat{\mathbf{A}}(n) - \mathbf{y}(n)\mathbf{y}^T(n)\hat{\mathbf{A}}(n)]$$

where $\alpha(n)$ is a sequence of positive scalars such that

(45)
$$\sum_{n=0}^{\infty} \alpha^2(n) = 0$$

(46)
$$\sum_{n=0}^{\infty} \alpha(n) = \infty$$

Equation 44 can be written in the form

(47)
$$\hat{\mathbf{A}}(n+1) = \hat{\mathbf{A}}(n) + \alpha(n)[\mathbf{F}(\hat{\mathbf{A}}(n)) + \mathbf{E}(\mathbf{x}(n), \hat{\mathbf{A}}(n))]$$

where we have defined

(48)
$$\mathbf{x}(n) = [x_1(n), ..., x_N(n)]$$

(49)
$$\mathbf{F}(\hat{\mathbf{A}}(n)) = \hat{\mathbf{A}}(n) - \mathbf{R}_{yy}(n)\hat{\mathbf{A}}(n)$$

(50)
$$\mathbf{E}(\mathbf{x}(n), \hat{\mathbf{A}}(n)) = -[\mathbf{y}(n)\mathbf{y}^T(n) - \mathbf{R}_{yy}(n)]\hat{\mathbf{A}}(n)$$

$x_j(n)$ being an observation of the random variable X_j at time n.

Equation (47) is a particular form of the Robins-Monro procedure to find the roots of $\mathbf{F}(\hat{\mathbf{A}})[3]$, and it is possible to show that it converges under fairly general assumptions (note, however, that the Robins-Monro procedure is normally stated as a vector recursion, and (47) represents a matrix recursion).

To show that (47) obeys the necessary conditions for convergence of the Robins-Monro procedure consider the following facts:

1. If $\mathbf{E}(\mathbf{x}, \hat{\mathbf{A}}) = 0$, (47) converges to $C(\hat{\mathbf{A}}) = 0$. This was shown in previous sections.

2. There is a Lyapunov function (the cost functional $C(\hat{\mathbf{A}}) = C^v(\hat{\mathbf{A}}^v)$) such that

$$(51) \qquad \frac{\partial C^v}{\partial \hat{\mathbf{A}}^v}^T \mathbf{F}^v(\hat{\mathbf{A}}^v) < 0$$

for any $\hat{\mathbf{A}}^v$ such that $C^v(\hat{\mathbf{A}}^v) > 0$ (denoting, as before, by $\mathbf{F}^v$ the vectorization of $\mathbf{F}$).

3. We have

$$(52) \quad E[\mathbf{E}(\mathbf{x}(n), \hat{\mathbf{A}}(n))] = E[[\hat{\mathbf{A}}(n)\mathbf{x}(n)\mathbf{x}^T(n)\hat{\mathbf{A}}^T(n) - \mathbf{R}_{yy}(n)]\hat{\mathbf{A}}(n)] = 0$$

4. One can show that there are positive constants k_1, k_2 such that

$$(53) \quad |\mathbf{F}^v(\hat{\mathbf{A}})|^2 + E[|\mathbf{E}^v(\mathbf{x}, \hat{\mathbf{A}})|^2] \leq k_1(1 + C^v(\hat{\mathbf{A}}^v)) - k_2 \frac{\partial C^v}{\partial \hat{\mathbf{A}}^v}^T \mathbf{F}^v(\hat{\mathbf{A}}^v)$$

for any $\hat{\mathbf{A}}^v$, where $|...|$ denotes the euclidean norm. In fact, it is a direct consequence of the definitions of $C(\hat{\mathbf{A}})$, $\mathbf{F}^v(\hat{\mathbf{A}})$, $\mathbf{E}^v(\mathbf{x}, \hat{\mathbf{A}})$ and $\frac{\partial C}{\partial \hat{\mathbf{A}}^v}$ that both sides of inequality (53) can be expressed as $6^{\underline{th}}$ order forms in the elements $\hat{a}_{ij}$, hence it is always possible to choose k_1 and k_2 such that (53) holds.

As conditions (1-4) hold, it is possible to show that (47) converges to the desired solution[3].

8. Distributed Network Implementation

In this section we show that the proposed stochastic algorithm can be implemented with a distributed network structure. Consider again equation (44), and rewrite it as

$$(54) \qquad \hat{a}_j(n+1) = \hat{a}_j(n)(1 + \alpha(n)) - \alpha(n)y_j(n)\sum_{k=1}^{N} y_k(n)\hat{a}_k(n)$$

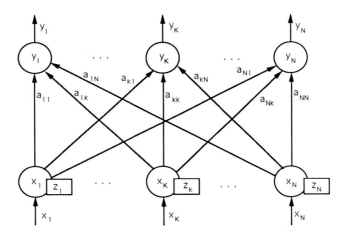

Figure 3: Distributed network implementation of the decorrelation algorithm

For the component $\hat{a}_{ji}$ of vector $\hat{a}_j(n)$, this can be written as

$$(55) \qquad \hat{a}_{ji}(n+1) = \hat{a}_{ji}(n)(1 + \alpha(n)) - \alpha(n)y_j(n)\sum_{k=1}^{N} y_k(n)\hat{a}_{ki}(n)$$

Now define $z_i(n)$ as

$$(56) \qquad z_i(n) = \sum_{k=1}^{N} y_k(n)\hat{a}_{ki}(n)$$

and rewrite (55) as

$$(57) \qquad \hat{a}_{ji}(n+1) = \hat{a}_{ji}(n)(1 + \alpha(n)) - \alpha(n)y_j(n)z_i(n)$$

Consider now the network structure represented in Fig.3, where:

1. $\hat{a}_{ji}$ represents the "weight" in the link between input unit i and output unit j.

2. The output variables y are given by

$$(58) \qquad y_j(n) = \sum_{k=1}^{N} \hat{a}_{jk}(n) x_k(n)$$

and so they can be obtained by propagation of input variables x from the input to the output layer.

3. The auxiliary variables z can be obtained by backpropagation of variables y from the output to the input layer (see (56)).

4. The adaptation of link $\hat{a}_{ji}$ can be obtained by multiplying its current value by $(1 + \alpha(n))$, and then subtracting from it the product $y_j(n) z_i(n)$, scaled by $\alpha(n)$ (see (57)).

Each iteration of the algorithm can be performed in three consecutive steps: forward propagation (computation of the y_i), backpropagation (computation of the z_i), and weight adaptation.

A similar distributed implementation can be used for the deterministic version of the algorithm (when working with finite training sets). In this case, the weight update is evaluated for each input sample following the same method described for the stochastic version. However, this weight update must be accumulated on a sweep over the whole training set, and the effective update is only performed after the presentation of all training samples (this method corresponds to the well known batch or deterministic training mode of conventional neural networks).

Comparing the orthogonalization procedure proposed here with the one proposed by Sanger [1], we note that an important feature of Sanger's "generalized Hebbian learning rule" is that it is able to reduce the dimensionality of the input data set by finding the principal components of the input data. But to achieve this result, the algorithm must perform the sequential computation (in the training phase) of the output for each unit of the second layer. As the output of the first unit converges to the first principal component (by means of the "normalized" Hebbian rule), its contribution is then subtracted from the input data, which enables the output of the second unit to converge to the second principal component. This procedure is repeated for the desired number of network outputs. To operate in this way, the computation of the weight update is performed once at a time for the links reaching a given output unit, and this implies that the network must to have some kind of sequential organization. If one considers distributed implementations, it is possible to say that, despite its local structure, the operation of Sanger's procedure is not fully parallelizable. The algorithm that we propose here is simply an orthogonalization technique, and it is not able to find the principal components of the input data. However, its operation is much more homogeneous in the training phase, enabling the fully parallel operation of all units in each of the three steps of the algorithm (forward computation, backward computation, and weight update). Therefore, if one wishes to find the principal components of the input data, Sanger's procedure must be used. However, if one just wishes to find a representation of the input data in term of orthogonal components, the simpler procedure proposed here can be used.

9. Conclusions

We have presented a new decorrelation and normalization algorithm. The algorithm was first presented with a deterministic formulation, and conditions for convergence in this case were derived. It was also shown that the algorithm can be seen as modified gradient procedure. A stochastic approximation version of the algorithm was then considered, and it was shown that it was a special case of the Robins-Monro procedure, which also converges to the desired solution if the step size α meets some additional conditions. Finally, a network structure for the distributed implementation of the algorithm was proposed.

Appendix A.   The eigenvalue recursion

To show that (21) converges to the identity matrix, one has only to show that all eigenvalues of $\mathbf{R}_{yy}(n)$ converge to 1, at least for some values of α. The eigenvalue evolution being defined by (29), we have only to study this polynomial recursion. To do this, we begin by defining the polynomial $P(\lambda)$ as

$$(59) \qquad P(\lambda) = (1 + \alpha)^2 \lambda - 2\alpha(1 + \alpha)\lambda^2 + \alpha^2 \lambda^3$$

and then we note that, if (29) converges to a limit, this limit can only be one of the roots of the equation $\lambda = P(\lambda)$, which are 0, 1, and $1 + 2/\alpha$.

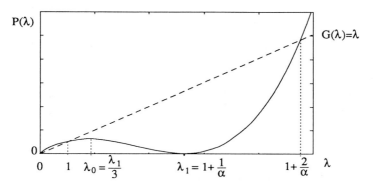

Figure 4: Eigenvalue recursion

Fig. 4 shows the graphical representations of $P(\lambda)$ and $G(\lambda) = \lambda$, which helps to understand this polynomial recursion. The set of necessary conditions that α must meet for (29) to converge is somewhat complex, hence we will state here only a set of sufficient conditions. Call $\lambda(n_0)$ a generic eigenvalue at a given step n_0 and $P'(\lambda)$ the derivative of $P(\lambda)$ in order to λ, which is given by

$$(60) \qquad P'(\lambda) = (1 + \alpha^2) - 4\alpha(1 + \alpha)\lambda + 3\alpha^2\lambda^2$$

The roots of $P'(\lambda)$ are $\lambda_0 = 1/3(1 + 1/\alpha)$ and $\lambda_1 = 1 + 1/\alpha$. Now consider the following facts:

- For (29) to converge in a vicinity of $\lambda = 1$, one must have $|P'(1)| < 1$. Since we have $P'(1) = 1 - 2\alpha$, one must set $\alpha < 1$.

- If $\lambda(n_0) < 1$, a sufficient condition for (29) to converge to 1 is that $\lambda_0 > 1$. In fact, with this condition, $P(\lambda) > \lambda$ for $\lambda \in {]}0,1{[}$ and, moreover, $P'(\lambda)$ does not change its sign in this interval. To make $\lambda_0 > 1$, one must set $\alpha < 1/2$.

- If $1 < \lambda(n_0) < \lambda_0$, (29) converges to 1. This is a direct consequence of having $|P'(\lambda)| < 1$ for $\lambda \in [1, \lambda_0{[}$ (see Fig. 4). As it is easily seen, the condition $1 < \lambda(n_0) < \lambda_0$ holds if $\alpha < 1/(3\lambda(n_0) - 1)$.

Since the above conditions must hold for all eigenvalues of $\mathbf{R}_{yy}(n_0)$, we can summarize them as follows. Denote by $\lambda_{max}(n_0)$ the largest eigenvalue of $\mathbf{R}_{yy}(n_0)$. Set $\alpha < 1/2$ and, if $\lambda_{max}(n_0) > 1$, set in addition $\alpha < 1/(3\lambda_{max}(n_0) - 1)$.

Note that, if $\lambda_{max}(n_0) > 1$, then its value will be decreasing and approaching 1 during the training procedure. Hence, if α meets the above conditions at step n_0, its value can probably be increased at step $n_0 + 1$ (up to the limit of $\alpha = 1/2$). On the other hand, if we have a given eigenvalue $\lambda(n_0)$ different from zero at step n_0, these conditions ensure that $\lambda(n_0+1)$ will be also different from 0. This shows that, if $\mathbf{R}_{yy}(n_0)$ is a positive definite matrix, $\mathbf{R}_{yy}(n_0 + 1)$ will be also positive definite. Therefore, to validate the above assumptions for any step n of the algorithm, it suffices to set $\mathbf{A}(0) = \mathbf{I}$ (with this choice, we will have $\mathbf{R}_{yy}(0) = \mathbf{R}_{xx}$) and to recall that $\mathbf{R}_{xx}$ is positive definite. Finally, note that by making $\mathbf{A}(0) = \mathbf{I}$, and considering the step 0 of the algorithm, the conditions of convergence stated in section 5 are the same as those listed above (since, in this case, $\lambda_{max}^X = \lambda_{max}(0)$).

A final remark of this study results from the direct observation of Fig. 4. As it can be easily seen, while the above conditions are sufficient for convergence, the procedure will very probably converge to the desired result if we set $\alpha < 1/2$ and $\alpha < 1/(\lambda_{max} - 1)$. This corresponds to a somewhat less restrictive condition for α, and will yield a faster convergence.

Appendix B.   Gradient Computation

Consider the gradient of $C(\hat{\mathbf{A}})$ relative to an arbitrary line of $\hat{\mathbf{A}}$, say $\hat{\mathbf{a}}_j$. Given (33), we get

$$
(61) \qquad \frac{\partial C}{\partial \hat{\mathbf{a}}_j} = \sum_{k=1}^{N} \sum_{\substack{l=1 \\ l \neq k}}^{N} 2r_{kl} \frac{\partial r_{kl}}{\partial \hat{\mathbf{a}}_j} - \sum_{k=1}^{N} 2(1 - r_{kk}) \frac{\partial r_{kk}}{\partial \hat{\mathbf{a}}_j}
$$

Noting that the cross-correlation r_{kl} is defined by (32), the partial gradient derivatives are easily computable. In fact, we have

$$
(62) \qquad \frac{\partial r_{kl}}{\partial \hat{\mathbf{a}}_j} = \begin{cases} \mathbf{R}_{xx}\hat{\mathbf{a}}_k & \text{if } j = l \\ \mathbf{R}_{xx}\hat{\mathbf{a}}_l & \text{if } j = k \\ 0 & \text{otherwise} \end{cases} \qquad \text{for } k \neq l
$$

and

$$(63) \qquad \frac{\partial r_{kk}}{\partial \hat{\mathbf{a}}_j} = \begin{cases} 2\mathbf{R}_{xx}\hat{\mathbf{a}}_k & \text{if} \quad j = k \\ 0 & \text{otherwise} \end{cases}$$

Substitution of (62) and (63) into (61) brings

$$(64) \qquad \frac{\partial C}{\partial \hat{\mathbf{a}}_j} = 2\sum_{\substack{k=1 \\ k \neq j}}^{N} r_{kj} 2\mathbf{R}_{xx}\hat{\mathbf{a}}_k - 2(1 - r_{jj})2\mathbf{R}_{xx}\hat{\mathbf{a}}_j$$

or, since $r_{kj} = r_{jk}$,

$$(65) \qquad \frac{\partial C}{\partial \hat{\mathbf{a}}_j} = 4\mathbf{R}_{xx}[\sum_{k=1}^{N} r_{jk}\hat{\mathbf{a}}_k - \hat{\mathbf{a}}_j]$$

which corresponds to the result (34).

References

[1] Terence D. Sanger, "Optimal Unsupervised Learning in Feedforward Neural Networks", Msc. Thesis, M.I.T., August 1988.

[2] B. Noble, "Applied Linear Algebra", Prenticce-Hall, New-Jersey, 1969.

[3] M. B. Nvel'son and R.Z. Has'minskii, "Stochastic Approximation and Recursive Estimation", pp. 79-93, American Mathematical Society , Providence, Rhode Island, 1973.

NEURAL NETWORKS: Advances and Applications
E. Gelenbe (Editor)
© Elsevier Science Publishers B.V. (North-Holland), 1991

Neural Networks & Combinatorial Optimization: a Study of NP-complete Graph Problems

b y

Laurent Hérault - Jean-Jacques Niez

C.E.A. / I.R.D.I. / Division L.E.T.I. / D.SYS / S.E.T.I.A. C.E.N.G., Avenue des Martyrs, 85X 38041 Grenoble Cedex, FRANCE

Abstract: This paper deals with the mapping of intractable optimization problems into artificial complex systems which mimic physical ones and are emulated with neural networks. The optimal solution of the problem is then identified with the ground state of a complex system. Many neural network methods have been proposed to approximate this ground state. Among them are the use of an Hopfield analog network, simulated annealing, mean field approximation, mean field annealing and some hybrid methods combining the previous ones. They are particularly well suited to graph problems which deal with cut and connectivity, morphisms and the extraction of a subgraph with particular properties. This paper focuses on K-partitioning of graphs, maximum subgraph matching and inclusion and the obtention of the largest maximal clique which are representative of these families of problems.

1.   Introduction

The study of complex systems is an interdisciplinary science which has emerged some years ago. It was born from a conjunction between computer science, statistical physics and non-linear dynamics [4, 7]. Many methods used in statistical physics can be applied to artificial systems involving a lot of degrees of freedom among which combinatorially hard graph optimization problems are to be found. Such methods are additionally easily mapped onto massively parallel architectures such as artificial neural networks.

Many optimization problems become intractable when the number of sub-optimal solutions grows exponentially with the size of the problem. Such problems belong to the class of np-complete problems, i.e. no algorithm is known which provides an exact solution to the problem in a computational time which is a polynomial in the size of the problem's input [16, 40]. There are several such problems in graph theory which may be classified into the following families: cut and connectivity problems, morphism problems, vertex labelling problems and problems of extraction of a subgraph with particular properties. Many applications are related to these problems in artificial intelligence, computer vision, pattern recognition, design of VLSI circuits, distributed processing, etc [21, 22, 23, 24, 25, 26, 27, 32, 33, 34].

Since the sixties, increasing efforts have been made in these areas. In the past, researchers have developed heuristic methods which provide sub-optimal solutions in a time that is proportional to a polynomial in the size of the problem. But searching dynamics in the solution space associated with an heuristic method is strongly restricted to a small part of the landscape when the problem facing us is np-complete. Thus the solutions provided by heuristic methods' are often unacceptable for problems involving large size graphs which are unfortunately the most frequent in practical applications. Moreover, each of the known heuristic methods is specific to a particular problem and a general implementation on fast parallel computers appears to be very difficult.

Recently, researchers have analysed the structure and the function of the human brain in order to determine some basic concepts and principles which could be applied to the analysis of artificial complex systems [13, 15, 45]. Thus, some fast and flexible neural network methods have been proposed to attempt to solve efficiently hard optimization problems. The problem adressed in this paper concerns the transcription of some of the most intractable graph optimization problems in terms of artificial complex systems to be mapped onto neural networks.

The paper is organized as follows. In section 2, we will review the numerical methods that are used to minimize the energy of a complex system in the context of neural networks. Section 3 deals with cut and connectivity problems and in particular with graph K-partitioning. Section 4 deals with morphism problems such as maximum subgraph matching. Section 5 concerns the search of a subgraph with specific properties such as the largest maximal clique.

2. Basic concepts on energy minimization of a complex system using neural networks

The basic concept is the encoding of the optimization problem in terms of states that are discrete variables in an Euclidean space. A real valued global energy is then defined over the set of all possible states. This energy depends on very complex interactions between the variables and has generally some physical meaning in the context of optimization. In fact, the optimal solution of the problem is the absolute minimum of this energy and one or more local minima can be considered as acceptable solutions to the problem. Convergence dynamics associated with the energy minimization process must satisfy the problem constraints as well as the optimization of the objective function of the problem.

Some neural methods have been proposed to minimize such a global energy function and differ from the previous heuristic methods by the following characteristics. One often introduces thermal noise in the dynamics of searching in order to be able to explore any part of the solution space. They are not specific to a particular optimization problem. Also, they can be easily implemented onto massively parallel architectures (such as neural networks or computers that emulate them). Finally, they give good results irrespectively of the number of variables and one can easily relax the constraints of the problem.

A network of formal neurons is a set of highly interconnected processing elements which mimic biological neurons. A formal neuron is defined by an internal state (similar to its output), connections with some other neurons or with the environment and a non-linear transfer function which allows to calculate the internal state as a function of the signals received on its inputs. A connection between two neurons is represented by a weighted link between the output of a neuron and the input of the other. Various topologies of neural networks have been defined in the literature [37], each one being specific to a class of problems. The model used in optimization is the highly interconnected network introduced by Hopfield [26, 27].

The first step in the mapping of a combinatorial optimization problem is the representation of the objective function as well as the problem constraints in the form of a simple function that is usually chosen to be quadratic and that we call the energy:

(2.1)
$$E = E_{objective} + \sum_{c} \lambda_c . E_{constraint\ c}$$

(2.2)
$$E = -\frac{1}{2} . \sum_{i=1}^{N} \sum_{j=1}^{N} T_{ij} . x_i . x_j + \sum_{i=1}^{N} I_i . x_i$$

where:

N is the number of neurons in the network,
x_i is associated with a variable of the problem and is referred as the binary output of the ith neuron,
T_{ij} is the connection weight between the neurons i and j,
I_i represents the bias external input for the neuron i.

However, more general non quadratic energy functions can be treated [14]. This energy can be considered as the energy of a complex physical system composed of magnetic moments in interaction. Consequently, several physical methods used for the study of this kind of complex systems are simulated in order to minimize E. Among them are the simulated annealing, the mean field approximation, the mean field annealing and some hybrid methods combining them. Other methods that are specific to neural networks have also been proposed including the Hopfield analog neural network.

2.1. Hopfield neural network (HNN)

The Hopfield network was first defined for information storage and retrieval and for learning. In this class of applications, the synaptic weights change during the convergence process of the network [24, 25]. In the field of optimization, the connection weights are completely specified by the energy to be minimized [26, 27].

The convergence process can be described as follows: the initial state of the network is randomly defined. Then the network evolves freely according to prescribed dynamics until it reaches a minimum of the energy E and stops.

The neural network used for this purpose is composed of either digital (two-state) or analog neurons. The dynamics associated with digital neurons is discrete in time and asynchronous. The input signal received by the neuron i at time t+1 is given by:

$$(2.3) \qquad u_i(t+1) = \sum_{j=1}^{N} T_{ij} \cdot x_j(t) - I_i$$

and the output of the digital neuron i is:

$$(2.4) \qquad x_i(t) = 0 \quad \text{if} \quad u_i(t) \leq 0$$
$$1 \quad \text{otherwise.}$$

It is essential to notice that the energy landscape can have many local minima because of the discretisation of the variable space which is an hypercube $(0,1)^N$.
The number of local minima is smaller when one uses an analog neural network whose state is constrained to belong to the interior of the hypercube $(0,1)^N$. Here, the proposed dynamics associated with an analog neural network is continuous in time (and synchronous). The input of the analog neuron i is given by the differential equation [26]:

$$(2.5) \qquad \frac{d u_i}{dt} = -\frac{u_i}{\tau} + \sum_{j=1}^{N} T_{ij} \cdot x_i - I_i$$

where τ is the characteristic time constant (=RC) generally set to 1 so that time is measured in units of τ.
The output of the analog neuron i is given by:

$$(2.6) \qquad x_i = \frac{1}{2} \cdot \left(1 + \tanh \frac{u_i}{x_0} \right)$$

which is a sigmoïd function. The parameter x_0 determines the slope of the sigmoïd function. Decreasing this parameter during the convergence process ensures that the local minima of the energy E correspond to the corners of the hypercube $(0,1)^N$.
One usually prefers to use analog networks rather then digital ones for two reasons. First, an analog network tends to avoid oscillations between stable states. Secondly, the solutions are much better than those provided by digital neural networks (without noise) because valleys of the energy landscape are generally wider and the neuron outputs are not restricted to the corners of the hypercube during convergence.

Nevertheless, the dynamics of this network tends to propose a solution which is the first local minimum found. As a consequence, the solutions obtained are often not good enough. This can be avoided by adding a noise term which allows to overcome barriers in the solution space [36]. This method builds a bridge between the neural network approach developped by Hopfield and Tank [26, 27] and the simulated annealing methodology described as follows. In the following, we will not use this method. We will restrict our investigations to simulated annealing, mean field approximation and mean field annealing.

2.2. Simulated annealing (SA)

A good way to find low energy states, called ground states, of a physical complex system is to heat the system up to some high temperature, then to cool it slowly. This process, called annealing, forces the system evolution into states of low energy, while not getting trapped in higher local minima. The basic idea of simulated annealing, due to Kirkpatrick [32, 33], consists in treating the system to be optimized as a physical system defined by the degrees of freedom $\{x_1, ..., x_N\}$ and the global energy E (equation 2.1). The absolute minimum (ground state) of this energy is reached by simulating the cooling process of a physical system from a temperature T that is high down to T near zero. These initial and final temperatures can be estimated theoretically [47]. The cooling process, defined initially by Metropolis [38], tends to prevent the system from being trapped in a thermodynamically metastable state that is a high local minimum of E by introducing a thermal noise that allows the system to reach any part of the configuration space. Moreover, some asymptotic convergence theorems have been established by many authors [18, 19, 34, 39]. They suppose a decreasing law of the temperature that is exponential. For example, if at the kth temperature step, the temperature satisfies the bound:

(2.7)
$$T(k) \geq \frac{c}{\log(1+k)}$$

where c is a constant independent of k, then Geman [18] has proved that the system converges to the absolute minimum when k tends to the infinite.

Let us consider an initial configuration of the $\{x_i\}$ that is random, a list of feasible elementary transformations Δx_i that determine the topology in which one wants to solve the problem and a law of temperature decrease. For a given temperature, one applies a sequence of random elementary transformations that is long enough to reach a near equilibrium state at this temperature. For each of these elementary transformations, one calculates the energy variation ΔE caused by the perturbation:

$$(2.8) \qquad \Delta E = E\,(x_i + \Delta x_i) \; - \; E\,(x_i).$$

Then, the transformation is accepted according to the following criterion [38]: if $\Delta E < 0$, the transformation is energetically favorable and is accepted; otherwise, it is accepted with a probability $\exp(-\Delta E /T)$. Once a transformation is accepted, one goes on from the new perturbated state. This Markovian process ensures that at the equilibrium, the states of the system are distributed according to a Boltzman probability law. Practically, when each elementary transformation has been proposed about 100 times at a given temperature, the equilibrium is considered to be reached. Then one repeats the Metropolis process for a new temperature that is slightly lower. Good results seem to be obtained when the decrease factor of the temperature is 0,93 between two steps. One stops when the temperature is small enough to consider that the system has reached a state near the ground state (the system is frozen). Then, the x_i neuron outputs provide a very good solution of the optimization problem. The simulated annealing algorithm is given in appendix A. Experience indicates that when it is used to solve graph optimization problems, the number of elementary transformations necessary to reach a near equilibrium state at each temperature closely depends on the graph homogeneity: the more non-homogeneous the graph, the smaller the necessary number of transformations because the slopes of the relevant energetic valleys are then more abrupt. The main drawback of simulated annealing is the large amount of computational time that is required because of the stochastic relaxation: it is necessary to perform a lot of elementary transformations at each temperature step to reach a near equilibrium state. Some attempts to speed up the convergence to near optimal solutions have been proposed by using a parallel formulation of the Metropolis criterion [1, 2, 34]. Another possibility consists in using the mean field theory.

2.3.   Mean field theory (MFT)

The minimization of the energy E (equation 2.2) where the x_i variables are constrained to be 0 or 1 is strictly equivalent to the minimization problem of the energy where the new neuron outputs σ_i are constrained to be -1 or +1 by using the following change of variables:

$$(2.9) \qquad \forall \, i \in <1, N>, \; x_i = \frac{\sigma_i + 1}{2} .$$

The new energy to be minimized is then:

$$(2.10) \qquad H(\sigma_1, ..., \sigma_i, ..., \sigma_N) = - \sum_{i=1}^{N} \sum_{j=1}^{N} J_{ij} . \sigma_i . \sigma_j \; + \; \sum_{i=1}^{N} \delta_i . \sigma_i .$$

This energy H has the same mathematical form as the Hamiltonian of magnetic materials described by an Ising model [4, 7, 30]. Let the atoms forming the material be the vertices of a graph. Each atom has a "spin " which is pointing either "up" or "down". We describe the spin value by σ_i. The term J_{ij} is the interaction energy between the spins i and j. The mean field approximation is a simple analytic manipulation which simplifies the study of the system state at the equilibrium by using a local approximation [21, 22, 42, 43].
At a given temperature, the Metropolis process of the simulated annealing makes the system evolve until it has reached a near equilibrium state. Then, we have:

$$(2.11) \qquad <H(\sigma_1, ..., \sigma_i, ..., \sigma_N)> = H_{equilibrium} \; (T)$$

$$= - \sum_{i=1}^{N} \sum_{j=1}^{N} J_{ij} . <\sigma_i . \sigma_j> \; + \; \sum_{i=1}^{N} \delta_i . <\sigma_i>.$$

The discrete probability to be in a particular configuration $(\sigma^0_1, ..., \sigma^0_N)$ at a given temperature is given by a Boltzman probability distribution (see section 2.2). Let us associate to each spin i a random binary variable X_i. Then:

(2.12) $\qquad \forall\, i \in\, <1, N>, \sigma_i \in \{-1,1\}\,,\; \sigma_i^0 \in \{-1,1\}$ and

$$P\,(X_1 = \sigma_1^0;\,...;X_N = \sigma_N^0)\; =\; \frac{\exp\left(-\dfrac{H\,(\sigma_1^0,\,...,\,\sigma_N^0)}{T}\right)}{\displaystyle\sum_{(\sigma_1,\,...,\,\sigma_N)}\exp\left(-\dfrac{H\,(\sigma_1,...,\,\sigma_N)}{T}\right)}\,.$$

In this expression, the summation run over all possible spin configurations. Experience indicates that low energy states are dominant at the equilibrium, i.e. that their probability is high.

The mean field approximation [46] consists in studying each spin i plunged in the field created on this spin by the other spins fixed in their mean state. Then, the discrete probability of the marginal state σ_i at the temperature T for all spin i is approximated by:

(2.13) $\qquad P\,(\,X_i = \sigma_i\,)\; =\; \dfrac{\exp\left(\dfrac{<h_i^{tot}>.\,\sigma_i}{T}\right)}{P\,(X_i = 1) + P\,(X_i = -1)}\;,\quad \sigma_i \in \{-1,1\}$

where

(2.14) $\qquad <h_i^{tot}> = <h_i> + h_i^{ext},$

(2.15) $\qquad <h_i> = 2\,.\displaystyle\sum_{j=1}^{N} J_{ij}\,.<\sigma_j>,$

(2.16) $\qquad h_i^{ext} = -\,\delta_i.$

The key approximation is in equation (2.15). $<h_i>$ may be considered as the mean field created on the spin i by the other spins j seen as frozen in the $<\sigma_i>$ states. h_i^{ext} may be considered as the external field viewed by the spin i. Thus, $<h_i^{tot}>$ is the total mean field existing on the spin i. Moreover, for a state dependent function F, one has:

$$(2.17) \qquad <F(X_i)> = \frac{P(X_i = 1) \cdot F(1) + P(X_i = -1) \cdot F(-1)}{P(X_i = 1) + P(X_i = -1)}.$$

Thus, from equations (2.13) and (2.17), one derives easily the mean state of the spins:

$$(2.18) \qquad \forall\, i \in <1,N>,$$

$$<\sigma_i> = \frac{(+1) \cdot \exp\left(\dfrac{<h_i^{tot}>}{T}\right) + (-1) \cdot \exp\left(-\dfrac{<h_i^{tot}>}{T}\right)}{\exp\left(\dfrac{<h_i^{tot}>}{T}\right) + \exp\left(-\dfrac{<h_i^{tot}>}{T}\right)} = \tanh\left(\frac{<h_i^{tot}>}{T}\right).$$

Then, for the neural network defined by the equation (2.10), one gets, from equations (2.14) to (2.18):

$$(2.19) \qquad \forall\, i \in <1, N>, \quad \mu_i = \tanh\left(\frac{2 \cdot \displaystyle\sum_{j=1}^{N} J_{ij} \cdot \mu_j - \delta_i}{T}\right)$$

where the digital neuron outputs σ_i have been replaced by their average values $\mu_i = <\sigma_i>$. It is a system of coupled non-linear equations. An analytical solution is difficult to find as soon as N is greater than 2 [40]. One notices that the energy landscape associated with this new analog neural network is smoother than the one of the simulated annealing. Thus the probability of being trapped in a high local minimum is smaller.

The system (2.19) can be solved iteratively:

$$(2.20) \qquad \forall\, i \in <1, N>, \quad \mu_i^{n+1} = \tanh\left(\frac{2 \cdot \displaystyle\sum_{j=1}^{N} J_{ij} \cdot \mu_j^n - \delta_i}{T}\right), \quad n \geq 1$$

where μ_i^n is an estimation of $<\sigma_i>$ at the iteration n.

The determination of the initial configuration of the system is trivial

when $\delta_1 = ... = \delta_N = 0$. In fact, $\mu_i(t=0) = 0$ for all spin i is an obvious solution of the system (2.19). Practically, one determines the initial
configuration of the system by adding noise on this trivial unstable
solution. For instance, μ^0_i values are randomly chosen between the
two values $(-10^{-5}, +10^{-5})$. When the δ_i values are not 0, one chooses
the same μ^0_i values. During the convergence, they will move towards -1 or +1.

Two modes of solutions are possible. At a new step in synchronous
mode, every μ_i is updated by using the μ_j which have been calculated at the previous step. In the case of asynchronous mode, one calculates the μ_i value of only one spin that is randomly selected. The
asynchronous mode produces better results because the convergence process is less subject to the oscillations which frequently exist in
synchronous mode. Practically, in an asynchronous mode, each μ_i
has to be updated no more than N times to reach the equilibrium
state of the network [40].

The solution of the optimization problem is quite obviously given by
equations (2.20). In fact, when one estimates that the system has
converged, all spin i for which μ_i is positive has a probability to be
+1 greater than 50%. Thus one derives a final decision process that
sets the spin values to -1 or 1 according to the average values μ_j.
The algorithm is given in appendix B.

Contrary to simulated annealing, this method is intrinsically parallel
by nature. The convergence process of the mean field algorithm is
perfectly deterministic and is controlled by a dynamical system. It
reduces the computational effort by as much as 10 times.

The main drawback of this method is the difficult choice of the parameter T. It has no major influence on the quality of the results
when it is chosen in a certain range. Also, one experimentally notices that the range of possible temperatures increases with the size
of the optimization problem. To avoid the difficult choice of the ambient temperature, mean field annealing has been proposed.

2.4.   Mean field annealing (MFA)

In the mean field approximation algorithm, the temperature is defi-
nitively fixed and a good one is quite difficult to estimate. An alternative approach consists in performing annealing during the convergence of the mean field approximation algorithm [8, 12, 21, 22].
The decrease process of the temperature may then be of two types.
First, the temperature can be slightly decreased from a high initial
value to a smaller one as soon as every neuron has been updated

once [21, 22]. The system does not reach a near equilibrium state at any temperature during the convergence process but when the temperature is small enough, the system is frozen in a good stable state. Consequently, the convergence time is reduced: the smaller the temperature, the more rapid the convergence of the dynamical system of equations (2.19).

Another approach [12] consists in noticing that during the temperature decrease, there is a critical temperature T_c such that at this temperature, some of the mean field variables μ_i begin to move significantly towards +1 or -1. The principle is then to estimate theoretically this critical temperature and to let the system evolve at this temperature until equilibrium is reached. Then one drops the temperature to near zero and iterates until the system has reached a near equilibrium state.

Once the system has converged in both cases, the neuron state probabilities $(\mu_i+1)/2$ are more discriminating than those provided by the mean field approximation algorithm: all the μ_i are near +1 or -1. Thus the determination of the solution of the optimization problem is made without ambiguity concerning the neuron state associated with each problem variable. Moreover, the annealing process does not alterate the quality of the results which is comparable to the one obtained by using the stochastic relaxation of simulated annealing. The convergence time may be for 2 to 5 times faster than that of MFT approach.

Eventually, in terms of quality of solution, the SA method is the best approach, followed by the MFT and the MFA algorithms. On the contrary, in terms of computation time, the MFA approach is the best, followed by the MFT and the SA methods.

3. Cut and connectivity problems - The graph K-partitioning

Among the cut and connectivity problems, one finds [16]: graph partitioning, acyclic partition, the maximum cut and the minimum cut into bounded sets problems. All these problems can be encoded and solved in a similar manner. As an example, we will study the graph K-partitioning problem [21, 22].

The problem is to partition the vertices of an undirected weighted graph into two or more disjoints subsets of specified sizes in such a way as to minimize the number of connections between the subsets of the partition. It has many potential applications. One of them concerns the optimal static assignment of distributed modules to several processors in order to minimize the cost of running a program [9]. This cost may be money, time or some other measure of resource usage. This problem also arises in the simulation of a large network of processors using a small set of different processors [6]. Another application is the layout of micro-electronic systems [35]: one wants to assign small circuits to packages (chips) of specified sizes in order to minimize a measure of interconnection between them. This problem also appears in the field of computer vision [29]: segment images are represented as graphs in which each vertex represents a segment and in which a weighted edge between two vertices is associated with a topological relationship between two segments in the image (left_of, right_of, colinear, ...).

Given an undirected graph $G=(V,w)$ in which V is a set of N vertices and w is a weighting function describing M positively weighted edges, one wants to partition this graph into K distinct vertex subsets of specified sizes $N_1,..., N_K$ in order to minimize the total weight of edges connecting vertices in distinct subsets. Let $A=(a_{ij})$ be its weighted adjacency matrix. Let us suppose that one wants to explore exhaustively the space of the possible distributions of $N.K$ vertices into K subsets of size N. The total number of feasible partitions is:

$$(3.1) \quad \frac{1}{K!} \cdot \binom{N.K}{N} \cdot \binom{N.K-N}{N} \cdot .... \cdot \binom{2.N}{N} \cdot \binom{N}{N} = \frac{(N.K)!}{K! \cdot (N!)^K} .$$

Typically, with $N.K=250$ and $K=10$, the number of possible configurations is greater than 10^{234}. Such an exploration would need thousands years of CPU time on the most powerful computers. Thus there is no hope of developing exhaustive methods to solve such a problem. Therefore, attempts to solve this problem have concentrated on finding heuristics which will yield approximate solutions in polynomial time. The best known heuristic is due to Kernighan [31] and produces a very good bipartition. The idea is the following: given an initial graph bipartition which is perfectly balanced, the optimal bipartition may be obtained by interchanging a vertex group of one subset of the bipartition with a vertex group of the other subset. In order to approximate those vertex groups, one executes a sequence of vertex permutations from one subset to the other so that globally the interconnection cost decreases. Thus the algorithm allows a temporary increase of the interconnection cost. For this reason, this method avoids being trapped at the first local

minimum: one is able to leave shallow valleys of the solution landscape. Its major drawback is its sensitivity to the quality of the initial partition. Kernighan [31] proposed to extend his approach to the
K-partitioning problem with $N_1 = ... = N_K = N/K$ by a dichotomic recursive procedure. Experimentally, this heuristic gives unsatisfacto-
ry results when the desired number of subsets is greater than 4
(see figures 1 and 2-a).

3.1. Transcription of the problem in terms of the mi-nimization of a global energy of a complex system

We associate with every vertex i a vector which specifies its localization in the partition:

$$(3.2) \qquad \vec{\sigma}_i = (\sigma_i^1, ..., \sigma_i^K)^T$$

where $\sigma_i^k = 1$ if the vertex i is in the subset k and $\sigma_i^k = -1$ otherwise.
The partition interconnection cost can be calculated by noticing that

$$(3.3) \qquad \forall (i,j) \in <1, N>^2, \ \forall k \in <1, K>,$$

$$a_{ij} \cdot \left(\frac{\sigma_i^k - \sigma_j^k}{2} \right)^2 = a_{ij}$$

if one and only one of the vertices i and j are in the subset k, and

$$a_{ij} \cdot \left(\frac{\sigma_i^k - \sigma_j^k}{2} \right)^2 = 0 \ \text{otherwise.}$$

The interconnection cost between the subset k and the other subsets is:

$$(3.4) \qquad I_k = \frac{1}{2} \cdot \sum_{i=1}^{N} \sum_{j=1}^{N} a_{ij} \cdot \left(\frac{\sigma_i^k - \sigma_j^k}{2} \right)^2$$

for all k in <1,K>.
After some algebraic manipulations, the total interconnection cost
between all the subsets, which we call the interconnection energy,

becomes:

$$(3.5) \quad E_{interconnection} = \frac{1}{2} \cdot \sum_{k=1}^{K} I_k$$

$$= -\frac{1}{8} \cdot \sum_{i=1}^{N}\sum_{j=1}^{N} a_{ij} \cdot \vec{\sigma}_i \cdot \vec{\sigma}_j + \frac{1}{8} \cdot \sum_{i=1}^{N}\sum_{j=1}^{N} a_{ij}$$

An energy function which expresses the imbalance of the partition can be defined. First it is noticed that if the partition is perfectly balanced, then in a subset k, N_k of the σ^k_i equal +1 and $N-N_k$ of the σ^k_i equal -1. Therefore:

$$(3.6) \qquad \forall\, k \in <1, K>, \ \sum_{i=1}^{N} \sigma_i^k = 2 \cdot N_k - N.$$

An imbalance measure in the subset k is defined by:

$$(3.7) \qquad D_k = \left(2 \cdot N_k - N - \sum_{i=1}^{N} \sigma_i^k \right)^2.$$

Therefore, after some algebra, the total partition imbalance, which we name imbalance energy, is given by:

$$(3.8) \quad E_{imbalance} = \sum_{k=1}^{K} D_k$$

$$= \sum_{i=1}^{N}\sum_{j=1}^{N} \vec{\sigma}_i \cdot \vec{\sigma}_j - 4 \cdot \sum_{i=1}^{N}\sum_{k=1}^{K} N_k \cdot \sigma_i^k - K \cdot N^2 + 4 \cdot \sum_{k=1}^{K} N_k^2.$$

The global energy to be minimized can be written as follows:

$$(3.9) \qquad E = E_{interconnection} + (\lambda / 8) \cdot E_{imbalance},$$

where λ is a parameter which allows to weigh the constraints. It is clear that it is not necessary to keep the constants and the multiplicative factors in this energy. After simplification, we minimize the following quadratic energy:

$$(3.10) \quad E \approx \sum_{i=1}^{N} \sum_{j=1}^{N} \sum_{k=1}^{K} (\lambda - a_{ij}) . \sigma_i^k . \sigma_j^k \quad - \quad 4 . \lambda . \sum_{i=1}^{N} \sum_{k=1}^{K} N_k . \sigma_i^k .$$

In order to statistically give the same importance to the balance constraint and to the interconnection cost minimization constraint, one can estimate the value of the parameter λ (using a similar argument as the one of Kirkpatrick [32]):

$$(3.11) \quad \lambda \approx \alpha . \frac{1}{N^2} . \sum_{i=1}^{N} \sum_{j=1}^{N} a_{ij}$$

where α is an adjustable parameter always close to 1.

3.2. Energy minimization using an analog Hopfield neural network

Let us define an analog Hopfield neural network with a N x K matrix organisation in which the output of the $(i,k)^{th}$ neuron expresses the σ_i^k value. This network is the neural transcription of the vectorial representation previously defined (equation 3.2). The main particularity of this approach is that the energy to be minimized has to be modified. It is derived from the equation (3.10) to which is added an energy term associated with a constraint which takes into account the structural organization of the network: each vertex of G has to belong to exactly one subset. Thus the global energy to be minimized is given by:

$$(3.12) \quad E = \sum_{i=1}^{N} \sum_{j=1}^{N} \sum_{k=1}^{K} (\lambda - a_{ij}) . \sigma_i^k . \sigma_j^k \quad - \quad 4 . \lambda . \sum_{i=1}^{N} \sum_{k=1}^{N} N_k . \sigma_i^k$$

$$+ \ B . \sum_{i=1}^{N} \left(2 - K - \sum_{k=1}^{K} \sigma_i^k \right)^2$$

where B is a positive real value.

After some algebra, this energy can be written as an Hopfield energy:

$$(3.13) \quad E = -\frac{1}{2} \cdot \sum_{i=1}^{N} \sum_{j=1}^{N} \sum_{k=1}^{K} \sum_{l=1}^{K} T_{ik,jl} \cdot \sigma_i^k \cdot \sigma_j^l - \sum_{i=1}^{N} \sum_{k=1}^{K} I_{ik} \cdot \sigma_i^k$$

where $T_{ik,jl} = -2 \cdot (\lambda - a_{ij}) \cdot \delta_{kl} - 2 \cdot B \cdot \delta_{ij}$

$I_{ik} = 2 \cdot B \cdot (2 - K) + 4 \cdot \lambda \cdot N_k.$

Convergence dynamics associated with such a network have been described in section 2.1.

3.3. Energy minimization using simulated annealing

Given the global energy to be minimized (equation 3.10), a set of elementary transformations and the associated energy variations can be defined as follows: an elementary transformation is the move of a vertex i from a subset k to a subset l. One gets:

$$(3.14) \quad \Delta E_i^{k \to l} = E(\sigma_i^k = -1, \sigma_i^l = 1) - E(\sigma_i^k = 1, \sigma_i^l = -1).$$

After some algebra, one obtains:

$$(3.15) \quad \Delta E_i^{k \to l} = 4 \cdot \sum_{j=1, j \neq i}^{N} (\lambda - a_{ij}) \cdot (\sigma_j^l - \sigma_j^k) + 8 \cdot \lambda \cdot (N_k - N_l).$$

The annealing process is decribed in section 2.2. The total number of possible elementary transformations is N.(K-1). At each temperature, the number of the Markov chain steps that are tested is 100.N.(K-1). Practically, when 10.N.(K-1) transformations have been accepted at a given temperature, the system is considered to have reach the equilibrium at this temperature. Then a new temperature which is slightly lower is applied on the system.

3.4. Energy minimization using the mean field theory

The mean energy of the system can be approximated by using the mean field approximation. The mean energy associated with each σ_i spin is:

$$(3.16) \qquad <E(\vec{\sigma}_i)> = - <\vec{h}_{i\,tot}>.<\vec{\sigma}_i>$$

where

$$\vec{h}_{i\,tot} = (h_{i\,tot}^1, ..., h_{i\,tot}^K)^T.$$

$<h^k_{i\,tot}>$ is the kth component of the total mean field existing on the vertex i. It is composed of $<h^k_i>$ which is the kth component of the field vector created on the vertex i by the other k^{th} spins seen as frozen in their mean state and h^k_{ext} which is the kth component of an external field in which the system is imbedded:

$$(3.17) \qquad <h^k_i> = -2.\sum_{j=1}^{N}(\lambda - a_{ij}).<\sigma_j^k>,$$

$$(3.18) \qquad h^k_{ext} = 4.\lambda.N_k ,$$

$$(3.19) \qquad <h^k_{i\,tot}> = <h^k_i> + h^k_{ext}.$$

The mean state of the vector of spins associated with the vertex i then has the following k^{th} component:

$$(3.20) \qquad \forall k \in <1,K>, \ \forall i \in <1,N>,$$

$$<\sigma_i^k> = \frac{\exp\left\{\frac{1}{T}.\left(<h^k_{i\,tot}> - \sum_{l=1,l\neq k}^{K}<h^l_{i\,tot}>\right)\right\} - \sum_{l=1,l\neq k}^{K}\exp\left\{\frac{1}{T}.\left(<h^l_{i\,tot}> - \sum_{m=1,m\neq l}^{K}<h^m_{i\,tot}>\right)\right\}}{\sum_{l=1}^{K}\exp\left\{\frac{1}{T}.\left(<h^l_{i\,tot}> - \sum_{m=1,m\neq l}^{K}<h^m_{i\,tot}>\right)\right\}}.$$

i.e.:

$$(3.21) \quad <\sigma_i^k> = \frac{\exp\left(2.\frac{<h_{i\,tot}^k>}{T}\right) - \sum_{l=1,\,l\neq k}^{K} \exp\left(2.\frac{<h_{i\,tot}^l>}{T}\right)}{\sum_{l=1}^{K} \exp\left(2.\frac{<h_{i\,tot}^l>}{T}\right)}$$

$$= \frac{2}{\sum_{l=1}^{K} \exp\left\{\frac{2}{T}.(<h_{i\,tot}^l> - <h_{i\,tot}^k>)\right\}} - 1.$$

After simplification, one obtains the following non-linear system:

$$(3.22) \qquad \forall\, k \in <1, K>,\ \forall\, i \in <1, N>,$$

$$<\sigma_i^k> = 2 \Big/ \sum_{l=1}^{K} \exp\left\{\frac{2}{T}.\left[4.\lambda.(N_l - N_k) - 2.\sum_{j=1}^{N}(\lambda - a_{ij}).(<\sigma_j^l> - <\sigma_j^k>)\right]\right\} - 1.$$

The solutions of the system (3.22) can be iteratively obtained thanks to the following equations:

$$(3.23) \qquad \forall\, k \in <1, K>,\ \forall\, i \in <1, N>,$$

$$\mu_i^{new} = 2 \Big/ \sum_{l=1}^{K} \exp\left\{\frac{2}{T}.\left[4.\lambda.(N_l - N_k) - 2.\sum_{j=1}^{N}(\lambda - a_{ij}).(\mu_j^{l\,old} - \mu_j^{k\,old})\right]\right\} - 1$$

where $\qquad\qquad \mu_i^k = <\sigma_i^k>.$

Once the system has converged according to a dynamics described in sections 2.3 or 2.4, each μ_i^k value is the approximated probability for the vertex i to belong to the class k. A decision procedure then puts the vertices in the subsets according to these probabilities.

3.5. Experimental results

We now give experimental results for the partitioning of a regular hexagonal graph with 324 vertices and 901 edges (see figure 1): the degree of a vertex , i.e. the number of vertices connected to this vertex, is 6 in the "interior" of the graph. We consider the partitioning of this graph in 5 subsets of equal sizes. The result provided by one of the most powerful heuristic methods (Kernighan heuristic [31]) is given in figure 2-a. Figure 2-b shows the results provided by simulated annealing. For most of the graphs, simulated annealing improves by about 20 % the interconnection cost. The running time necessary to obtain a good solution on a conventional sequential computer is high: about 2 CPU hours on a SUN 4-260. Nevertheless the time complexity increases linearly with the size of the problem. One notices that the quality of the results is also very good when random or non-homogeneous graphs are to be partitioned [21, 22].

Mean field theory provides partitions that are comparable to those given by simulated annealing but are obtained in a CPU time 10 to 20 times smaller (about 15 minutes on a SUN 4-260). To determine the initial configuration of the system when $N_1 = \ldots = N_K$, let us notice that if $\sigma^k(t=0) = 2/K\text{-}1$ for all vertex components, then the components σ^k_i are solutions of the system (3.21). Practically, one determines the initial configuration of the system by adding noise on this trivial solution: for instance, the σ^k_i are randomly chosen between the two values $(2/K\text{-}1\text{-}10^{-5}, 2/K\text{-}1+10^{-5})$. Figure 3 shows the partitions obtained with the mean field approximation and with the mean field annealing algorithms. Figure 4 and 5 shows the evolution of the μ^k_i probabilities of all the vertices to belong to a particular subset during the convergence process.

It is obvious that these approaches are powerful enough to solve cut and connectivity problems.

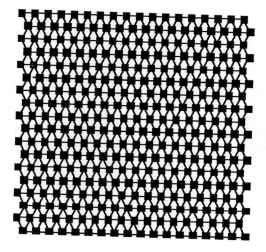

figure 1: regular hexagonal graph: 324 vertices and 901 edges.

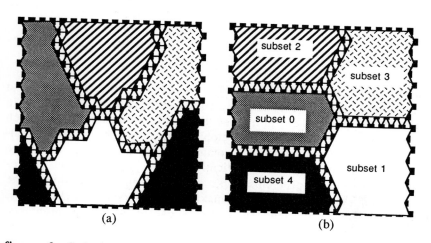

(a)

(b)

figure 2: Balanced 5-partitioning of the graph of figure 1: (a) Kernighan method. The interconnection cost is 107 and the subsets are well balanced. (b) Simulated annealing: the interconnection cost is 84. The initial temperature is 40, the final one is 0,378. The distribution of vertices is the following: 60 vertices in subset 0, 74 in 1, 62 in 2, 69 in 3 and 59 in 4.

186

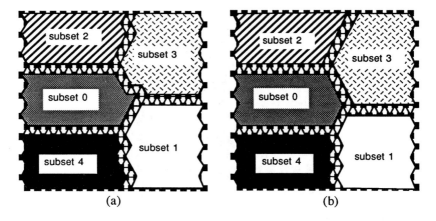

(a)   (b)

figure 3: Balanced 5-partitioning of the graph of figure 1: (a) Kerhighan method. The interconnection cost is 107 and the subsets are well balanced. (b) Simulated annealing : the interconnection cost is 84. The initial temperature is 40, the final one is 0,378. The distribution of vertices is the following: 60 vertices in subset 0, 74 in 1, 62 in 2, 69 in 3 and 59 in 4.

4.   Morphism problems

One of the most general method for describing the real world is to use stuctural description, i.e. the description of a certain object in terms of its parts, their properties and their mutual relations. Such a description is called variously graph, colored graph, weighted multigraph, relational structure or semantic network. Starting from two such descriptions, practical applications may induce a lot of np-complete morphism problems [16]: the subgraph isomorphism, the largest common subgraph, the maximum subgraph matching, the digraph D-morphism, and the multiple choice matching problems. Some other problems adressed in this paper problems deal with inclusion between graphs: graph inclusion, subgraph inclusion and maximum subgraph inclusion. These problems may be treated by using the same kind of encoding and methodology. We will focus on some of the most difficult but interesting problems: maximum subgraph matching and maximum subgraph inclusion.

The aim is to determine what two or more structural descriptions have in common and particularly which parts of the descriptions are topologically identical or included. This problem is fundamental

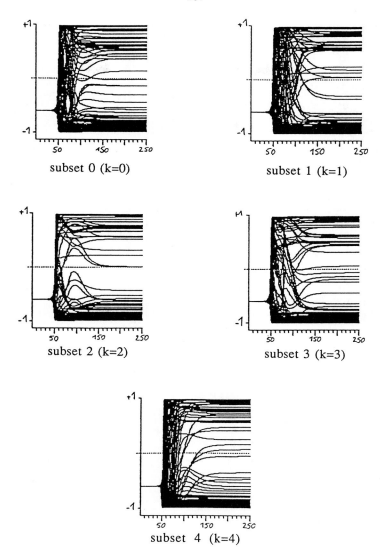

subset 0 (k=0)

subset 1 (k=1)

subset 2 (k=2)

subset 3 (k=3)

subset 4 (k=4)

figure 4: *Mean field approximation: curves giving $< \sigma^k_i >$ as a function of the scan number ($k = 0,...,4$ and $i = 0,...,323$).*

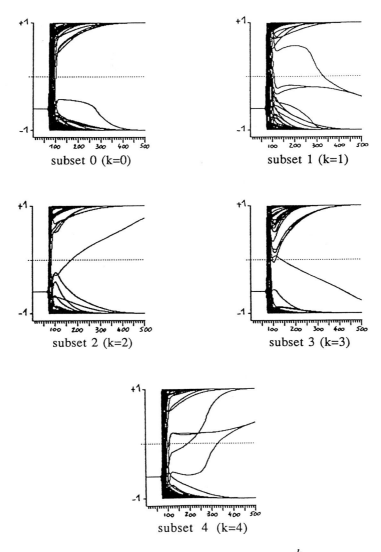

figure 5: Mean field annealing: curves giving $< \sigma^k_i >$ as a function of the scan number ($k = 0,...,4$ and $i = 0,...,323$).

in various fields and especially in the fields of image analysis and computer vision. For example, this problem is encountered in stereo correspondence and pattern recognition [3, 23, 28, 29]. Many heuristic solutions has been published in the past (for a survey, see [17, 44]). We propose neural approaches which identify the problem with a physical complex system.

A structural description can be represented as a multigraph which is directed and weighted (arcs and vertices). A multigraph is a graph with several arcs between two vertices. A graph is an ordered pair (V,w) where V is the set of vertices and w is a weighting function which gives a non negative integer value $w(v_i, v_j)$ to each pair of vertices (v_i, v_j). It may be described thanks to its adjacency matrix. Let $A = (a_{ij})$ be this matrix. It is such that a_{ij} is non zero if there exists an arc from v_i to v_j in the graph. An undirected graph is a graph whose adjacency matrix is symmetric. A diagonal element of the matrix represents a vertex weight, and the others the arc weights. The graph is said to be unweighted when the weights are binary. In order to simplify the explanation, we will first consider the case of simple directed unweighted graphs. Then, a straightforward generalisation to weighted multigraphs will be described.

Given structural descriptions A and B, we will study the following problems that are of increasing difficulty, each one being a generalization of the preceding one.

(i) Graph isomorphism: does an isomorphism exist between A and B? If they both have N vertices and obviously the same number of edges, the number of configurations in the solution space is N!. This problem is not proved either to be np-complete or to have an efficient algorithm that solves it in a polynomial time [16].

(i') Graph inclusion: if A and B are structural descriptions with N vertices, is A included in B ? i.e. do all the mutual relations of A exist in B ? The complexity of this problem is the same as in problem (i).

(ii) Subgraph isomorphism: does an isomorphism exist between A and a subgraph of B? If N and M are respectively the vertex number of A and B and M greater than N, the size of the solution space is:

$$\binom{M}{N} . N!$$

This problem is known to be np-complete.

(ii') Subgraph inclusion: is A included in a subgraph of B ? i.e. if N and M are respectively the vertex number of A and B and M greater than N, do all the mutual relations of A exist in a subgraph of B ? The complexity of this problem is the same as in problem (ii).

(iii) Maximum subgraph matching: find the maximum isomorphic pair (A',B') such that A' is a subgraph of A and B' a subgraph of B. If M and N are respectively the number of vertices of B and A and M greater than N, then the size of the solution space is:

$$\sum_{i=1}^{N} \binom{N}{i} \cdot \binom{M}{i} \cdot i!$$

This problem is np-complete.

(iii') Maximum subgraph inclusion: find the maximum pair (A', B') where A' is a subgraph of A , B' is a subgraph of B and A' is included in B' i.e. all the mutual relations of A' exist in B'. The complexity of this problem is the same as in problem (iii).

An important remark is that the following methodology may ⁎be used to solve vertex labelling problems such as [16]: the bandwidth, the directed bandwidth, the optimal linear arrangement, the directed optimal linear arrangement and the minimum cut linear arrangement problems.

4.1. Transcription of the morphism problem in terms of the minimization of the global energy of a complex system

4.1.1. Isomorphism between simple unweighted directed graphs

Let $G_A = (V_A, w_A)$ and $G_B = (V_B, w_B)$ be two simple unweighted graphs with N vertices. Let $A=(a_{ij})$ and $B=(b_{ij})$ be their adjacency matrices. The graph isomorphism problem is to find a bicontinued one-to-one correspondence Π between $V_A = \{v_1, ..., v_N\}$ and $V_B = \{v'_1, ..., v'_N\}$ which minimizes a distance, i.e. maximizes the overlap between G_A and G_B. We will use the following classical criterion as a distance:

$$(4.1) \qquad J(\Pi) = \sum_{k=1}^{N} \sum_{l=1}^{N} [w_A(v_k, v_l) - w_B(\Pi(v_k), \Pi(v_l))]^2 .$$

This expression means that if the connectivity between the vertices v_k and v_l in G_A is different from the connectivity between $\Pi(v_k)$

and $\Pi(v_l)$ in G_B, then the distance $J(\Pi)$ is high.

Let P be a N x N permutation matrix defined as follows:

(4.2) $\qquad \forall\,(k, i) \in\, <1,N>^2,\ p_{ki} = 1 \quad \text{if } \Pi(v_k) = v'_i$

$\qquad\qquad\qquad\qquad\qquad\qquad = 0 \quad \text{otherwise.}$

One notices that:

(4.3) $\quad \forall\,(k, l) \in\, <1, N>^2,\quad w_B(\Pi(v_k), \Pi(v_l)) = \sum_{i=1}^{N}\sum_{j=1}^{N} p_{ki} \cdot b_{ij} \cdot p_{lj}.$

It is the coefficient (k, l) of $P.B.P^T$. Then, by using the classical Euclidean norm:

(4.4) $\qquad \forall\ M = (m_{kl})_{(k, l)\in <1, N>^2},\quad \| M \|^2 = \sum_{k=1}^{N}\sum_{l=1}^{N} m_{kl}^2,$

the problem (i) is reduced to the problem of finding the permutation matrix P that minimizes the distance J (P) defined as follows:

(4.5) $\qquad\qquad\qquad J(P) = \| A - P.B.P^T \|^2.$

4.1.2. Inclusion between simple unweighted directed graphs

Let $G_A=(V_A, w_A)$ and $G_B=(V_B, w_B)$ be two simple unweighted graphs with N vertices. The problem of inclusion of G_A in G_B is to find a morphism Ω between $V_A=\{v_1, \dots, v_N\}$ and $V_B = \{v'_1, \dots, v'_N\}$ which maximizes the criterion:

(4.6) $\qquad\qquad K(\Omega) = \sum_{k=1}^{N}\sum_{l=1}^{N} w_A(v_k, v_l) \cdot w_B(\Omega(v_k), \Omega(v_l)).$

This criterion means that if there exists a relation between the vertices v_k and v_l in G_A, then there must be a relation between $\Omega(v_k)$ and $\Omega(v_l)$ in G_B.

By using the permutation matrix as defined in section 4.1.1, the problem (i') is to find P which minimizes K(P) defined by the scalar product:

(4.7) $K(P) = - <A \mid P.B.P^T>.$

4.1.3. Subgraph isomorphism between simple unweighted directed graphs

Let G_A and G_B be two simple unweighted graphs with respectively N and M vertices, M being greater than N (M>N). The subgraph isomorphism problem is to find a bicontinued one-to-one correspondence Π between $V_A = \{v_1, \dots, v_N\}$ and a subset of $V_B = \{v'_1, \dots, v'_M\}$. If A and B are the adjacency matrices of G_A and G_B, the problem can be formulated as the minimization of J(P) given by equation (4.5) but where P is a N x M binary rectangular matrix that represents the correspondence Π and has the properties:

(4.8) $\forall k \in <1, N>, \displaystyle\sum_{i=1}^{M} p_{ki} = 1$ and $\forall i \in <1, M>, \displaystyle\sum_{k=1}^{N} p_{ki} = 0$ or $1.$

The equation (4.8) means that each vertex of G_A has exactly one correspondent in G_B and each vertex of G_B has no more than one correspondent in G_A. The continuity constraint is ensured by J(P)=0. From equation (4.5), J(P) can be written:

(4.9) $J(P) = \|A\|^2 + \|P.B.P^T\|^2 - 2.<A \mid P.B.P^T>$

where $\|A\|^2$ is a constant term.

In this expression, we have:

(4.10) $\|P.B.P^T\|^2 = \displaystyle\sum_{k=1}^{N}\sum_{l=1}^{N}\left(\sum_{i=1}^{M}\sum_{j=1}^{M} p_{ki}.b_{ij}.p_{lj}\right)^2$

$$= \sum_{k=1}^{N}\sum_{l=1}^{N}\sum_{i=1}^{M}\sum_{j=1}^{M} p_{ki}.b_{ij}.p_{lj}$$

and

$$(4.11) \qquad < A \mid P.B.P^T > = \sum_{k=1}^{N}\sum_{l=1}^{N}\sum_{i=1}^{M}\sum_{j=1}^{M} a_{kl} \cdot p_{ki} \cdot b_{ij} \cdot p_{lj}.$$

By associating with each matrix coefficient of P a binary neuron of a neural network, the problem (ii) is equivalent to the minimization problem on the p_{ij} variables of the following energy derived from equations (4.9) to (4.11):

$$(4.12) \qquad E_J = \sum_{k=1}^{N}\sum_{l=1}^{N}\sum_{i=1}^{M}\sum_{j=1}^{M} (1 - 2. a_{kl}) \cdot p_{ki} \cdot b_{ij} \cdot p_{lj}.$$

One notices that:

$$(4.13) \qquad \forall\, k \in\, <1, N>, \forall\, i \in\, <1, M>, \ p_{ki} = \delta_{v_i' \Pi(v_k)}.$$

Thus, by using the notation:

$$(4.14) \qquad \text{if } \Pi\ (v_k) = v'_i, \text{ then } v'_i = v'_\Pi\ (k)$$

one can write:

$$(4.15) \qquad E_J = \sum_{k=1}^{N}\sum_{l=1}^{N} (1 - 2. a_{kl}) \cdot b_{\Pi(k)\Pi(l)}.$$

The absolute minimum of E_J corresponds to a maximum topological overlap between G_A and G_B. If E_J is zero, then G_A and $\Pi(G_A)$ are iso - morphic. A staightforward generalisation to the manipulation of weighted multigraphs can be formulated (see section 4.1.5.).

4.1.4. Subgraph inclusion between simple unweighted directed graphs

Let G_A and G_B be two simple unweighted graphs with respectively N and M vertices, M being greater than N (M>N). The subgraph inclusion problem is to find a morphism Ω between $V_A = \{v_1, \dots, v_N\}$ and a subset V'_B of $V_B = \{v'_1, \dots, v'_M\}$ such that V_A is included in V'_B. If A and B are the adjacency matrices of G_A and G_B, the problem can be formulated as the minimization of K(P) given by equation (4.7) but where P is a N x M binary rectangular matrix of the same type as in section 4.1.3 that represents the correspondence Ω.

By associating with each matrix coefficient of P a binary neuron of a neural network, the problem (ii') is equivalent to the minimization problem on the p_{ij} variables of the following energy derived from equation (4.7) and (4.11):

$$(4.16) \qquad E_K = - \sum_{k=1}^{N} \sum_{l=1}^{N} a_{kl} \cdot b_{\Omega(k),\Omega(l)} \cdot$$

The absolute minimum of E_K corresponds to a maximum topological inclusion between G_A and G_B. If E_K is zero, then G_A is a part of G_B. A staightforward generalisation to the manipulation of weighted multigraphs can be formulated.

4.1.5. Subgraph isomorphism and inclusion between two general structural descriptions

Let us define two weighted directed multigraphs G_A and G_B with respectively N and M vertices (M>N). The arcs are weighted and each weight can be considered as a mutual relation between two parts of the structural description. Let R_1, ..., R_S be these relations. For each relation R_s, the following subgraph of G_A, specified by its adjacency matrix is defined:

$$(4.17) \qquad (a^s_{kl})_{k \in <1, N>, l \in <1, N>} \text{ with } a^s_{kl} = 1 \text{ if } a_{kl} = R_s,$$
$$= 0 \text{ otherwise.}$$

Such subgraphs are also defined for G_B. Then, the objective is to find the correspondence that tends to minimize the criterion E_J (equation 4.15) or E_K (equation 4.16) associated with each relation R_s. The energies to be minimized are given by:
- case of the isomorphism problem:

$$(4.18) \qquad E_J = \sum_{s=1}^{S} \lambda_s \sum_{k=1}^{N} \sum_{l=1}^{N} (1 - 2 \cdot a^s_{kl}) \cdot b^s_{\Pi(k)\Pi(l)},$$

- case of the inclusion problem:

$$(4.19) \qquad E_K = \sum_{s=1}^{S} \lambda_s \sum_{k=1}^{N} \sum_{l=1}^{N} a_{k\,l}^{s} \cdot b_{\Omega(k)\,\Omega(l)}^{s}$$

where $(\lambda_1, ..., \lambda_s, ..., \lambda_S) \in (\mathfrak{R}^+)^S$.

The λ's values are determined arbitrarily and each one expresses the relative weight of the associated relation in the structural description.

4.1.6. Maximum subgraph matching and inclusion

To solve the problem (iii) and (iii'), we propose an heuristic approach that uses the neural network methodology. Let us suppose that G_A has less vertices than G_B. The first step consists in extracting a subgraph MO (maximum overlap) from G_B that has a high probability to contain the desired subset and that has the same vertex number as G_A. We choose MO such that the overlap between G_A and MO is maximum. This can be done by using the approach described in section 4.1.5: one mimimizes E_J or E_K (equations 4.18 and 4.19). The second step consists in looking for the largest subgraph of G_A included or isomorphic to a subgraph of MO. This heuristic method does not ensure that we have obtained the optimal solution of the global problem. Nevertheless, the results seem to enforce its credibility. Let us describe the second step. The objective is to find the biggest subgraph $G'_A = (V'_A, w'_A)$ of G_A such that G'_A and its correspondent by the morphism in MO verify the desired property (isomorphism or inclusion) and the morphism is a continued application. Thus the morphism has to verify the following condition:
- case of the isomorphism problem:

$$(4.20) \qquad D_J = \sum_{s=1}^{S} \sum_{v_k \in V'_A} \sum_{v_l \in V'_A} [\, w_A^s (v_k, v_l) - w_B^s (\Pi(v_k), \Pi(v_l)) \,]^2 = 0 .$$

- case of the inclusion problem:

$$(4.21) \qquad D_K = \sum_{s=1}^{S} \sum_{v_k \in V'_A} \sum_{v_l \in V'_A} w_A^s (v_k, v_l) \cdot w_B^s (\Omega(v_k), \Omega(v_l)) = 0 .$$

Thus, to find G'_A, the following criterion is applied to each vertex v_k of G_A:

- case of the isomorphism problem: calculate D_k given by:

$$(4.22) \qquad D_k = \sum_{s=1}^{S} \sum_{v_l \in V_A'} [\, w_A^s(v_k, v_l) - w_B^s(\Pi(v_k), \Pi(v_l)) \,]^2 .$$

If D_k is non zero, then v_k is not in G'_A.

- case of the inclusion problem: calculate D_k given by:

$$(4.23) \qquad D_k = \sum_{s=1}^{S} \sum_{v_l \in V_A'} w_A^s(v_k, v_l) \cdot w_B^s(\Omega(v_k), \Omega(v_l)) .$$

If D_k is non zero, then v_k is not in G'_A.

Then, G'_A is the largest isomorphic or included subgraph between G_A and MO and is asserted to be a very good common subgraph between G_A and G_B.
The energy minimization associated with the first step is proceeded by using the methods that are described in section 2.
We now want to illustrate algorithmic methods through the subgraph isomorphism or inclusion problems.

4.2. Energy minimization using an analog Hopfield neural network

Let us define an analog Hopfield neural network with N x M matrix organisation in which the output of the $(k,i)^{th}$ neuron expresses the p_{ki} value. The energy to be minimized using this network is given by equations (4.5) and (4.7), but two energetic terms associated with constraints which takes into account the structural organization of the network have to be added. They expresses that:

(1) each vertex of G_A has exactly one correspondent in G_B,
(2) each vertex of G_B has no more than one antecedent in G_A.

Energetic terms that correspond to those constraints are added to the energy given by equation (4.5) or (4.7). The new energy can be viewed as the energy of an Hopfield neural network:

$$(4.24) \qquad E = -\frac{1}{2} \cdot \sum_{k=1}^{N} \sum_{l=1}^{N} \sum_{i=1}^{M} \sum_{j=1}^{M} T_{ki,lj} \cdot p_{ki} \cdot p_{lj}.$$

In the case of the isomorphism problem, the synaptic weights are given by:

$$(4.25) \qquad \forall \, (k,l) \in <1,N>^2, \; \forall \, (i,j) \in <1,M>^2,$$

$$T_{ki,lj} = 2. \sum_{s=1}^{S} \lambda_s . [(1 - 2.a_{kl}^s). b_{ij}^s + C.\delta_{ij}.(1 - \delta_{kl}) + D.\delta_{kl}.(1 - \delta_{ij})]$$

with $(C,D) \in (\Re^-)^2$.

In the case of the inclusion problem, we obtain:

$$(4.26) \qquad \forall \, (k,l) \in <1,N>^2, \; \forall \, (i,j) \in <1,M>^2,$$

$$T_{ki,lj} = 2. \sum_{s=1}^{S} \lambda_s . [a_{kl}^s . b_{ij}^s + C.\delta_{ij}.(1 - \delta_{kl}) + D.\delta_{kl}.(1 - \delta_{ij})]$$

with $(C,D) \in (\Re^-)^2$.

The constants C and D are empirically determined. Convergence dynamics associated with such a network have been described in section 2.1.

4.3. Energy minimization using simulated annealing

The subgraph isomorphism and inclusion problems can be described as a complex system whose energy is given by equations (4.15) and (4.16). To minimize it by using simulated annealing, some elementary transformations have to be defined.

Let $G_A = (V_A, w_A)$ and $G_B = (V_B, w_B)$ be two structural descriptions in which S relations $R_1, \dots, R_S$ exist. First, let Φ be the correspondence function to be found ($\Phi = \Pi$ or Ω). If G_A has N vertices and G_B has M vertices, M being greater than N, the following Φ and Σ functions are introduced:

(4.27)
$$\Phi : V_A \rightarrow V_B$$
$$v_k \rightarrow \Phi(v_k) = v'_i$$

and

$$\Sigma : V_B \rightarrow V_A \cup \{v_{N+1}\}$$

$v'_i \rightarrow \Sigma(v'_i) = v_k$ if there exists v_k in V_A such that $\Phi(v_k) = v'_i$,

$= v_{N+1}$ otherwise

where v_{N+1} is a vertex of degree zero which is artificially added to the V_A set. Thus, one adds a column and a line of zeros in each of the adjacency matrices (a^s_{ij}) associated with each relation R_s of the structural descriptions.

Given the previous definitions, the elementary transformations are defined as follows:

1) Select at random a vertex v_k of V_A . Let $v'_i = \Phi(v_k)$ its corres - pondent in V_B.

2) Select in a random way a vertex v'_j of V_B that is different from v'_i.

3) Exchange $\Sigma(v'_i)$ and $\Sigma(v'_j)$ in V_A:

$$\Sigma^{new}(v'_i) = \Sigma^{old}(v'_j)$$
$$\Sigma^{new}(v'_j) = \Sigma^{old}(v'_i).$$

The number of elementary transformations is N.(M-1) .

After some algebra, the energy variation associated with such an elementary transformation becomes:

- case of the isomorphism problem:

(4.28)
$$\Delta E_J = 2. \sum_{s=1}^{S} \lambda_s . \{ (b^s_{ij} - b^s_{ji}).(a^s_{kl} - a^s_{lk})$$

$$+ \sum_{m=1, \, m \neq k,l}^{N} [(b^s_{i\Pi(m)} - b^s_{j\Pi(m)}).(a^s_{km} - a^s_{lm})$$

$$+ (b^s_{\Pi(m)i} - b^s_{\Pi(m)j}).(a^s_{mk} - a^s_{ml})] \}.$$

If G_A and G_B are undirected, then ΔE is simpler:

$$(4.29) \qquad \Delta E_J = 4. \sum_{s=1}^{S} \lambda_s . \sum_{m=1, \, m \neq k, l}^{N} (b^s_{i\Pi(m)} - b^s_{j\Pi(m)}).(a^s_{km} - a^s_{lm}) .$$

- case of the inclusion problem:

$$(4.30) \qquad \Delta E_K = \Delta E_J / 2 .$$

One notices that the energy variation associated to the isomorphism problem is 2 times the energy variation associated to the inclusion problem. Thus, the two problems are quite similar.

At each temperature, the length of the Markov chain of transitions which are tested is $100.N.(M-1)$. Practically, when $10.N.(M-1)$ transformations have been accepted at a given temperature, the system is considered to have reached the equilibrium at this temperature. One notices that no constraint induced by the simulated annealing method has to be added to the energy to be minimized. In the mean field approximation algorithm, one has to take into account a constraint in the energy to be minimized.

4.4. Energy minimization using mean field theory

In this approach, the energy to be minimized is given by equation (4.15) or (4.16) but has to be slightly modified. In fact, the correspondence function to be found must be a surjective mapping. Thus, one has to ensure that in each column of the permutation matrix P, there is no more than one coefficient p_{ki} that is 1 and all the others are 0. To perform this constraint, an energetic term is added to E_J or E_K:

$$(4.31) \qquad - C. \sum_{s=1}^{S} \lambda_s \sum_{k=1}^{N} \sum_{l=1}^{N} \sum_{i=1}^{M} \sum_{j=1}^{M} \delta_{ij} . (1 - \delta_{kl}) . p_{ki} . p_{lj}$$

where $(\lambda_1, ..., \lambda_s, ..., \lambda_S) \in (\mathfrak{R}^+)^S$ and $C \in \mathfrak{R}^-$.
C is empirically determined.

In order to associate with each problem variable a spin which is either +1 or -1, the following variable change is performed:

$$(4.32) \qquad \forall \, k \in <1, N>, \forall \, i \in <1, M>, \ \sigma_{ki} = 2 . p_{ki} - 1 .$$

Then, the mean energy associated with each spin k can be approximated by using the mean field approximation:

(4.33) $$<E(\vec{\sigma}_k)> = -<\vec{h}_{k\,tot}>.<\vec{\sigma}_k>$$

where $$\vec{h}_{k\,tot} = (h^{tot}_{k1}, ..., h^{tot}_{ki}, ..., h^{tot}_{kM})^T$$

and $$\vec{\sigma}_k = (\sigma_{k1}, ..., \sigma_{ki}, ..., \sigma_{kM})^T.$$

In this expression h_{ki}^{tot} may be considered as the ith component of the total field vector existing on the vertex v_k of G_A. It is the sum of the ith components of the field created on the vertex v_k by the other vertices and of the external field in which the system is plunged:

(4.34) $$\forall k \in <1, N>, \forall i \in <1, M>, <h^{tot}_{ki}> = <h^{int}_{ki}> + h^{ext}_{ki}.$$

- case of the isomorphism problem:

(4.35) $$<h^{int}_{ki}> = 2.\sum_{s=1}^{S}\frac{\lambda_s}{4}\sum_{l=1}^{N}\sum_{j=1}^{M}\{(1-2.a^s_{kl}).b^s_{ij} + C.\delta_{ij}.(1-\delta_{kl})\}.<\sigma_{lj}>.$$

(4.36) $$h^{ext}_{ki} = \sum_{s=1}^{S}\frac{\lambda_s}{4}\sum_{l=1}^{N}\sum_{j=1}^{M}\{(1-2.a^s_{kl}).b^s_{ij} + (1-2.a^s_{lk}).b^s_{ji} + 2.C.\delta_{ij}.(1-\delta_{kl})\}.$$

- case of the inclusion problem:

(4.37) $$<h^{int}_{ki}> = 2.\sum_{s=1}^{S}\frac{\lambda_s}{4}\sum_{l=1}^{N}\sum_{j=1}^{M}\{a^s_{kl}.b^s_{ij} + C.\delta_{ij}.(1-\delta_{kl})\}.<\sigma_{lj}>.$$

(4.38) $$h^{ext}_{ki} = \sum_{s=1}^{S}\frac{\lambda_s}{4}\sum_{l=1}^{N}\sum_{j=1}^{M}\{a^s_{kl}.b^s_{ij} + a^s_{lk}.b^s_{ji} + 2.C.\delta_{ij}.(1-\delta_{kl})\}.$$

The mean state of the spins are easily derived from equations

(4.32) and (4.33). They are the solutions of the following system of non linear equations of the kind described in section 2.3:

(4.39) $$\forall\, k \in <1, K>, \quad \forall\, i \in <1, M>,$$

$$<\sigma_{ki}> = \frac{\exp\left\{\frac{1}{T}\left(<h^{tot}_{ki}> - \sum_{j=1, j\neq i}^{M} <h^{tot}_{kj}>\right)\right\} - \sum_{r=1, r\neq i}^{M} \exp\left\{\frac{1}{T}\left(<h^{tot}_{kr}> - \sum_{j=1, j\neq r}^{M} <h^{tot}_{kj}>\right)\right\}}{\sum_{r=1}^{M} \exp\left\{\frac{1}{T}\left(<h^{tot}_{kr}> - \sum_{j=1, j\neq r}^{M} <h^{tot}_{kj}>\right)\right\}}.$$

i.e.:

(4.40) $$<\sigma_{ki}> = \frac{\exp\left(2.\frac{<h^{tot}_{ki}>}{T}\right) - \sum_{r=1, r\neq i}^{M} \exp\left(2.\frac{<h^{tot}_{kr}>}{T}\right)}{\sum_{r=1}^{M} \exp\left(2.\frac{<h^{tot}_{kr}>}{T}\right)}$$

$$= \frac{2}{\sum_{r=1}^{M} \exp\left\{\frac{2}{T}.(<h^{tot}_{kr}> - <h^{tot}_{ki}>)\right\}} - 1.$$

One notices that this equation ensures that each vertex of G_A has exactly one correspondent in G_B. Thus, it is not necessary to add this constraint in the expression of the energy to be minimized. The system (4.40) can now be solved iteratively:

- case of the isomorphism problem:

(4.41) $\forall\, k \in\, <1, N>, \forall\, i \in\, <1, M>,$

$$<\sigma_{ki}^{new}> = -1 + 2 \,/ \sum_{r=1}^{M} \exp \left\{ \sum_{s=1}^{S} \frac{\lambda_s}{2.T} \sum_{l=1}^{N} \sum_{j=1}^{M} [2.(\,(b_{rj}^s - b_{ij}^s).(1-2.a_{kl}^s) \right.$$

$$+ C.(\delta_{rj} - \delta_{ij}).(1-\delta_{kl})\,).<\sigma_{lj}^{old}>$$

$$+ (b_{rj}^s - b_{ij}^s).(1-2.a_{kl}^s)$$

$$+ (b_{jr}^s - b_{ji}^s).(1-2.a_{lk}^s)$$

$$+ 2.C.(\delta_{rj} - \delta_{ij}).(1-\delta_{kl})\ \}.$$

- case of the inclusion problem:

(4.42) $\forall\, k \in\, <1, N>, \forall\, i \in\, <1, M>,$

$$<\sigma_{ki}^{new}> = -1 + 2 \,/ \sum_{r=1}^{M} \exp \{ \sum_{s=1}^{S} \frac{\lambda_s}{2.T} \sum_{l=1}^{N} \sum_{j=1}^{M} [2.(\,(b_{rj}^s - b_{ij}^s).a_{kl}^s$$

$$+ C.(\delta_{rj} - \delta_{ij}).(1-\delta_{kl})\,).<\sigma_{lj}^{old}>$$

$$+ (b_{rj}^s - b_{ij}^s).a_{kl}^s + (b_{jr}^s - b_{ji}^s).a_{lk}^s$$

$$+ 2.C.(\delta_{rj} - \delta_{ij}).(1-\delta_{kl})\ \}$$

and $$<p_{ki}>^{new} = \frac{<\sigma_{ki}>^{new} + 1}{2}.$$

Once the system has converged according to the dynamics described in sections 2.3 or 2.4, each $<p_{ki}>$ value represents the probability for the vertex v_k of G_A to correspond to the vertex v'_i of G_B. Then, a decision process puts to 1 each variable that has a probability to be +1 greater than 50 %.

4.5. Experimental results

Let us suppose that one is searching for a graph G_A of 23 vertices describing the "Eiffel Tower" (figure 6-a) in a very complicated random multigraph G_B of 250 vertices with a mean vertex degree of 10 (figure 6-b) (problem described in section 4.1.5). These structural descriptions are using eight relations.

On figure 7-a, we show the solution to the subgraph isomorphism problem provided by the simulated annealing algorithm, when G_B contains exactly G_A (isomorphism problem). The one-to-one correspondence found here is optimal.

On figure 7-b, we show the solution to the maximum subgraph matching problems provided by our heuristic approach when G_B contains the "Eiffel Tower" without the right leg (problem described in section 4.1.6). Once more the solution here is optimal.

The solutions provided by the other neural approaches are comparable in quality. Obviously, these approaches are very efficient to solve intractable problems of morphism between complicated graphs.

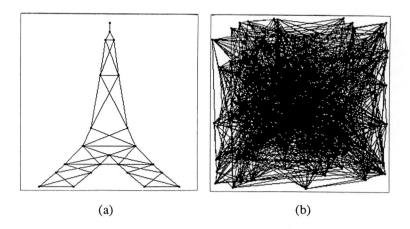

(a)   (b)

figure 6: (a) G_A : Structural description of the "Eiffel Tower": 23 vertices, 8 relations. (b) G_B : Complicated graph which contains the "Eiffel Tower": 250 vertices, mean vertex degree of 10, 8 relations.

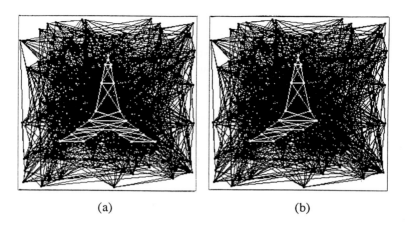

(a)   (b)

figure 7: Simulated annealing (with the λ's values egal to 1): (a) So-lution to the subgraph isomorphism problem. (b) Solution to the maximum subgraph matching when G_B contains the "Eiffel Tower" without the right leg.

5.   Problems of subset extraction with particular properties

Neural techniques are well adapted to extract from an undirected graph some sets of vertices with particular properties such as [16]: the clique, the independent set, the balanced complete bipartite subgraph, the transitive subgraph, the minimum K-connected sub-graph, the cubic subgraph, the kernel, the K-closure problems. Among these problems, that of listing all the maximal cliques of a graph is np-complete [11]. If the graph has N vertices, the number of subgraphs to be tested is:

$$\sum_{i=1}^{N} \binom{N}{i}$$

This approach is generally used to find the largest maximal clique. Neural methodology proposes an alternative approach to find the largest maximal clique that avoids enumerating all the maximal cliques. The desired subgraph is given by the absolute minimum of a global energy.

One notices that the morphism problem between two structural descriptions can be easily transformed into that of finding the largest maximal clique of an undirected graph which combines the two structural descriptions [5, 10, 28].

5.1. Transcription of the subgraph extraction problem in terms of the minimization of the energy of a complex system (case of an undirected graph)

Let $G = (V, w)$ be a simple undirected graph with N vertices and (a_{ij}) its adjacency matrix. Let us associate with each vertex of the graph a neuron output x_i that is 1 if the vertex is in the desired subset or 0 otherwise. An energetic term which expresses that the desired subset is a clique is:

$$(5.1) \qquad E_{clique} = \frac{1}{2} \cdot \sum_{i=1}^{N} \sum_{j=1}^{N} (1 - a_{ij}) \cdot x_i \cdot x_j - \frac{1}{2} \cdot \sum_{i=1}^{N} x_i.$$

The second part of this expression is induced by the diagonal terms of the adjacency matrix. If the vertices v_i and v_j are in the clique, then this energy is minimum if they are connected. Moreover, if E_{clique} is zero, then the desired subset is a clique. An energetic term which tends to maximize the number of vertices in the clique is:

$$(5.2) \qquad E_{max} = \left(N - \sum_{i=1}^{N} x_i \right)^2 = \sum_{i=1}^{N} \sum_{j=1}^{N} (1 - x_i) \cdot (1 - x_j).$$

The global energy to be minimized combines E_{clique} and E_{max} :

$$(5.3) \qquad E = \lambda \cdot E_{max} + E_{clique}$$

where λ is an adjustable positive real parameter. One notices that the λ value does not noticeably influence the quality of the experimental results. After some algebra, the energy to be minimized becomes:

$$(5.4) \quad E(\vec{x}) = \sum_{i=1}^{N} \sum_{j=1}^{N} \left(\lambda + \frac{1 - a_{ij}}{2} \right) . x_i . x_j - \left(2.\lambda.N + \frac{1}{2} \right) . \sum_{i=1}^{N} x_i$$

where $\vec{x} = (x_1, ..., x_i, ..., x_N)$.

5.2. Energy minimization using simulated annealing

An elementary transformation is defined as the move of a vertex either from the desired subset to the "exterior" or from the "exterior" to the "interior" of the desired subset:

$$x^{new} = 1 - x^{old}.$$

The energy variation associated with an elementary transformation involving the vertex v_i becomes, after some algebra:

$$(5.5) \quad \Delta E = (1 - 2.x_i) . \left[\sum_{j=1, j \neq i}^{N} (2.\lambda + 1 - a_{ij}) . x_j - (2.N - 1) . \lambda \right].$$

The convergence dynamics is described in section 2.2.
The calculations for the MFT, MFA and Hopfield nets are of the same type as previously.

5.3 Energy minimization using mean field theory

In this approach, the energy to be minimized is given by the equation (5.4). In order to associate with each problem variable a spin which is either +1 or -1, the following variable change is performed:

$$(5.6) \quad \forall i \in <1, N>, \quad x_i = \frac{\sigma_i + 1}{2} \quad \text{where} \quad \sigma_i \in \{-1, +1\}.$$

Then, the energy to be minimized becomes:

$$(5.7) \quad E = -\sum_{i=1}^{N} \sum_{j=1}^{N} \frac{1}{4} . \left(\lambda + \frac{1 - a_{ij}}{2} \right) . \sigma_i . \sigma_j + \sum_{i=1}^{N} \frac{1}{4} . \left(N.(1 - 2.\lambda) - 1 - \sum_{j=1}^{N} a_{ij} \right) . \sigma_i$$

From the equations (5.7) and (2.19), the system of coupled non-linear equations to be solved is given by:

(5.8) $\qquad \forall\, i \in <1, N>,\ \mu_i = <\sigma_i>$ and

$$\mu_i = \tanh\left\{\frac{1}{T}\left[\sum_{j=1}^{N} -\frac{1}{2}.\left(\lambda + \frac{1-a_{ij}}{2}\right).\mu_j\ -\frac{1}{4}.\left(N.(1-2.\lambda)-1-\sum_{j=1}^{N} a_{ij}\right)\right]\right\}.$$

It is solved iteratively (see sections 2.3 and 2.4). Once the system has converged, each $< x_i >$ given by:

(5.9) $\qquad < x_i > = (\mu_i + 1)/2$

represents the probability for the vertex v_i to belong to the largest maximal clique. Then, a decision process puts to 1 each variable that has a probability to be +1 greater than 50%.

5.4.   Experimental results

One generates a random graph of 100 vertices with a mean vertex degree of 10 and which contains a maximal clique of a specified size which is the largest maximal to be found (figure 8-a). Whatever the size of the clique, simulated annealing provides the optimal solution using the same λ value (figure 8-b). The solutions provided by the other neural approaches are comparable in quality. Thus, they are efficient to extract subgraphs with particular properties.

6. Conclusion

Neural approaches such as SA, MFT and MFA are powerful statistical physics methods to solve families of intractable graph problems including cut and connectivity problems, morphism problems, labelling problems and problems of extraction of subsets with particular properties. We have focused on graph K-partitioning, the maximum subgraph matching and the largest maximal clique which are representative problems of these families.
In terms of the quality of solutions, the SA method is the best approach, followed by the MFT and the MFA algorithms. On the contrary, in terms of computational time, the MFA approach is the best, followed by the MFT and the SA methods. To provide a near optimal solution to the 5-partitioning of large graphs (300

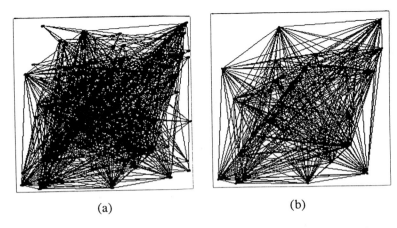

(a)   (b)

figure 8: *(a) Random graph of 100 vertices: mean vertex degree of 10. (b) The largest maximal clique extracted of the graph of figure 8-a with λ=0,01.*

vertices), simulated annealing needs about 2 CPU hours on a SUN 4-260, while mean field annealing produces a comparable solution in a CPU time which is less than 10 minutes.

Appendix A

In this appendix, we describe the simulated annealing algorithm. We use the encoding defined in section 2.2. The algorithm is the following:

1. Get an initial configuration of the system.

2. Fix the initial temperature.
   Fix the number of elementary transformations to be tested at each temperature: NET.
   If NET is the number of possible elementary transformations, then L = 100.NET.

3. Get the initial number of accepted transformations at the temperature T: NTaccept = 0.
   Repeat L times:
   a) Pick at random an elementary transformation.
   b) Calculate the associated energy variation ΔE.
   c) If ΔE is negative, then:
      i. the elementary transformation is accepted:

NTaccept --> NTaccept + 1

ii. operate the transformation by updating the optimization variables.

d) If ΔE is positive, the elementary transformation is accepted with a probability $P = \exp (-\Delta E / T)$.

4. If NTaccept $= L/10$, then consider that the equilibrium is reached at T: update the ambient temperature:

$T_{new} = 0,93 \cdot T_{old}$ and go to step 3.

If NTaccept is between N and $L/10$, the system is freezing; update the ambient temperature $(T_{new} = 0,965 \cdot T_{old})$ and go to step 3.

If NTaccept is lower than N (the system is considered to be frozen), then stop: the final solution is obtained.

Appendix B.

In this appendix, we describe the mean field approximation algorithm. We use the encoding defined in section 2.3. The algorithm is the following:

1. Fix the mode:

synchronous --> fct $= 0$

asynchronous --> fct $= 1$.

Fix the temperature T.

Fix the scan number of the optimization variables: Nbscan.

Get, for all i, the μ_i variables randomly chosen between the values $(-10^{-5}, +10^{-5})$.

2. Repeat Nbscan times:

a. Scan randomly the graph vertices in such a way that every vertex is updated once.

Update every μ_i seen in the scan:

.calculate μ_i^{new} according to equation (2.20).

.if fct $= 1$, update the spin i: $\mu_i^{old} = \mu_i^{new}$.

b. if fct $= 0$, update for all spin i: $\mu_i^{old} = \mu_i^{new}$.

3. Test if the system has converged.

If the system has not converged, either the temperature T is too high, or Nbscan is too small. Go to step 1.

If the system has converged, then for all optimization variable i:

if μ_i is positive, then $\sigma_i = 1$, else $\sigma_i = -1$.

Appendix C.

The mean field annealing algorithm is similar to the mean field approximation one:

1. Fix the mode:
       synchronous --> fct = 0
       asynchronous --> fct = 1.
   Fix the initial temperature $T = T_0$.
   Fix the decreasing coefficient of the temperature between two consecutive scans: decT = 0,995.
   Fix the scan number of the optimization variables: Nbscan.
   Get, for all i, the μ_i variables randomly chosen between the values $(-10^{-5}, 10^{-5})$.

2. Repeat Nbscan times:
   a. Scan randomly the graph vertices in such a way that every vertex is updated once.
      Update every μ_i seen in the scan:
           .calculate μ_i^{new} according to equation (2.20).
           .if fct = 1, update the spin i: $\mu_i^{old} = \mu_i^{new}$.
   b. if fct = 0, update for all spin i: $\mu_i^{old} = \mu_i^{new}$.
   c. T --> decT . T.

3. Test if the system has converged.
   If the system has not converged, either the temperature T is too high, or Nbscan is too small. Go to step 1.
   If the system has converged, then for all optimization variable i:
      if μ_i is positive, then $\sigma_i = 1$, else $\sigma_i = -1$.

References

1. E.H. Aarts, F.M.J. de Bont, E.H.A. Habers, P.J.M van Laarhoven: "A parallel statistical cooling algorithm" Lecture Note in Computer Science 210, pp 87, 1986.
2. J.R.A. Allwright, D.B. Carpenter : "A distributed implementation of simulated annealing for the travelling salesman problem" Parallel Computing 10, pp 335, North Holland, 1989.
3. H.S. Baird: "Model Based Image Using Location" Cambridge M.A: MIT Press, 1985.
4. F. Barahona: "On the computational complexity of Ising spin glass

models" J. Phys. A : Math. Gen. 15, 3241-3253, 1982.

5. H.G. Barrow, R.M. Burstall : "Subgraph isomorphism, matching relational structures and maximal cliques" Information Processing Letters, Vol.4, Numb.4, Jan.1976.

6. S.K. Bhaskar, A. Rosenfeld : "Simulation of processors by smaller ones" in Evaluation of multicomputers for image processing, Academic Press, 1986

7. I. Bieche, R. Maynard, R. Rammal, J.P. Uhry : "On the ground states of the frustration model of a spin glass by a matching method of graph theory" J. Phys. A: Math. Gen. 13, 2553-2576, 1980.

8. G.L. Bilbro, W.E. Snyder : "Range image restoration using mean field annealing" presented at IEEE Conf. on Neural Information Processing Systems, denver, Nov. 1988.

9. S.K. Bokhari : "Assignement problems in parallel and distributed computing" Kluwer Academic publishers, 1987.

10. R.C. Bolles : "Robust feature matching through maximal cliques" Proc. SPIE Technical Symposium on Imaging and Assembly, Washington, D.C. April 1979.

11. R. Bolles, R.A. Cain : "Recognizing and locating partially visible objects, the local-feature-focus method" International Journal of Robotics research, 1(3), pp 57, 1982.

12. D.E. van den Bout, T.K. Miller : "Graph partitioning using annealed neural networks", IJCNN, Washington, June 1989.

13. J.P. Changeux : "L'homme neuronal", Ed. Fayard, Pluriel, 1983.

14. T.S. Chiang, C.T. Hwang, S.J. Shin: "Diffusion for global optimization in R^n", SIAM Journ. Control and Optimization, Vol 25, No 3, pp 737, May 1987.

15. F. Crick, C. Asanuma : "Certains aspects of the anatomy and physiology of the cerebral cortex" in "Parallel Distributed Processing", Vol 2, Chap 20, pp 333, The MIT Press, Cambridge, Massachussets, 1986.

16. M. Garey, D. Johnson: "Computers and intractability: a guide to the theory of NP-completeness", W.H. Freeman, 1979

17. G. Gati: "Further annotated bibliography on the isomorphism disease" Journal of Graph Theory, Vol.3, pp 95, 1979.

18. S. Geman, D. geman: "Stochastic relaxation, Gibbs distributions and the bayesian restoration of images", IEEE Proc. Pattern Analysis and Machine Intelligence, PAMI-6, pp 721, 1984.

19. B. Gidas: "Non stationary Markov chains and convergence of the annealing algorithms", Journ. Statist. Phys. 39, pp 73, 1985.

21. L. Herault, J.J. Niez: "How neural networks can solve hard combinatorial optimization problems: a performance study on the graph

K-partitioning", 2nd Intern. Work. on Neural Networks and their Applications, Nîmes, France, Nov. 1989.

22. L.Hérault, J.J. Niez : " Neural networks & graph K-partitioning " Complex Systems 3 (1989).

23. L. Hérault, F. Veillon, R. Horaud, J.J. Niez: "Symbolic Image Matching by simulated annealing", submitted at Int. Conf. on Comp. Vision, Osaka, 1990.

24. J. Hopfield : "Neural networks and physical systems with emergent collective computational abilities", Proc. Nat. Acad. Sci. USA 79, pp 2554, 1982.

25. J. Hopfield: "Neurons with graded response have collective computational properties like those of two-state neurons", Proc. Nat. Acad. Sci. USA 81, pp 3088, 1984.

26. J. Hopfield, D. Tank: "Neural computation of decisions in optimization problems", Biol. Cyber. 52, pp 141, 1985.

27. J. Hopfield, D. Tank: "Computing with neural circuits: a model", Science 233, pp 625, 1986.

28. R. Horaud, F. Veillon, T. Skordas : "Finding geometric and relational structures in an image", 1rst European conference on comuter vision, Antibes, France, 1990.

29. R. Horaud, T. Skordas : "Stereo-correspondence through feature grouping and maximal cliques", IEEE Transactions on Pattern Analysis and Machine Intelligence, Vol. 11, No. 11, November, 1989.

30. E. Ising : "Geitrag zur theorie des ferromagnetismus", Z. Phys. 31, 253-258, 1925.

31. B.Kernighan, S.Lin : "An efficient heuristic procedure for partitioning graphs" The Bell System Technical Journal, Feb. 1970

32. S. Kirkpatrick, C.D. Gelatt, M.P. Vecchi: "Optimization by simulated annealing", Science 220, pp 671, 1983.

33. S. Kirkpatrick : "Optimization by simulated annealing: quantitative studies", Journ. Statist. Phys. 34, pp 974, 1984.

34. P.J.M. van Laarhoven, E.H.L. Aarts: "Simulated Annealing: theory and applications", D. Reidel Publishing Company, 1987.

35. E.L. Lawler : "Electrical Assemblies with a minimum number of interconnections" IEEE Transactions on Electronic Computers, Vol. EC-11, 1962.

36. B.C. Levy, M.B. Adams: "Global optimization with stochastic neural networks" IEEE International Conference on Neural Networks, San Diego, pp III-681, 1987.

37. R.P. Lippman : "An introduction to computing with neural networks", IEEE Acoustics, Speech and Signal Processing, Vol 4, No 2, pp 4, Apr. 1987.

38. N. Metropolis, A. Rosenbluth, M. Rosenbluth, A. Teller, E. Teller: "Equation of state calculations by fast computing machines", Journ. Chem. Phys. 21, pp 1087, 1953.

39. D. Mitra, F. Romeo, A.L. Sangiovanni Vincentelli: "Convergence and finite-time behavior of simulated annealing", Proc 24th Conf. on Decision and Control, Ft. Lauderdale, pp 761, Dec. 1985.

40. P. Peretto, J.J. Niez : "Stochastic dynamics of neural networks" IEEE Trans. on Systems, Man, and Cybernetics, Vol. SMC-16, No. 1, January/February, 1986.

41. C.H. Papadimitriou, K. Steiglitz: "Combinatorial optimization: algorithms and complexity", Prentice Hall, New York, 1982

42. C. Petersen, J.R. Anderson : "Neural networks and NP-complete optimization problems: a performance study on the graph bisection problem", Complex Systems 2, pp 59, 1988.

43. C. Petersen, J.R. Anderson : " A mean field theory learning algorithm for neural networks", Complex Systems 1, pp 995, 1987.

44. R.C. Read, D.G. Corneil: "The graph isomorphism disease" Journal of Graph Theory, Vol.1, pp 339, 1977.

45. T.J. Sejnowski : "Open questions about computation in cerebral cortex" in "Parallel Distributed Processing", Vol 2, Chap 21, pp 372, The MIT Press, Cambridge, Massachussets, 1986.

46. H.E. Stanley : "Introduction to Phases Transitions and Critical Phenomena" The International Series of monographs on Physics, Oxford university Press, 1971.

47. S.R. White "Concepts of scale in simulated annealing" CH2080-0/84/0000/0646S01.00, pp 646, IEEE 1984.

NEURAL NETWORKS: Advances and Applications
E. Gelenbe (Editor)
© Elsevier Science Publishers B.V. (North-Holland), 1991

Merging Multilayer Perceptrons and Hidden Markov Models: Some Experiments in Continuous Speech Recognition

H. Bourlard [t,‡] & N. Morgan [‡]

(‡) International Computer Science Institute
1947 Center Street, Suite 600
Berkeley, CA 94704, USA

(t) Philips Research Laboratory Brussels
Av. Van Becelaere 2, Box 8,
B-1170 Brussels, Belgium

Abstract: The statistical and sequential nature of the human speech production system makes automatic speech recognition difficult. **Hidden Markov Models (HMM)** have provided a good representation of these characteristics of speech, and were a breakthrough in speech recognition research. However, the a priori choice of a model topology and weak discriminative power limit HMM capabilities. Recently, connectionist models have been recognized as an alternative tool. Their main useful properties are their discriminative power and their ability to capture input-output relationships. They have also proved useful in dealing with statistical data. However, the sequential character of speech is difficult to handle with connectionist models.

We have used a classical form of connectionist system, the **Multilayer Perceptron (MLP)**, for the recognition of continuous speech as part of an HMM system. We show theoretically and experimentally that the outputs of the MLP approximate the probability distribution over output classes conditioned on the input i.e., the **Maximum a Posteriori (MAP)** probabilities. We also report the results of a series of speech recognition experiments. By using contextual information at the input of the MLP, frame classification performance can be achieved which is significantly improved over the corresponding performance for simple Maximum Likelihood probabilities, or even MAP probabilities without the benefit of context.

However, it is not easy to improve the recognition of words in continuous speech by the use of an MLP, although it is clear that the classification at the frame and phoneme levels was better than could be achieved with our HMM system. We present several modifications of the original methods that were required to achieve comparable performance at the word level. Preliminary results are reported for a 1000 word vocabulary, phoneme based, speaker-dependent continuous speech recognition system embedding MLP into HMM.

1. Introduction

The statistical and sequential nature of the human speech production system makes automatic speech recognition difficult. **Hidden Markov Models (HMM)** have provided a good representation of these characteristics of speech, and were a breakthrough in speech recognition research. However, their discriminant properties are weak if they are trained using the **Maximum Likelihood Estimate (MLE)** [Brown, 1987]. An algorithm based on another criterion, **Maximum Mutual Information (MMI)** [Brown, 1987] provides more discrimination, but the mathematics are complex, and many constraining assumptions must be made. Finally, the a priori choice of a model topology limits HMM capabilities; the incorporation of acoustic or phonetic contextual information requires a complex HMM and a large (possibly prohibitive) storage capacity.

Recently, connectionist models have been recognized as an alternative tool for pattern recognition problems such as speech recognition. Their main useful properties are their discriminative power and their ability to capture input-output relationships. Additionally, contextual information can easily be incorporated. They have also proved useful in dealing with statistical data. Using the interpolative capabilities of connectionist models, statistical pattern classification can be performed over an undersampled pattern space [Niles et al., 1989] without many restrictive simplifying assumptions (such as the independence of input features). However, the sequential character of speech is difficult to handle with connectionist models. If the connections are supplied with delays, feedback loops can be added providing dynamic and implicit memory. Several authors [Jordan, 1986; Watrous, 1987; Elman, 1988] have proposed original architectures of this type. However, these architectures are not suited for dealing with connected speech unit recognition. In other words, they are not able to explain (properly) time-varying input patterns in terms of a sequence of output classes. As an alternative, we propose here a hybrid approach exploiting the discriminative and interpolating capabilities of connectionist models while using HMM formalism to capture the dynamics of speech and to segment continuous speech into a succession of words.

We have used a classical form of connectionist system, the **Multilayer Perceptron (MLP)**, for the recognition of continuous speech as part of an HMM system. We show theoretically and experimentally that the outputs of the MLP approximate the probability distribution over output classes conditioned on the input i.e., the **Maximum a Posteriori (MAP) probabilities**. We also report the results of a series of speech recognition experiments. By using contextual information at the input of the MLP, frame classification performance can be achieved which is significantly improved over the corresponding performance for simple MLE, or even MAP probabilities without the benefit of context. Our frame classification results [Bourlard et al., 1990] are consistent with other research showing the capabilities of MLPs trained with back-propagation-styled learning schemes for the recognition of voiced-unvoiced speech segments [Gevins & Morgan, 1984], isolated phonemes [Watrous & Shastri, 1987; Waibel et al., 1988; Makino et al., 1983], or of isolated words [Peeling & Moore, 1988]. These results indicate that "neural network" approaches can, for some problems, perform pattern classification at least as well as traditional statistical approaches. However, this is not particularly mysterious. When traditional statistical assumptions (distribution, independence of multiple features, etc.) are not valid, systems which do not rely on these assumptions can work better (as discussed in [Niles et al., 1989]). Furthermore, networks provide an easy way to incorporate multiple sources of evidence (multiple features, contextual windows, etc.) without restrictive assumptions.

However, it is not easy to improve the recognition of words in continuous speech by the use of an MLP, although the classification at the frame and phoneme levels can be better than what can be achieved with a standard HMM system. Several modifications and improvements of the initial ideas were necessary to achieve comparable performance at the word level. For instance, while it has been shown that the outputs of a feedforward network can be used as emission probabilities in an HMM [Bourlard et al., 1990], the corresponding word recognition performance can be very poor. This is true even when the same network demonstrates extremely good performance at the frame or phoneme levels. The modifications necessary for good performance are presented here, and preliminary results are reported for a 1000 word vocabulary, phoneme based, speaker-dependent continuous speech recognition system embedding MLP into HMM. For a preliminary experiment, this hybrid MLP-HMM algorithm appears to exceed performance of the same HMM system using standard statistical approaches to estimate the emission probabilities. This was only possible after the original algorithm was modified in ways that did not necessarily maximize the frame recognition performance for the training set. We will describe these modifications below, along with experimental results.

2. Hidden Markov Models

In the **Hidden Markov Model (HMM)** formalism, the speech signal is hypothesized to be produced by a particular finite state automaton built up from a set of states $Q = \{q_1, q_2, \ldots, q_K\}$ governed by statistical laws. In that case, each speech unit (e.g. each vocabulary word or each phoneme) is associated with a particular HMM made up of L states $q_\ell \in Q$, with $\ell = 1, \ldots, L$, according to a predefined topology.

A preprocessor extracts vectors of acoustic parameters from the speech waveform at regular intervals, typically every 10-ms. In this way, the speech signal is transformed into a sequence of acoustic vectors $X = \{x_1, x_2, \ldots, x_N\}$. Moreover, in discrete HMM, each acoustic vector x_n ($n = 1, \ldots, N$) is quantized by replacing it by the closest (in the Euclidean sense) prototype vector y_n selected in a predetermined finite set $\mathcal{Y}$ of cardinality I.

The training and recognition criteria are based on the **MLE** probability $P(X|M)$ of observing the acoustic vector sequence X given a particular sequence M of HMMs. During training, the model parameters (defined below) are optimized for maximizing $P(X|M)$, where M is the Markov model associated with X. Thus, if X is a training sentence, M is the Markov model obtained by concatenating elementary HMMs according to the constituting sequence of words or phonemes.

Let q_ℓ^n denote the state q_ℓ observed at time $n \in [1, N]$. Events q_ℓ^n are mutually exclusive so that probability $P(X|M)$ can be written for any arbitrary n:

$$P(X|M) = \sum_{\ell=1}^{L} P(q_\ell^n, X|M) , \qquad (1)$$

where $P(q_\ell^n, X|M)$ represents the probability that X is produced by M while associating x_n with state q_ℓ.

Maximization of (1) can be conducted by the forward-backward recurrences of the Baum-Welch algorithm [Baum, 1972; Bourlard et al., 1985; Brown, 1987]. However, it is sometimes preferred to replace the maximization of $P(X|M)$ (the actual MLE) by a **Viterbi criterion** which is an approximation in which only the most probable state sequence capable of producing X is taken into account. To explicitly show all possible paths, (1) can be rewritten as

$$P(X|M) = \sum_{\ell_1=1}^{L} \cdots \sum_{\ell_N=1}^{L} P(q_{\ell_1}^1, \ldots, q_{\ell_N}^N, X|M) .$$

The Viterbi criterion is obtained by replacing all summations by a "max" operator. The probability (1) is then approximated by:

$$\overline{P}(X|M) = \max_{\ell_1, \ldots, \ell_N} P(q_{\ell_1}^1, \ldots, q_{\ell_N}^N, X|M) . \qquad (2)$$

In both cases (MLE and Viterbi), it can be shown that probabilities $P(X|M)$ and $\overline{P}(X|M)$ can be expressed in terms of $p[q_\ell^n, x_n|Q_1^{n-1}, X_1^{n-1}, M]$, where X_k^n is the acoustic vector sequence $\{x_k, x_{k+1}, \ldots, x_n\}$ and Q_k^n a particular state sequence $\{q_{\ell_k}^k, \ldots, q_{\ell_n}^n\}$. In the following, only the Viterbi criterion will be considered. In that case, if we assume that HMMs are first order Markov chains (i.e. the influence of past states on the current state is restricted to the immediately preceding state alone), (2) can be computed by the following **Dynamic Programming (DP)** recurrences [Ney, 1984; Bourlard et al., 1985] of the Viterbi algorithm:

$$\overline{P}(q_\ell^n, X_1^n|M) = \max_{k} \left[\overline{P}(q_k^{n-1}, X_1^{n-1}|M) \, p(q_\ell^n, x_n|q_k^{n-1}, X_1^{n-1}, M) \right] . \qquad (3)$$

The global probabilities $\overline{P}(q_\ell^N, X|M)$ for all ℓ are computed by using (3) recursively. The optimal final state is associated with that particular ℓ which maximizes the global probability (also referred to as matching score); the associated best path (and, consequently, the optimal state sequence) can be recovered by backtracking. Each training vector is then uniquely associated with only one particular transition. In order to reduce the number of free parameters, a further necessary simplification is to assume that the acoustic vectors are not correlated. In that case, probability $p(q_\ell^n, x_n|q_k^{n-1}, X_1^{n-1})$ in (3) reduces to $p(q_\ell^n, x_n|q_k^{n-1})$ and are referred to as **local probabilities**, or also **local contributions**. If $n_{ik\ell}$ denote the number of times each prototype vector y_i has been associated with a transition $\{q_k \rightarrow q_\ell\}$ between two states $\in \mathcal{Q}$ on all the training sequences, the estimates of those local probabilities used in standard HMMs and which guarantee the convergence of the **Viterbi training** [Jelinek, 1976; Bourlard et al., 1985] are given by:

$$\hat{p}[q_\ell^t, y_i|q_k^{t-1}] = \frac{n_{ik\ell}}{\sum_{j=1}^I \sum_{m=1}^K n_{jkm}}, \quad \forall i \in [1, I], \quad \forall k, \ell \in [1, K]. \tag{4}$$

These local probabilities are often split into a product of a **transition probability** and an **emission probability** (transition emitting models) [Jelinek, 1976] which are respectively estimated by:

$$\hat{p}[q_\ell^t|q_k^{t-1}] = \frac{\sum_{j=1}^I n_{jk\ell}}{\sum_{j=1}^I \sum_{m=1}^K n_{jkm}},$$

and

$$\hat{p}[y_i|q_\ell^t, q_k^{t-1}] = \frac{n_{ik\ell}}{\sum_{j=1}^I n_{jk\ell}}.$$

A further and usual simplification is to assume that the emission probabilities only depend on the current state q_ℓ (state emitting models); its estimate is then

$$\hat{p}[y_i|q_\ell] = \frac{n_{i\ell}}{\sum_{j=1}^I n_{j\ell}}, \tag{5}$$

where $n_{i\ell}$ is now simply the number of times prototype y_i has been observed on state q_ℓ.

If the models are trained by using this formulation of the Viterbi algorithm, no discrimination is taken into account. Indeed, criterion (1) and estimates (4) and (5) are not discriminant and do not minimize the error rate, either at the word level or at the acoustic vector level. For example, local probabilities (4) or (5) are not the correct criterion for labeling a prototype vector y_i, i.e. to find the most probable state given a current input vector (and a specified previous state). Indeed, the optimal decision should be based on the MAP probability, (also referred to here as the Bayes probability) where the most probable state q_{opt} is defined by

$$opt = \underset{\ell}{\operatorname{argmax}} \; p[q_\ell^t | y_i, q_k^{t-1}] \,, \tag{6}$$

or by

$$opt = p[q_\ell | y_i]$$

if the transitions are not taken into account. It is easy to prove that the estimates of the Bayes probabilities in (6) are:

$$\hat{p}[q_\ell^t | y_i, q_k^{t-1}] = \frac{n_{ik\ell}}{\sum_{m=1}^{K} n_{ikm}} \,. \tag{7}$$

Thus, the optimal criterion, minimizing the decoding error rate at the word or at the frame level, should be based on the MAP. This assertion and the role of other probabilities used in stochastic speech recognition were clearly explained in [Nadas et al., 1988]. It was also shown that the MAP estimate appears safer for the training of speech recognizers when the language model is poor, for instance when the a priori word probabilities are poorly estimated. However, those conclusions were only valid for isolated word recognition, and did not apply to local probabilities used in the lower level decoding process (i.e., frame probabilities used in an HMM for continuous speech recognition).

In conclusion, notwithstanding their undoubted efficiency, HMMs suffer from several weaknesses, namely:

- Poor discrimination due to the training algorithm that maximizes $P(X_j | M_j)$, if M_j is the model associated with X_j, but does not minimize $P(X_j | M_k)$, for all $k \neq j$, i.e. the probability to produce X_j by rival models (actually, the discrimination problem follows from the fact that the training criterion is based on $P(X | M)$ and not on $P(M | X)$ which is the optimal criterion).

- A priori choice of model topology and local probability density functions, e.g. assuming that the distribution of the acoustic vectors observed on each state can be represented as a mixture of multivariate Gaussian densities.

- Assumption that the state sequences are first-order Markov chains.

- No contextual information is taken into account; the possible correlation of the successive acoustic vectors is thus overlooked, which permits the multiplication of local probabilities.

Regarding the last two points, it was recalled in [Poritz, 1988] that the output probabilities should depend on a fixed window back into the recent past on both states and observations, which is certainly not the case in standard HMM.

3. Statistical inference in Multilayer Perceptrons

Both HMMs and MLPs are systems which can "learn", i.e., can be trained. However, MLPs are good at simultaneously forcing the acceptance of training patterns into their own classes and their rejection by rival classes. Furthermore, it has been proved that MLPs are able to approximate any kind of nonlinear discriminant functions [Lippmann, 1987; White, 1988]. In fact, by performing nonlinear and nonparametric regression, they extract input features that are relevant to classification without any assumption about the underlying probability density functions. If the training set is large enough to determine the correct discriminant features, these connectionist models will exhibit "generalization" properties, i.e. they will be able to correctly classify unseen data. In the following, we show that these machines allow us to overcome some of the HMM's drawbacks previously explained. It is shown that the output values of an MLP are estimates of MAP-like probabilities, i.e., (5) (or something more general if there is feedback from higher layers to the input field). Using an MLP with this feedback and extending the input field to include context, output probabilities can be generated which depend on a fixed temporal window on both states and observations.

Let q_k, with $k = 1, \ldots, K$, be the output units of an MLP associated with different classes (each of them corresponding to a particular state of $\mathcal{Q}$), and let us assume that the training set consists of a labeled sequence of N quantized acoustic vectors $\{y_{i_1}, y_{i_2}, \ldots, y_{i_N}\}$, where each y_{i_k} belongs to $\mathcal{Y}$. At time t, the input pattern of the MLP is a binary code of the label associated with y_{i_t} (generally the index of the corresponding prototype) and is known to be associated with a particular state (or class) q_k^t. The training of the MLP parameters is usually based on the minimization of the following **Mean Square Error criterion (MSE)**:

$$E = \frac{1}{2} \sum_{n=1}^{N} \sum_{k=1}^{K} [g_k(y_{i_n}) - d_k(y_{i_n})]^2 , \qquad (8)$$

where $g_k(y_{i_n})$ represents the output value of unit k given y_{i_n} at the input and $d_k(y_{i_n})$ is the associated target value and, in classification mode, is 1 if the input is known to belong to class q_k and 0 otherwise. Expanding summations to collect all terms depending on the same y_i, (6) can be rewritten as:

$$E = \frac{1}{2} \sum_{i=1}^{I} \sum_{k=1}^{K} \sum_{\ell=1}^{K} n_{ik} \cdot [g_\ell(y_i) - d_\ell(y_i)]^2 , \qquad (9)$$

where n_{ik} is the number of times y_i has been observed in class (or state) q_k. Thus, whatever the MLP topology may be, i.e. the number of its hidden layers and of units per layer, the optimal output values $g_{k,opt}(y_i)$ are obtained by setting to zero the partial derivative of E with respect to $g_k(y_i)$. It can easily be proved that the optimal values for the outputs are then

$$g_{k,opt}(y_i) = \frac{n_{ik}}{\sum_{\ell=1}^{K} n_{i\ell}} = \hat{p}[q_k|y_i] , \tag{10}$$

which are the estimates of the Bayes probabilities (not including transition probabilities). If the MLP is provided with a feedback from the output units to the input field it has been shown [Bourlard & Wellekens, 1990] that the optimal output values are then equal to (7), including the transition probabilities as well. However, these optimal values can only be reached if the MLP contains enough parameters, does not get stuck at a local minimum during the training, and is trained long enough to reach the global minimum.

These results follow directly from the minimized criterion, not from the topology of the model. In fact, the same optimal values (10) may also result from other criteria, such as the entropy or relative entropy of the targets with respect to the output [Bourlard & Wellekens, 1990]. This solution, obtained by cancelling the partial derivative of the error criterion (MSE or entropy) versus the output vector g, is the optimal set of values that could be reached by the algorithm actually used for the training of the MLP, the **Error Back-Propagation algorithm (EBP)** [Werbos, 1974; Rumelhart et al., 1986]. In this procedure, a gradient estimate is used to cancel the partial derivatives of the error versus the weight parameters W. Indeed:

$$\frac{\partial E}{\partial w_{ij}} = (\nabla_g E)^t \cdot \frac{\partial g}{\partial w_{ij}} \quad , \ \forall i, j ,$$

where t signifies the transpose operation. Thus, a minimum in the output space ($\nabla_g E = 0$) is also a minimum in the parameter space ($\partial E/\partial w_{ij} = 0, \ \forall i, j$). However, it is also clear that $\partial E/\partial w_{ij} = 0, \ \forall i, j$, does not necessarily lead to $\nabla_g E = 0$ which then implies that the network has converged to a local minimum of the error function. In this case, the outputs will not be the MAP probabilities. In fact, it is no longer guaranteed that the output values will look like probabilities, e.g., that they sum up to unity. An elegant way to circumvent this problem is to replace the classical sigmoidal function applied at the output units by a "softmax" function [Bridle, 1989] defined, for any i, as:

$$g_k(y_i) = \frac{e^{x(i,k)}}{\sum_{\ell=1}^{K} e^{x(i,\ell)}} , \tag{11}$$

where $x(i,k)$ is the output value of unit k before the nonlinearity for an input y_i. This function generalizes the sigmoid and has a nice relationship with the Gibbs distribution [Bridle, 1989].

The previous conclusions have been obtained for a discrete-input MLP used for classification with "one-from-K coding", i.e. one output for each class, with all targets zero except for the correct class where it is unity. If there are enough parameters in the system and if the training does not get stuck at a local minimum, the output values of the MLP will approximate the a posteriori probabilities. Section 4 will show some empirical evidence for this assertion. However, this conclusion can also be generalized to continuous inputs. It is known by regression theory that an MSE criterion (as well as other criteria , including the entropy) converges, if there is enough training data, to the conditional expectation of the output given the input. That is, the estimate will converge to $E[d(x_t)|x_t]$, where x_t stands for the input vector at time t and $d(x_t)$ the associated desired output. In classification mode, as $d(x_t)$ is a "one-from-K coding", we have then $E[d(x_t)|x_t] = P[d(x_t)|x_t]$, i.e., the probability distribution over classes conditioned on the input.

Since these results are independent of the topology of the models, they remain valid for linear discriminant functions. In practice, performance is limited by the number of parameters, so it is not guaranteed that the optimal values given in equation 8 can be reached, even if we can escape from local minima. However, it can be shown [Devijver & Kittler, 1982, pp. 171-172] that the discriminant functions obtained by minimizing an MSE criterion retains the essential property of being the best approximation to the Bayes probabilities (in the sense of mean-square-error).

The outputs of the MLP thus approximate MAP probabilities, which are known to lead to the optimal classification; they are discriminant by nature and minimize the classification error rate. These optimal outputs (10) are related, by the Bayes rule, to the emission probabilities (5) of standard HMMs; if they are divided by the prior probabilities of the classes observed on the training set, they may be used as emission probabilities in usual HMMs.

4. Classification at the frame level

4.1. Database and standard approaches

In the following experiments, the speech signal has been sampled at a rate of 16 kHz, and 30 points of smoothed, "mel-scaled" logarithmic spectra (over bands from 200 to 6400 Hz) were calculated every 10-ms from a 512-point FFT over a 25-ms window. The mel spectrum and the energy were vector-quantized to pointers into a single speaker-dependent table of prototypes.

Two independent sets of vocabularies for training and test were used. The training data-set consisted of two sessions of 100 sentences per speaker. These two sessions of 100 sentences are phonetically segmented on the basis of 50 phonemes. However, as

	training set (26767 patterns)	test set (27702 patterns)
Full Gaussian	65.1	64.9
MLE	45.9	44.8
MAP	53.8	53.0

Table 1: Classification rates at the frame level obtained by standard approaches

the phonetic segmentation of the test set were not available, only the first session of the training set was used for training the MLP while the other one was used for testing the generalization capabilities and also as the stopping criterion (cross-validation). The test set consisted of one session of 200 sentences per speaker. The recognition vocabulary contained 918 words, including the 'silence' word. The overlap between training and recognition was 51 words, which were mostly articles, prepositions and other structural words. The acoustic vectors were coded using an alphabet of 132 prototype-vector labels. These prototype vectors were calculated from the training data by using a standard cluster-analysis technique (K-means).

In Table 1, results obtained with Maximum Likelihood Estimates (MLE) and Maximum a Posteriori (MAP) probabilities are given. In these cases, the parameters have been obtained by standard methods for estimating discrete probabilities (i.e., simply by counting). Since we know the phonemic transcription and segmentation of the training set, we can count the frequencies $F(i, j)$ of observation of label y_i, $i = 1, \ldots, 132$ within a state q_j. In our case, each phoneme is associated with a single state and, consequently, $j = 1, \ldots, 50$. The MLE of phoneme j is then given by:

$$p(y_i|q_j) = \frac{F(i, j)}{N_j}$$

where N_j is the overall frequency of phoneme j, and the MAP is:

$$p(q_j|y_i) = \frac{F(i, j)}{N_i}$$

where N_i is the overall frequency of prototype y_i in the training set. For comparison, results obtained with a Gaussian classifier described by a full covariance matrix for each class are also given in Table 1 ("Full Gaussian"). In this case the results were very good, perhaps because the continuous mel-spectra were classified directly without losing any information through the vector quantization process.

4.2. MLP approach

As shown in Section 3, the MLP can at best approximate Bayes (MAP) probabilities. The MLP is potentially preferable to counting as in (7) and (10), because it generates interpolated estimates when there is insufficient training data for the input space, e.g., when the input is highly-dimensioned through the use of multiple frames as contextual input. This fact is clearly illustrated in the following experiments.

Vector-quantized mel spectra were used as binary input to a hidden layer. Multiple input frames provided context to the network. While the size of the output layer was kept fixed at 50 units, corresponding to the 50 phonemes to be recognized, the width of the contextual input and the number of hidden units were varied. The acoustic vectors were coded as one of 132 prototype vectors by a simple binary vector with only one bit 'on', so the input field contained $132 \times a$ bits where a represents the number of frames in the input field. In that case, the total number of possible inputs was equal to 132^a. There were 26767 training patterns and 26702 independent test patterns. Of course, in the case of contextual inputs, this represented only a small fraction of the possible inputs, so that generalization was potentially difficult.

Training was done by the EBP algorithm [Werbos, 1974; Rumelhart et al., 1986], first minimizing an entropy criterion [Hinton, 1987] and then the standard least-mean-square error [Rumelhart et al, 1986]. In each iteration, the complete training set was presented, and the parameters were updated after each training pattern. To avoid overtraining of the MLP, improvement on the test set was checked after each iteration. If the classification rate on the test set was decreasing, the adaptation parameter of the gradient procedure was decreased, otherwise it was kept constant. After several reductions of learning rate, performance on the test set ceased to improve and training was stopped. In another experiment, this approach was checked by splitting the data in three parts: one for the training, one for the above cross-validation, and a third one absolutely independent of the training procedure for final testing. No significant difference was observed between classification rates for the cross-validation and test data. The important idea in this procedure was that we stopped iterating by any one particular criterion when that criterion was leading to no new cross-validation set performance. This appeared to ameliorate the effects of over-fitting that had been observed in our earlier experiments, and greatly improved classification for frames of continuous speech.

Results obtained for different MLP architectures are given in Table 2; here "MLP$a \times b$-c-d" stands for an MLP with a blocs of b (binary) input units, c hidden units and d output units. The size of the output layer is kept fixed at 50 units, corresponding to the 50 phonemes to be recognized. For the binary input case, b is the number of prototype vectors (equal to 132 in our case). If c is missing, there are no hidden units.

	training set (26767 patterns)	test set (27702 patterns)
MLE	45.9	44.8
MLP5×132-20-50	65.5	59.0
outputs/priors	60.2	51.7
MLP9×132-5-50	62.8	54.2
outputs/priors	61.5	51.9
MLP9×132-20-50	75.7	62.7
outputs/priors	72.1	57.5
MLP9×132-50-50	86.4	61.4
MLP9×132-200-50	86.9	59.4
MLP9×132-50	76.9	65.0
outputs/priors	67.7	54.5
MLP15×132-50-50	83.6	64.2
outputs/priors	86.8	64.9
MLP21×132-20-50	93.0	64.0
outputs/priors	89.7	59.1
MLP21×132-50-50	95.0	67.7
outputs/priors	95.4	66.1
MLP21×132-50	92.6	68.6
outputs/priors	87.8	62.7
MLP25×132-20-50	92.8	62.7

Table 2: Classification rates at the frame level for different MLPs

Results reported in Table 2 clearly show that it is possible to improve the classification rates (at the frame level) over those obtained by classical approaches (e.g. MLE). This has been done by providing context to the network, which is a potential advantage of the MLP. For simple relative frequency (counting) methods, it is not possible to use contextual information, because the number of parameters to be learned would be too large. Therefore, in Table 1 and MLE in Table 2, the input field was restricted to a single frame. This restriction explains why the Bayes classifier (MAP, in Table 1), which is inherently optimal for a given pattern classification problem, is shown in Table 2 yielding a lower performance than the potentially suboptimal MLPs. Frame performance is also shown for the cases where the MLP outputs were divided by the respective a priori class probabilities (see "outputs/priors" in Table 2). While this generally degraded

# hidden units	parameterization ratio	training	test
MLP9×132-5-50	.23	62.8 (1.010)	54.2 (1.012)
MLP9×132-20-50	.93	75.7 (1.030)	62.7 (1.035)
MLP9×132-50-50	2.31	86.4 (1.018)	61.4 (1.000)
MLP9×132-200-50	9.3	86.9 (1.053)	59.4 (0.995)
MLE	.25	45.9	44.8
MAP	.25	53.8	53.0
MLP1×132-50-50	.34	53.5 (1.011)	52.7 (1.012)

Table 3: Classification rates and MAP approximation at the frame level

classification performance, we believed that it might lead to improved word recognition. This was later verified, as described in Section 5.

For some simple examples, we now have some empirical evidence that the MLP is estimating MAP probabilities. In Table 3 we have reported the results obtained with a fixed contextual input window (9 frames) for a hidden layer which varied from 5 to 200 units. The numbers in parentheses give the average sum, over all the training or test patterns, of the MLP output values. Since these outputs should approximate MAP probabilities, their sum should be approximately 1. The average error between the output values obtained with the MLP with no contextual input (MLP1×132-50-50) and the actual MAPs, which can be obtained by counting in the case of no contextual inputs, is also reported: for the training and the test sets, this is equal to 2.78×10^{-4} and 2.93×10^{-4} respectively and the standard deviation is 1.15×10^{-2} in both cases, which leads to the confidence interval:

$$P(|g(i,k) - p(q_k|y_i)| > 0.04) < 0.001 ,$$

using the standard assumption of normality. For that case (the only one we can compare with), it can also be observed that the MLP solution converges to the optimal MAP performance (53.5 and 53.8 for the training set and 52.7 and 53.0 for the test set). All these results clearly suggest that the training did not get stuck in a very suboptimal local minimum (since the optimal global minimum can be proven to correspond to Bayes probabilities at the output of the MLP). Therefore, we infer that an MLP can be useful in estimating Bayes probabilities associated with acoustic vectors in a temporal context which is too large for the training of a classical HMM.

In Table 3, it is also interesting to notice that large values for the parameterization ratio (# parameters / # training measurements) only corresponds to a slight degradation of generalization performance (3.3% over a factor of 10 in number of parameters). The iterative estimation process was stopped when generalization degraded for an independent data set (cross-validation) [Morgan & Bourlard, 1990], which explains the insensitivity of test set classification scores to the net size. This will be further discussed in Section 5.2.

4.3. Feature dependence

An MLP can sometimes be useful without any contextual input. For example, in the SRI speech recognizer [Murveit & Weinstraub, 1988], one of the best large vocabulary, speaker independent, continuous speech recognition system, each acoustic vector is described by 4 features, the mel-cepstrum (f_1), the delta mel-cepstrum (f_2), the energy (f_3) and the delta energy (f_4). These features are independently described by 256, 256, 25 and 25 prototypes, respectively. Even without contextual information from the input field, it is impossible to directly estimate the probability of observing a set of 4 features given a class (or a state) q_k without an independence assumption (as there are $256 \times 256 \times 25 \times 25$ or 4×10^7 possible inputs). Therefore, assuming independence, the joint probability estimate is

$$p(f_1, f_2, f_3, f_4 | q_k) = \prod_{i=1}^{4} p(f_i | q_k) \ . \tag{12}$$

Using Bayes' rule, the MAP estimate can then be calculated:

$$\hat{p}(q_k | f_1, f_2, f_3, f_4) = \frac{\prod_{i=1}^{4} p(f_i | q_k).p(q_k)}{p(f_1, f_2, f_3, f_4)} \ . \tag{13}$$

If we now consider an MLP with four input groups, each of them coding a particular feature ($256 + 256 + 25 + 25 = 562$ input units), the $k - th$ output will approximate, in theory, the MAP probability $p(q_k | f_1, f_2, f_3, f_4)$ without the independence assumption. In this way, the system has the potential to extract and make use of the input feature correlation to improve classification performance. However, as before, the training procedure is not guaranteed to reach the optimal solution.

5. Recognition at the word level

5.1. Integrating an MLP into an HMM

For speech recognition problems, the major weakness of the connectionist formalism is its difficulty in coping with time-varying input patterns. Indeed, in the feedforward architecture described in the previous section, the successive acoustic vectors are classified independently of each other. There is no representation of the sequential character of the speech signal, except in the sense of the time-space mapping which was done to use the context of multiple time frames in the classification of each frame. The system thus has no short-term memory and successive classifications can be contradictory. This phenomenon does not appear in HMM since the preceding classifications are effectively used and since only some state sequences are permitted. One popular way to attack the temporal pattern recognition problem is to turn it into a spatial recognition problem in which the entire input sequence to be recognized is stored in a buffer at the input of the MLP [Peeling & Moore, 1988; Landauer et al., 1987]. In that case, each speech unit of the lexicon is associated with a particular output unit of the MLP. However, this approach does not seem to be appropriate to the recognition of connected speech units or, in other words, to find the best explanation of an input pattern in terms of a sequence of output classes. Moreover, the buffer must be large enough to accommodate the longest possible input sequence, which increases the number of parameters and, consequently, the number of required training examples. Thus, the buffer model is not a viable solution to continuous speech recognition.

However, given the current state of the art, training and recognition of connected speech does not seem possible solely by training connectionist networks with supervised learning algorithms. In particular, a target function has to be defined, which is difficult if training is carried out on connected speech units where the segmentation is generally unknown or, at least unsure. Even for training isolated units, there is no principled method for selecting the target function, which is usually chosen as a linear ramping function [Watrous & Shastri, 1987]. This problem does not appear in the HMM approach, in which only the sequence of speech units must be available. From a recognition point of view, when **Dynamic Time Warping (DTW)** [Jelinek, 1976; Ney, 1984] is used for decoding HMM, it tackles the variability of speech pronunciation. It is also an efficient tool for connected speech recognition and segmentation. This latter property seems to be difficult to achieve with a completely connectionist algorithm. Even assuming a perfect dynamical system taking the entire past into account, the output values would still represent the scores for states (or output classes) at the current time, but would not give any idea about the underlying segmentation (as the output values alone do not carry the information needed to recover the best interpretation). For example, in the HMM approach, even if we were able to build a high order Markov model, some kind of time warping process would still be necessary. Thus, avoiding explicit DTW for a continuous speech recognition task remains an open problem. On the other hand, it is also questionable whether it is even desirable to replace the DTW algorithm, as this process is very effective, and also has efficient hardware implementations [Murveit & Brodersen, 1986]. Moreover, a neural net architecture, called the "Viterbi Net", which can implement a DTW decoder, has been defined in [Lippmann & Gold, 1987].

To circumvent those problems, a hybrid approach using an MLP to estimate local probabilities of HMMs and Viterbi matching (a particular form of DTW) to integrate over time has been suggested in [Bourlard & Wellekens, 1988; Bourlard & Wellekens, 1990].

5.2. Methods

As shown by the above theoretical and experimental results, MLP output values may be considered to be estimates of MAP probabilities for pattern classification. Either these, or some other related quantity (such as the output normalized by the prior probability of the corresponding class) may be used in a Viterbi search to determine the best time-warped succession of states (speech sounds) to explain the observed speech measurements. This hybrid approach has the potential of exploiting the interpolating capabilities of MLP while using the DTW procedure to capture the dynamics of speech. In this way, most of the drawbacks of standard HMMs (i.e. lack of discrimination, a priori choice of probability density functions, poor contextual information) are tackled by the MLP while the temporal character is handled by the HMM formalism. For continuous speech training, an iterative process alternating MLP training and Viterbi matching can be used to improve initial segmentation points. In that case, Viterbi matching provides us with a segmentation of the training material and, consequently, with the target function needed for training the MLP. Convergence of this process has been proved in [Bourlard & Wellekens, 1990].

However, to achieve word level performance comparable to what we had achieved at the frame level, the following modifications of this basic scheme were necessary [Bourlard & Morgan, 1990; Morgan & Bourlard, 1990b]:

- MLP training methods - a new cross-validation training algorithm was designed in which the stopping criterion was based on performance for an independent validation set [Morgan & Bourlard, 1990a]. In other words, training was stopped when performance on a second set of data began going down, and not when training error leveled off. This greatly improved generalization, which could be further tested on a third independent test set. This has already been mentioned in Section 4.2.

- probability estimation from the MLP outputs - In the original scheme [Bourlard & Wellekens, 1990], MLP outputs were used as MAP probabilities for the HMM directly. While this helped frame performance, it hurt word performance. This may have been due at least partly to a mismatch between the relative frequency of phonemes in the training sets and test (word recognition) sets. Division by the prior class probabilities as estimated from the training set removed this effect of the priors on the DTW. This led to a small decrease in frame classification performance, but a large (sometimes 10 - 20%) improvement in word recognition rates (see Table 4 and accompanying description).

- word transition costs for the underlying HMM - word transition penalties had to be increased for larger contextual windows to avoid a large number of insertions. This was shown to be equivalent to keeping the same word transition cost but scaling the log probabilities down by a number which reflected the dependence of neighboring frames. A reasonable value for this can be determined from recognition on a small number of sentences (e.g., 50), choosing a value which results in insertions at most equal to the number of deletions.

- segmentation of training data - much as with HMM systems, an iterative procedure was required to time align the training labels in a manner that was statistically consistent with the recognition methods used. In our most recent experiments, we segmented the data using an iterative Viterbi alignment starting from a segmentation based on average phoneme durations, and terminated at the segmentation which led to the best performance on an independent test set. For one of our speakers, we had available a more accurate frame labeling (produced by an automatic but more complex procedure [Aubert, 1987]) to use as a start point for the iteration, which led to even better performance. These techniques improved our concomitant word recognition to be better than we could achieve either with the earlier MLP-HMM technique or the pure HMM technique (using, for both cases, HMMs with a single distribution for each phoneme, and a single vector-quantized feature).

6. Word recognition results

The output values of the MLP were evaluated for each frame, and (after division by the prior probability of each phoneme) were used as emission probabilities in a discrete HMM system. In this system, each phoneme was modeled with a single conditional density, repeated $D/2$ times, where D was a prior estimate of the duration of the phoneme. Only self-loops and sequential transitions were permitted. A Viterbi decoding was then used for recognition of the first hundred sentences of the test session (on which word entrance penalties were optimized), and our best results were validated by a further recognition on the second hundred sentences of the test set. Note that this same simplified HMM was used for both the MLE reference system (estimating probabilities directly from relative frequencies) and the MLP system, and that the same input features were used for both.

| system | size of | % correct | |
method	context	test	validation
MLP	1	27.3	
MLP/priors	1	49.7	
MLP	9	40.9	
MLP/priors	9	51.9	52.2
ML	1	52.6	52.5
MLP/priors (0 hidden)	9	53.3	

Table 4: Word recognition, speaker m003

Table 4 shows the recognition rate (100% - error rate, where errors includes insertions, deletions, and substitutions) for the first 100 sentences of the test session. All runs except the last were done with the 20 hidden units in the MLP, as suggested by the results above. Note the significant positive effect of division of the MLP outputs, which are trained to approximate MAP probabilities, by estimates of the prior probabilities for each class (denoted "MLP/priors" in Table 4).

Not shown here are the earlier improvements required to reach this level of performance, which were primarily the modifications to the learning algorithm described above. Additionally, word transition probabilities were optimized for both the Maximum Likelihood and MLP style HMMs. This led to a word exit probability of 10^{-8} for the MLE and for 1-frame MLP's, and 10^{-14} for an MLP with 9 frames of context. After these adjustments, performance was essentially the same for the two approaches. Performance on the last hundred sentence of the test session (shown in the last column of Table 4) validated that the two systems generalized equivalently despite these tunings.

An initial time alignment of the phonetic transcription with the data (for this speaker) had previously been calculated using a program incorporating speech-specific knowledge [Aubert, 1987]. This labeling had been used for the targets of the frame-based training described above. We then used this alignment as a "bootstrap" segmentation for an iterative Viterbi procedure, much as is done in conventional HMM systems. As with the MLP training, the data was divided into a training and cross-validation set, and the segmentation corresponding to the best validation set frame classification rate was used for later training. For both cross-validation procedures, we switched to a training set of 150 sentences (two repetitions of 75 sentences) and a cross-validation set of 50 sentences (two repetitions of 25 each). Finally, since the best performance in Table 5

method	context	test
MLP/priors (0 hidden)	9	65.3
ML	1	56.9

Table 5: Word Recognition using Viterbi segmentation, speaker m003

was achieved using no hidden layer, we continued our experiments using this simpler network, which also required only a simple training procedure (entropy error criterion only). Table 5 gives the performance for the full 200 recognition sentences (test + validation sets for Table 5), which shows a distinct improvement from the contextual integration of the MLP.

Two of the more puzzling observations in this work were the need to increase word entrance penalties with the width of the input context and the difficulty to reflect good frame performance at the word level. MLPs can make better frame level discriminations than simple statistical classifiers, because they can easily incorporate multiple sources of evidence (multiple frames, multiple features) without simplifying assumptions. However, when the input features within a contextual window are roughly independent, the Viterbi algorithm will already incorporate all of the context in choosing the best HMM state sequence explaining an utterance. If emission probabilities are estimated from the outputs of an MLP which has a $2c+1$ frame contextual input, the probability to observe a feature sequence $\{f_1, f_2, \ldots, f_N\}$ (where f_n represents the feature vector at time n) on a particular HMM state q_k is estimated as:

$$\prod_{i=1}^{N} p(f_{i-c}, \ldots, f_i, \ldots, f_{i+c}|q_k),$$

where Bayes' rule has already been used to convert the MLP outputs (which estimate MAP probabilities) into MLE probabilities. If independence is assumed, and if boundary effects (context extending before frame 1 or after frame N) are ignored (assume $(2c+1) \ll N$), this becomes:

$$\prod_{i=1}^{N} \prod_{j=-c}^{c} p(f_{i+j}|q_k) = \prod_{i=1}^{N} [p(f_i|q_k)]^{2c+1},$$

where the latter probability is just the classical Maximum Likelihood solution, raised to the power $2c+1$. Thus, if the features are independent over time, to keep the effect of transition costs the same as for the simple HMM, the log probabilities must be scaled down by the size of the contextual window. Note that, in the more realistic case where dependencies exist between frames, the optimal scaling factor will be less than $2c + 1$, down to a minimum of 1 for the case in which frames are completely dependent (e.g., same within a constant factor); the scaling factor should thus reflect the time correlation of the input features. An equivalent effect is achieved by increasing the word entrance penalties, so that they are raised to a power that is comparable to the scaling of the log probabilities.

Thus, if the features are assumed independent over time, there is no advantage to be gained by using an MLP to extract contextual information for the estimation of emission probabilities for an HMM Viterbi decoding. In general, the relation between the MLP and MLE solutions will be more complex, because of interdependence over time of the input features. However, the above relation may give some insight as to the difficulty we have met in improving word recognition performance with a single discrete feature (despite large improvements at the frame level). More positively, our results show that the probabilities estimated by MLPs can be used at least as effectively as conventional estimates and that some advantage can be gained by incorporating more information for the estimation of these probabilities.

7. Segmentation of training data

A problem in applying MLP methods to speech is the apparent requirement of hand-labeled frames for MLP training. To remove this obstacle, we have worked on embedding the MLP training in a Viterbi algorithm iteratively improving an initial segmentation as suggested earlier in [Bourlard & Wellekens, 1990]. Preliminary results show that we can generate a segmentation from a linear initialization, much as is done in conventional HMM systems.

As we still want to use cross-validation techniques for the MLP training and for the Viterbi matching in an unsupervised way, several modifications of the original scheme were necessary, and are briefly described here. Starting only with the phonetic transcription of the training and cross-validation sets, these two sets of sentences are linearly segmented, respectively providing the MLP output targets for the training set as well as for the cross-validation set. The MLP can then be trained (using cross-validation), which provides new weights and, consequently, new emission probabilities for the Viterbi matching. Using this newly trained MLP, Viterbi matching is performed on the training and cross-validation sets, providing us with new segmentations and consequently, with new output targets for MLP training and cross-validation. This process is iterated until the score (product over all the optimal path probabilities) on the cross-validation set (and not on the training set) begins to decrease. Thus, two cross-validations take place in this process: one for the MLP itself, and one for the Viterbi matching. This new

speaker	MLE	MLP
m003	54.4	59.7
m001	47.4	51.9
w010	54.2	54.3

Table 6: Word Recognition for 3 speakers, simple initialization

Viterbi training has been observed to converge to segmentations very close to the boot-strap segmentation. In particular, for 200 sentences, less than 4% of the frames were labeled differently by this automatic procedure than they had been by careful frame classification of the frames using the bootstrap procedure. This result, showing the effectiveness of embedding MLP training in a Viterbi segmentation, appears to have removed a major handicap of MLP use, the requirement for hand-labeled speech.

However, up to now, this embedded training has not yet been proved yielding better word recognition performance than the method presented in Section 6 (MLP trained on the segmentation obtained from a standard Viterbi algorithm initialized from bootstrap segmentations). This might be due to the weak correlation problem explained in Section 6. However, since the previous method also did not rely on hand-labeled speech, we still can conclude that hand-labeled examples are not required for MLP training.

We duplicated our recognition tests for two other speakers from the same data base. Since bootstrap segmentation data were not available for these speakers, we labeled each training set (from the original male plus a male and a female speaker) using a standard Viterbi iteration initialized from a time-alignment based on a simple estimate of average phoneme duration. This reduced all of the recognition scores, illustrating the effect of a good start point for the Viterbi iteration. However, as can be seen from the Table 6 results (measured over the full 200 recognition sentences), the MLP-based methods appear to do at least as well as the simpler estimation technique. In particular, the MLP system performed significantly better than the MLE ($p < 0.01$) for two out of three speakers, as well as for a multispeaker comparison over the three speakers (in each case using a normal approximation to a binomial distribution for the null hypothesis that the two systems were equivalent).

8. Conclusion

It is now clear, both from a theoretical perspective and from empirical measurements, that the outputs of an MLP (when trained for pattern classification) approximate MAP probabilities or, in other words, the class probabilities conditioned on the input.

The experimental results that have been presented here show some of the improvement for MLPs over conventional HMMs which one might expect from the frame level results (Table 2). MLPs can make better frame level discriminations than simple statistical classifiers, because they can easily incorporate multiple sources of evidence (multiple frames, multiple features), which is difficult to do in HMMs without major simplifying assumptions. However, the relation between the MLP and MLE word recognition is more complex, because of interdependence over time of the input features. Part of the difficulty with good recognition may also be due to our choice of discrete, vector-quantized features, for which no metric is defined over the prototype space. The features we have been using were chosen for their effectiveness in HMM systems, and different combinations may prove to be better for MLP inputs. In particular, we would expect that feature combinations which have not been vector-quantized should have more useful dependencies (both within-frame and over time) which the MLP may be able to learn and exploit. Despite these limitations, it now appears that the probabilities estimated by MLPs may offer improved word recognition through the incorporation of context in the estimation of emission probabilities.

Interestingly, our best results were obtained using an MLP with no hidden layer. This suggests that, for the case of a single VQ feature, a single Perceptron model is rich enough for the probabilistic estimation. This network can also be trained more easily than networks with one or more hidden layers, particularly when an entropy criterion is used.

Furthermore, the effectiveness of Viterbi segmentation in labeling training data for an MLP has been shown. This result appears to remove a major handicap of MLP use, i.e. the requirement for hand-labeled speech, and allows us to handle more complex HMMs.

Finally, is the MLP simply accomplishing a nice interpolation for the joint density estimates we seek? Perhaps so, and other smoothing techniques (kernel estimators, for instance) may work as well. Nonetheless, MLP approaches appear to offer a reasonable way of incorporating information from multiple sources of phonetic evidence into a continuous speech recognizer.

References

Aubert, X., "Supervised Segmentation with Application to Speech Recognition", in *Proc. Eur. Conf. Speech Technology*, Edinburgh, p.161-164, 1987.

Baum, L.E., "An Inequality and Associated Maximization Techniques in Statistical Estimation of Probabilistic Functions of Markov Processes", *Inequalities*, 3:1-8, 1972

Bourlard, H., Kamp, Y., Ney, H. & Wellekens, C.J., "Speaker Dependent Connected Speech Recognition via Dynamic Programming and Statistical Methods", in *Speech and Speaker Recognition*, Ed. M.R.Schroeder, pp. 115-148, Karger (Basel), 1985.

Bourlard, H., & Wellekens, C.J. "Links between Markov Models and Multilayer Perceptrons", *Advances in Neural Information Processing 1*, Ed. D. Touretzky, Morgan Kaufmann, pp. 502-510, 1988.

Bourlard, H. & Morgan, N., "A Continuous Speech Recognition System Embedding MLP into HMM", to be published in *Advances in Neural Information Processing Systems II*, Morgan Kaufmann, 1990.

Bourlard, H., Morgan, N. & Wellekens C.J., "Statistical Inference in Multilayer Perceptrons and Hidden Markov Models with Applications in Continuous Speech Recognition", to appear in *Neuro Computing, Algorithms, and Applications*, NATO ASI Series, 1990.

Bourlard, H. & Wellekens, C.J., "Links between Markov models and multilayer perceptrons", to be published in *IEEE Trans. on Pattern Analysis and Machine Intelligence*, 1990.

Bridle, J.S., "Probabilistic Scoring for Back-Propagation Networks, with Relationships to Statistical Pattern Recognition", *Neural Network for Computing*, Snowbird, UT, 1989.

Brown, P., "The Acoustic-Modeling Problem in Automatic Speech Recognition", *Ph.D. thesis*, Comp. Sc. Dep., Carnegie-Mellon University, 1987.

Devijver, P.A. & Kittler, J., *Pattern Recognition: A Statistical Approach*, Prentice Hall International, 1982.

Elman, J.L., "Finding Structure in Time", *CRL Tech, Report 8801*, University of California, San Diego, 1988.

Gevins, A. & Morgan, N., "Ignorance-Based Systems", *Proc. IEEE Intl. Conf. on Acoustics, Speech, & Signal Processing*, Vol. 3, 39A5.1-39A5.4, San Diego, 1984.

Hinton, G.E., "Connectionist Learning Procedures", *Technical Report CMU-CS-87-115*, Carnegie Mellon University, 1987.

Jelinek, F., "Continuous Speech Recognition by Statistical Methods", *Proceeding of the IEEE*, vol. 64, no. 4, pp. 532-555, 1976.

Jordan, M.L., "Serial Order: A Parallel Distributed Processing Approach", UCSD, Tech. Report 8604, 1986.

Landauer, T.K., Kamm, C.A. & Singhal, S. " Teaching a minimally structured back propagation network to recognize speech", *Proceedings of the Ninth Annual Conference of the Cognitive Science Society*, pp. 531-536, 1987.

Lippmann, R.P., "An Introduction to Computing with Neural Nets", *IEEE ASSP Magazine*, **3**, pp. 4-22, 1987.

Lippmann, R.P. & Gold, B., "Neural Classifiers Useful for Speech Recognition", *First Int. Conf. on Neural Networks*, pp. IV-417, San Diego, CA, 1987.

Makino, S., Kawabata, T. & Kido, K., "Recognition of consonants based on the Perceptron Model", *Proc. IEEE Intl. Conf. on Acoustics, Speech, & Signal Processing*, Vol. 2, pp. 738-741, Boston, Mass., 1983.

Morgan, N. & Bourlard, H., "Generalization and Parameter Estimation in Feedforward Nets: Some Experiments", to be published in *Advances in Neural Information Processing Systems II*, Morgan Kaufmann, 1990a.

Morgan, N. & Bourlard, H., "Continuous Speech Recognition using Multilayer Perceptrons with Hidden Markov Models", *Proc. IEEE Intl. Conf. on Acoustics, Speech, & Signal Processing*, Albuquerque, New Mexico, 1990b.

Murveit, H. & Brodersen, R.W., "An Integrated-Circuit-Based Speech Recognition System", *IEEE Trans. ASSP*, vol. 34, no. 6, pp. 1465-1472, 1986.

Murveit, H. & Weintraub, M., "1000-Word Speaker-Independent Continuous-Speech Recognition Using Hidden Markov Models", *Proc. IEEE Intl. Conf. on Acoustics, Speech, & Signal Processing*, pp. 115-118, New York, 1988.

Nadas, A., Nahamoo, D. & Picheny, M.A. "On a Model-Robust Training Method for Speech Recognition", *IEEE Trans. on ASSP*, vol. 35, no.9, pp. 1432-1436, 1988.

Ney, H. "The use of one-stage dynamic programming algorithm for connected word recognition", *IEEE Trans. on ASSP*, vol. 32, pp. 263-272, 1984.

Niles, L., Silverman, H., Tajchman, G. & Bush, M., "How Limited Training Data Can Allow a Neural Network Classifier to Outperform an 'Optimal' Statistical Classifier", *Proc. IEEE Intl. Conf. on Acoustics, Speech, & Signal Processing*, Vol. 1, pp. 17-20, Glasgow, Scotland, 1989.

Peeling, S.M. & Moore, R.K., "Experiments in Isolated Digit Recognition Using the Multi-Layer Perceptron", Royal Speech and Radar Establishment, Technical Report 4073, Malvern, Worcester, 1988.

Poritz, A.B., "Hidden Markov Models: A Guided Tour", *Proc. Int. Conf. on ASSP-88*, pp. 7-13, New York, 1988.

Rumelhart, D.E., Hinton, G.E. & Williams, R.J., "Learning Internal Representations by Error Propagation", *Parallel Distributed Processing. Exploration of the Microstructure of Cognition. vol. 1: Foundations*, Ed. D.E.Rumelhart & J.L.McClelland, MIT Press, 1986.

Waibel, A., Hanazawa, T., Hinton, G., Shikano, K. & Lang, K., "Phoneme Recognition: Neural Networks vs. Hidden Markov Models", *Proc. IEEE Intl. Conf. on Acoustics, Speech, & Signal Processing*, pp. 107-110, New York, 1988.

Watrous, R.L. & Shastri, L., "Learning Phonetic Features Using Connectionist Networks: an Experiment in Speech Recognition", *1st Int. Conf. on Neural Networks*, pp. IV-381-388, San Diego, CA, 1987.

Werbos, P.J., "Beyond Regression: New Tools for Prediction and Analysis in the Behavioral Sciences", *Ph.D. thesis*, Dept. of Applied Mathematics, Harvard University, 1974.

White H., "Multilayer feedforward networks can learn arbitrary mappings: connectionist nonparametric regression with automatic and semi-automatic determination of network complexity", Discussion Paper, University of California, San Diego, Department of Economics, 1988.

NEURAL NETWORKS: Advances and Applications
E. Gelenbe (Editor)
© Elsevier Science Publishers B.V. (North-Holland), 1991

Introduction to Neural Networks and their Application to Process Control

Ersin Tulunay
Electrical and Electronic Engineering Department
Middle East Technical University
06531 Ankara - Turkey

Abstract In this paper, neural networks, backpropagation and perceptual learning algorithms are considered and reviewed from the process control point of view. Various control application examples are considered. A method is proposed in order to use a neural network as a domain knowledge generator in expert systems.

1 Introduction

An *artificial neural network* is a system of interconnected computational elements operating in parallel, arranged in patterns similar to biological neural nets and modeled after the human brain [1].

The earliest roots of the parallel distributed processing can be found in the works of neurologists, such as Jackson in 1869 [2] (see Luria [3]). Neural network research has been popular since 1960s. Recently interest in this field has increased mainly because of the developments in very large scale integrated circuit technology, optical devices and new learning paradigms which make rapid and inexpensive implementation possible.

Neural networks are finding applications in various fields including *adaptive pattern recognition, adaptive signal processing, adaptive dynamic modeling, adaptive control, optimization, expert systems*. Some other specific applications include control of robot arm, diagnosis, numeric to symbolic conversion. In this paper the application of neural networks to process control is considered.

After the introduction in Section 1, the nature and basic topics of control and general information concerning *process control* and *intelligent control* are given in Sections 2, 3, 4 respectively. Basic structures and properties of neural networks are given in Section 5. Summary information concerning the basic learning algorithms used is given in Section 6. Section 7 deals with process control applications. The

Fuzzy logic approach and neural networks are considered in Section 8. Short information about hardware implementation, and remarks concerning the future work and concluding remarks are provided in Sections 9, 10 and 11.

2   The Nature and Basic Topics of Control

Broadly speaking control is the set of actions taken to make a system behave in a manner as close as possible to what we desire. It involves the variables which human beings are directly interested in. Actions to be taken for satisfactory control of complex processes also need direct human involvement. However in the 1940's the novelty of control systems was based mainly on the degree of machine-like functioning of controllers. The need for using human knowledge and expertise was considered a negative point for the control system. In recent years the interlinking of human expertise with the control system has been one of the most challenging areas of control [4, 5].

Controlling a dynamical system involves several fundamental processes:

- *modeling* of the system based on physical laws;

- *system identification* based on experimental data

- *signal processing* of the output by *filtering, prediction, state estimation*, etc.,

- *generating the control input* and applying it to the system.

Some of the basic areas of system control can be listed as

- *Adaptive, self tuning, self adjusting control*
  The plant model has a known form, but unknown parameters. The adaptive feedback loop attempts to reduce the uncertainty by on-line parameter estimation. Parameter estimates are then used to continuously retune the controller.

- *Nonlinear control*
  Most of the systems used in practice are nonlinear.

- *Control of distributed parameter systems*
  Most of the systems used in industrial processes and large systems are distributed parameter in nature; furthermore the variables are functions of time and space. They are represented by partial differential equations.

Most reel systems are complicated in nature and work under unpredictable conditions. Therefore exact mathematical description of the dynamics of such systems is extremely difficult or even impossible [5]. With this difficulty in mind some of the important issues of control can be listed as

- *Robust control*
  A control system should be stable and accomplish performance objectives not for one typical model but for a set of models covering expected uncertainties about the model parameters and disturbances. Controllers which have this property are called robust. The controllers are required to be robust with respect to modeling uncertainty and to adapt to slow variations in the system parameters.

- *Fault tolerant control*
  The control system should work even if there is some fault in the system. The system should be designed to be tolerant especially to sensor, actuator and perhaps to some other component failures; this may require real time reconfiguration of the feedback control structure [5].

  Theories for the design of fault tolerant feedback control systems are lacking. Such theories involve a blend of *numerical* and *symbolic* manipulations. Concepts of control theory and *artificial intelligence* (AI) must be blended [5].

- *Intelligent control*
  Although they are similar to adaptive systems, intelligent control systems work under much larger variations in uncertainties. Concepts in AI are not powerful enough for control applications, because control problems are much more dynamic and stochastic [5].

- *Control of systems with discrete variables and discrete events*
  The systems studied traditionally involve continuous variables and can be characterized by differential or difference equations. In some *hybrid* situations the state of the system involves both continuous and discrete variables. Also in an *intelligent rule based* system the controller first executes a series of diagnostic or decision tests, and then executes a traditional type of control involving numerical operations. This is also a hybrid case and the state of the system consists of a set of real numbers together with a set of logical or Boolean variables.

  Complicated man made dynamical systems which can be characterized not by differential equations but by the intricate interaction of discrete events are called discrete event dynamical systems. Examples of such systems are flexible manufacturing systems, computer communication networks and traffic systems. The discrete events are the completion of a task or arrival of a message.

3 Process Control

Process control basically deals with the industrial processes and power plants which may contain hundreds of loops. The processes to be controlled are usually distributed parameter and nonlinear in nature with extensive process and disturbance uncertainties. Large numbers of signals coming from the sensors and actuators have to be processed. Under such circumstances in general adaptive, robust fault tolerant, intelligent controllers are needed. In process control applications even a small improvement in the product can be very significant economically and from the environmental pollution view-point. Thus they cause accumulative inverse effects on the environment if they are not controlled under very strict requirements.

A general block diagram of a process control system with cascade feedback and feedforward loops is shown in Figure 1.

Mathematical modeling is an important step in control studies. The physical and chemical properties of the process are considered and the following basic principle can be applied for modeling:

(1)   inflow - outflow = accumulation

Most of the processes can be considered as a generalized flow process as shown in the example of Figure 2. Here fluid is assumed to flow through a cylindrical pipe, and during this passage, the fluid properties change as a result of transfer of energy mass and momentum between the fluid and its surroundings. Application of equation (1) to the generalized flow process yields the following partial differential equation [6]:

$$(2) \qquad \underbrace{\frac{\partial u(x,t)}{\partial t}}_{(I)} + \underbrace{\frac{\partial h(x,t)}{\partial x}}_{(II)} + \underbrace{r(x,t)}_{(III)} = \underbrace{\frac{\partial}{\partial x}\left[D(x,t)\frac{\partial u(x,t)}{\partial x}\right]}_{(IV)}$$

where

t and x are the time and space variables.

u is the generalized charge density,

h is the generalized charge flow per unit area or generalized current density,

r is the rate of disappearance of generalized charge per unit volume due to transfer to other systems or due to transformation from one form to another in case of chemical reactions.

v is the generalized potential,

D is the diffusion coefficient.

It is assumed that there is no radial dependence. In equation (2) terms I, II and III correspond to accumulation, transport and transfer processes respectively. Term IV represents the diffusion process. Equation (2) is very general and can be applied to almost any process provided that the terms involved can be determined for the specific process under consideration. However in general exact mathematical formulation is almost impossible because of the complicated and uncertain nature of processes and disturbances, because industrial processes have to operate in changing environmental conditions caused by the variations in the raw materials, fuels, load levels, environmental conditions etc. Therefore large ranges of uncertainties occur in the process parameter values, disturbances and signal inputs.

Even though a mathematical formulation is available to find the solution for these equations, the nonlinear case is extremely difficult. Control of distributed parameter systems is one of the topics of current and future interest [4, 5]. Therefore on line process identification and updating of control parameters, and the use of expert knowledge are very important in process control applications.

4 Intelligent Control

Control theory presently deals with well defined classes of problems, where physical variables to be controlled and the control objectives have an established mathematical description. Classical linear theory also tries to provide some robustness. But this robustness is functional over a relatively small range of uncertainties.

However process control systems operate under large process and disturbance uncertainties and therefore need direct human intervention for proper functioning. Direct human involvement is unacceptable in many real-time applications.

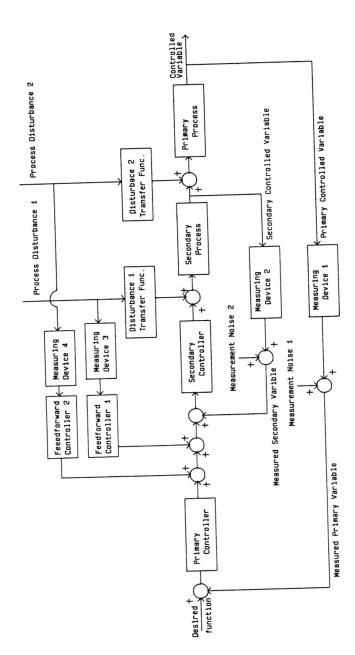

Figure 1: A general block diagram of a process control system.

Automatic control techniques for handling uncertainty must be developed. Adaptive, robust, fault tolerant control techniques are in this category.

Intelligent control systems are needed for satisfactory operations when a greater range of uncertainties occur as it is the case in practice. Artificial intelligence processes are slow and therefore they cannot be used in high speed real-time control applications [7]. It is thus realized that there is a need for real-time intelligent control techniques and components. Three approaches that have the potential for intelligent control are [7]:

(1) expert systems as adaptive elements in a control system,

(2) *fuzzy calculations* as decision producing elements in a control system,

(3) neural networks as compensation elements in control systems.

On the other hand large number of processes which operate under real life conditions involve information that is inherently rule based. Therefore rule based techniques are more suitable for the control of such processes. In many complex situations, rule based systems are slow and provide coarse solutions missing desirable fine detail.

Classical expert systems are logic based and involve sequential reasoning. Therefore neural nets have advantages for rule based control. Because they are taught by example, they are fast and they deal effectively with interacting parameters [7].

Fuzzy logic approach and neural nets will be considered in Section 8.

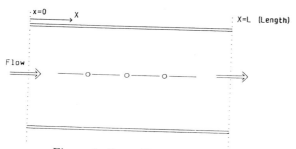

Figure 2: Generalized flow process.

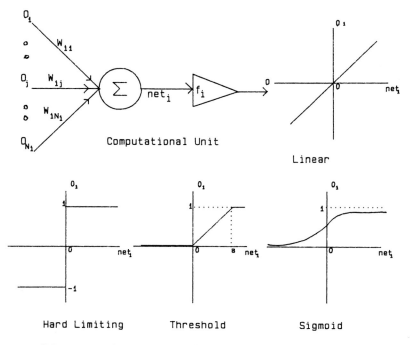

Figure 3: Schematics of a computing element together with typical activation functions.

5 Basic Structure and Properties of Neural Networks

5.1 Introduction

Individual neurons are characterized by [1]:

$$(3) \qquad O_i = f_i(x_i)$$

and

$$(4) \qquad x_i = \text{net } _i = \sum_{j=1}^{N_i} w_{ij}O_j + \Theta_i$$

where O_i is the output of neuron i, x_i is the total input to or *net output* from neuron i, $f_i(\bullet)$ is the input to output or net output to output, or *activation function* of neuron i, w_{ij} is the weight of the arc from neuron j to neuron i, O_j is the output from jth neuron of the previous layer. It is also the input to neuron i from neuron j. Θ_i is the *internal threshold, bias or offset* for node i, and N_i is the number of inputs to neuron i. A neuron thus forms a weighted sum of N_i inputs and passes the result through a linear or nonlinear activation function as shown in Figure 3. A node with a hard limiting activation function is sometimes called a *thresholding unit*.

Activation functions in Figure 3 can be expressed as

(5) Linear $f_i(\text{net}_i)$ = net_i

(6) Hard limiting (Activation func- $f_i(\text{net}_i)$ = $\begin{cases} 1 & \text{net}_i > 0 \\ 0 & \text{net}_i \leq 0 \end{cases}$
tion for linear threshold unit)

(7) Thresholding $f_i(\text{net}_i)$ = $\begin{cases} 0 & \text{net}_i \leq 0 \\ \text{net}_i & \text{net}_i \leq a \\ 1 & \text{net}_i > a \end{cases}$

(8) Sigmoid or logistic activation $f_i(\text{net}_i)$ = $\frac{1}{1+e^{-\text{net}_i}}$
function (squashing function)

Sigmoid units are more complicated but more powerful than hard limiting units because the sigmoid is an increasing function. It has non-zero derivatives which makes it useful in gradient descent learning methods [1].

The linear model has limitations and is not useful in *hidden layers*, because a linear multilayer neural network can always be represented as an equivalent linear single layer network [1]. Therefore nonlinear activation functions which we call *semilinear* are used. A semilinear activation function is one for which the output of a unit is a nondecreasing and differentiable function of the net output. Notice that linear threshold units do not satisfy the requirement because their derivative is infinite at the threshold and zero elsewhere.

A new class of random neural networks with negative and positive signals and product form solution was proposed and its relationship to standard connectionist models was discussed [8].

5.2 Multi layer neural feed forward network

A layered neural network with three hidden layers is shown in Figure 4.

The capabilities of multi-layer neural networks can be understood as a result of a theorem proved by Kolmogorov [9, 10] based on the 13th problem of Hilbert. This theorem states that any continuous function of N variables $f(x_1, \ldots, x_N)$ can be written using only linear summations and nonlinear but continuously increasing

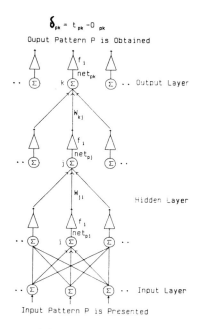

Figure 4: Schematics of a multilayer neural network.

functions $\phi_{pq}(x_p)$ in only one variable [9, 10].

$$(9) \qquad f(x_1, \ldots, x_N) = \sum_{q=1}^{2N+1} g_q \left(\sum_{p=1}^{N} \phi_{pq}(x_p) \right)$$

Thus it is seen that any continuous function of N variables can be computed by using a three-layer network with $N(2N+1)$ nodes having continuously increasing nonlinearities. However the theorem does not show how weights and nonlinearities must be selected or how sensitive the output function is to variations in the weights and internal functions [9].

Virtually all multi-layer applications have used two hidden layers or less [11]. As the number of layers increases data storage efficiency, ability of the network to generalize, and the fail-safe nature of the network increases. A more layered and more highly connected network can generally store the same data in fewer neurons.

The capabilities of perceptrons can be seen by investigating the decision regions they can form in the space defined by the inputs. As a simple example consider the single unit i in Figure 3 defined by equations (4) and (6) for the case of two inputs O_1 and O_2. It is seen from equations (4) and (6) that this unit divides the O_1, O_2

plane into two decision regions separated by the line

$$(10) \qquad \text{net}_i = \sum_{i=1}^{N_i} w_{ji} O_j + \Theta_i = w_{1i} O_1 + w_{2i} O_2 + \Theta_i = 0$$

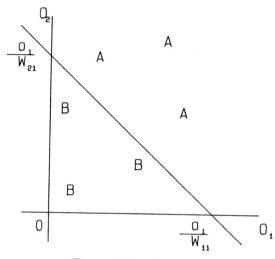

Figure 5: Decision regions.

as shown in Figure 5. Suppose input pattern A causes the right hand side of equation (4) to be positive. Then the output of the unit is 1. If input pattern B causes the right hand side to be negative then the unit will output 0. Thus the unit decides whether the input pattern belongs to class A or class B as shown in Figure 5. In general net$_i$ in (10) is the equation of an N_i dimensional hyperplane. This hyperplane partitions the space defined by the inputs to that node into two parts. Any point on one part of this hyperplane corresponds to the input class which causes output 1 and any point on the other part corresponds to the input class which causes output 0.

The effect of the weights w_{ji} is to stretch or compact the axes of the hyperspace. The offset or threshold Θ_i corresponds to the minimum distance the partitioning hyperplane passes from the origin [11].

By using nonlinear but continuous sigmoid units as activation functions various useful curves can be created for partitioning the hyperspace [11]. Further useful variations in partitions can be obtained by using multiple output nodes.

In multi-layer feed-forward neural networks there are connections between the elements of successive layers. There are no interlayer connections. In a *cyclic or feedback network* the output of one or more neurons is fed back into the network. This can affect the inputs to the same nodes. Cyclic networks have dynamic properties which cannot be obtained by non-cyclic networks [11].

5.3 Basic properties of neural networks

Current conventional signal processing techniques are algorithmic in nature. However neural networks can perform non-algorithmic signal processing [7].

Neural nets provide high computation rates because of their massively parallel nature. Provided that suitable hardware is available, neural networks can be implemented. Thus on-line operations may be possible.

Neural nets provide a greater degree of robustness, fault tolerance or *fail safety* compared to classical sequential computing systems, because the information is contained in the weighted wiring diagram in the distributed form with nodes having primarily local connections. Presentation of information often contains redundancies. Thus any damage in a few nodes or links or any invalid information contained in these does not impair overall performance significantly.

Associative storage and retrieval of knowledge is possible in neural networks [1, 12].

Unlike other classical large scale dynamic systems, the uniform rate of convergence toward a steady state of neural networks is essentially independent of the number of neurons in the network [12, 13].

There are also at present some problems associated with using or designing neural networks:

1. There is no general way of deciding about the network topology to perform a certain task.

2. The convergence of most of the important learning algorithms used in neural networks is not guaranteed.

It is also important to see that the necessary hardware is not presently ready to be used for taking full benefit of the high speed of neural computation.

The problem areas for which neural networks may provide some advantages can be pinpointed by considering the advantages and disadvantages of neural networks. The problems involving complexity, redundancy and speed can be solved more satisfactorily by using neural networks. So far results involving neural networks have been reported in the areas of learning, associative memory, decisions in optimization, adaptive pattern recognition, fuzzy sets, expert systems, adaptive filtering, numeric to symbolic conversion and control.

6 Basic Learning Algorithms

So far the most widely used learning algorithm has been the backpropagation algorithm [1] and its slightly modified forms [14]. The perceptron learning algorithm has also found some applications [15]. In this section the backpropagation and perceptron algorithms are briefly presented.

6.1 The backpropagation algorithm

The backpropagation algorithm [1] is a *gradient descent* or *steepest descent* method using the mean square error of the system over a given set of input output pairs, where the net change in the weights after one complete cycle of pattern presentations is proportional to the derivative of the overall measure of output error squares. This is strictly true only if the values of the weights are not changed during the pattern presentation cycle. By changing weights after each pattern is presented one departs to some extent from a true gradient descent in mean square error of the system over a given set of input-output pairs. Provided that the learning rate, to be explained in equation (13), is sufficiently small, this departure will be negligible and the "delta rule" will implement a very close approximation to gradient descent in sum squared error. In particular with small enough learning rate, the delta rule will find a set of weights minimizing this error function [1]. Learning internal representations by error propagation is considered in a more detail below.

The generalized delta rule

This learning procedure involves the presentation of a set of pairs of input and output patterns or *exemplars*. The system first uses the input vector to produce its own output vector and then compares this with the *desired output*, or *target* vector for generating the error.

The main steps of the generalized delta rule algorithm are given below.

First phase: forward pass

The input pattern p is presented and propagated forward through the network to compute output O_{pj} for each unit. The error signal δ_{pj} for output elements is calculated as

$$(11) \qquad\qquad \delta_{pj} = (t_{pj} - O_{pj})f'_j(\text{net}_{pj})$$

where t_{pj} is the required target output,

$$(12) \qquad\qquad f'_j(\text{net}_{pj}) = \frac{\partial O_{pj}}{\partial \text{net}_{pj}}$$

is the derivative of the squashing function.

Second phase: backward pass

Weight changes $\Delta_p w_{ji}$ for all of the connections that feed into the final layer are computed as

$$(13) \qquad\qquad \Delta_p w_{ji} = \eta \delta_{pj} O_{pi}$$

where η is the *step length* or *learning rate* and O_{pi} is the input to element j coming along the arc ji from element i and O_{pi} is known as a result of the forward pass.

Calculate δ for layers other than output recursively starting with the layer one level below the output.

$$(14) \qquad\qquad \delta_{pj} = f'_j(\text{net}_{pj}) \sum_k \delta_{pk} w_{kj}$$

where δ_{pk} is the error of the output elements calculated in equation (11). The weight w_{kj} is calculated by adding the w_{kj} value of forward pass and the weight change $\Delta_p w_{ji}$ calculated in equation (13).

The algorithm is usually started by using arbitrary initial values for weights and offsets Θ_i. A suitable value usually in the range 0 - 30 is chosen for η. The weights w_{ji} and offset Θ_i are updated as a result of error backpropagation.

The procedure is a gradient descent method and therefore has the problems of any hill climbing procedure. In the case of learning, it can lead to local minima rather than to the global ones. This implies that even if there exists a valid solution to the learning problem, the algorithm is still not guaranteed to find it. Another point is that the number of iterations needed for satisfactory learning is large. In some cases this situation causes difficulties for real time applications.

This algorithm may be particularly useful if the input space must be divided into decision regions which are separated by curved borders as simply demonstrated in

Figure 5. It has been reported in [16] that an alternative to this algorithm, called the selective update backpropagation algorithm has been introduced [17] and shown to work in cases where the backpropagation algorithm will not.

The backpropagation algorithm cannot be directly applied when the error has to pass through a process since its parameters cannot be varied according to the training algorithm. In this case a slight modification is done [18] as will be explained in Section 7.

Extension of the backpropagation algorithm to systems with feedback has also been reported [19].

Another algorithm called the perceptron algorithm is also well-known [9]. Weights and the thresholds are initialized by setting $w_i(0)$ $(0 \leq i \leq N - 1)$ and Θ to small random values. Here $w_i(t)$ is the weight from input i at time t and Θ is the threshold at the output node.

New input values $x_0, x_1, \ldots, x_N$ and the desired output $d(t)$ are presented.

Actual output is calculated as

(15)
$$y(t) = f\left(\sum_{\ell=0}^{N-1} w_i(t)x_i(t) - \Theta\right)$$

(16)
$$w_i(t+1) = w_i(t) + \eta[d(t) - y(t)]x_i(t) \quad 0 \leq i \leq N - 1$$

(17)
$$d(t) = \begin{cases} +1 & \text{if input from class A} \\ -1 & \text{if input from class B} \end{cases}$$

where η is a positive gain fraction less than 1 and $d(t)$ is the desired correct output for the current input. It is seen that when the correct output is provided by the network the weights are not changed.

In general, these algorithms can only place equilibrium states at the desired positions [13].

The performance of any learning system including the algorithms covered here depends highly on its input presentation [20].

Commercial software packages such as the systems from Nestor, HNC and SAIC have been reported [21].

7 Process Control Applications

There are types of control problems for which neural nets provide benefits such as fast adaptation rate, simpler controller structure and adaptation over both discrete and continuous parameter domains [13].

The ability of adaptive learning by example is an advantage.

Easy implementation, robustness, ability to accommodate defective hardware and changing conditions are other useful features of neural networks.

Stand-alone neural nets can be used as a real time controllers because of their speed, or they can be used to fine tune and supervise the action of existing controllers.

The problem of control in general can be considered as the mapping of measured variables into a corrective signal. A change occuring in the controlled variable at the output of the process mainly as a result of change occurring in the disturbance as shown in Figure 1 [7].

We propose here another way of looking at the problem based on interpreting the overall loop as an adaptive disturbance filter. Neural nets may be a suitable candidate for such an application since they can be used as adaptive noise filters [14].

In process control there are uncertainties in the plant and in the environment. The plant is usually nonlinear and the number of variables to be processed is usually high. Under these conditions two important areas of interest are system identification and adaptive control. Neural networks are becoming attractive for process control mainly because of their self modeling and organization capabilities which allow a process to be remodeled quickly so as to optimize the controller parameters for varying process and environmental conditions or degraded equipment. In this section a short review of some of the process control applications is given.

The controller output signal u must be generated such that, the process output y is equal to the desired output d when u is applied to the process as a corrective signal. Therefore the controller should produce u when d is inputted. This means that the controller dynamics must be the inverse of the plant dynamics.

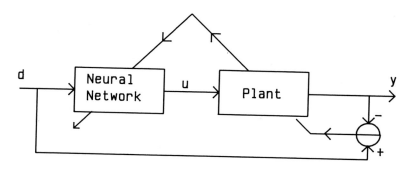

Figure 6: Specialized learning architecture.

7.1 Learning and operation modes of neural network controller

Specialized learning architecture [18]

An architecture called specialized learning is shown in Figure 6. Desired response d is given as the input to the neural network. It produces an output u given to the plant. The difference between the desired response d and actual response y of the plant is used to train the neural network. In this architecture, plant output y is used instead of neural network output u for training. This means that the error $d - y$ is propagated back through the plant. Therefore the plant itself must also be considered as part of the neural network. In this case equation (14) of the backpropagation algorithm must be modified [18]. Suppose $P_i(\bar{u})$ denotes the ith element of the plant output for plant input $\bar{u}$. Equation (14) is then modified as

(18)
$$\delta_a^n = f_a'(P_a^n) \sum_i \delta_i^p \frac{\partial P_i}{\partial u_a}$$

where

(19)
$$\delta_a^p = d_a - y_a$$

Usually the plant is a function of unknown form. Therefore each input to the plant is slightly disturbed around the operating point and corresponding changes with respect to the previous values are measured. Then the partial derivative in (18) is approximated as

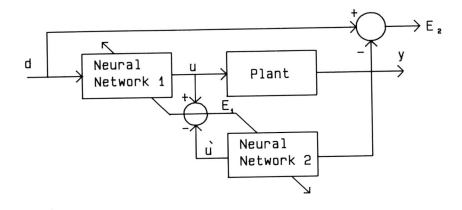

Figure 7: Indirect learning architecture.

$$(20) \qquad \frac{\partial P_i}{\partial a_j} = \frac{P_i(\bar{u} + \delta u_j \hat{\imath}_j) - P_i(\bar{u})}{\delta u_j}$$

where $\hat{\imath}_j$ is a unit vector.

This training is called specialized because the neural net is trained to behave as the inverse plant when it receives an input signal close to the desired output d. It may be trained on-line and it can fine tune itself while actually performing useful work [18].

Indirect learning architecture [18]

Backpropagation of the error through the plant itself can be avoided by using the indirect learning architecture which is shown in Figure 7. The desired plant output d is given to neural network 1 as input. Network output u is fed as input to the plant and actual plant output y is obtained. Normally error E_2 would be back propagated as in Figure 6. But it involves the backpropagation of error through the process which was considered above. Therefore actual process output y is inputted to neural network 2 and false process input u' is obtained at the output of neural net 2. Input u' is false because we do not know whether y is produced when we feed u' to the process. The error $u - u'$ is then back propagated to train the network as an inverse plant.

We consider the network 1 and 2 to be of same structure since they both try to represent the inverse of the plant. Thus when the error is propagated back for training network 2, network 1 is also trained.

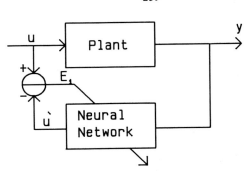

Figure 8: Generalized learning architecture.

In this method error E_1 is reduced instead of the plant error E_2. This situation causes difficulty. Neural network 1 may map all d's to a single $u = u_0$ which is mapped to $u' = u_0$ by the plant. In this case error E_1 is zero even thout the error of interest E_2 is obviously not zero.

Generalized learning architecture [18]

In specialized and indirect learning methods the training is carried out around the desired output. In generalized learning shown in Figure 8, an input u is selected and applied to the plant which produces the output y. Actual plant output y is then applied to the neural network. The difference between the plant input and neural net output u' is used to train the network as an inverse plant. The success of training to provide the generalization ability of the network is very important in this method. The network must respond correctly to inputs it was not specifically trained for, because in general the plant inputs u which forces the plant to produce the desired output d is not known. The combination of general and specialized learning methods may be a solution to this problem.

The three methods explained above have been used in various control studies [15, 22, 23].

7.2   Applications

In [22] a three layer neural network trained by the backpropagation algorithm is employed to identify the inverse plant. A linear activation function is used. From equation (3) we have:

(21)
$$O_{pi} = f(\text{net}_{pi}) = K \ \text{net}_{pi}$$

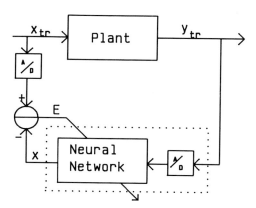

Figure 9: The external architecture block diagram for adaptation mode which uses generalized learning architecture.

where K is the proportional gain of neurons. The neural net is used as a controller. Simulations studies were carried out for online training and control on a second order system. The following observations were made.

An increase in the learning rate which is the gain of the activation function increases the speed of response but oscillations may start as is the case for a classical proportional controller. However the system still converges to a desired plant output within a short time. Therefore if a high gain is used in the activation function, the learning rate of the network must be large, and vice versa.

Under certain conditions, the increase in the number of neurons used in the hidden layer can increase the speed of convergence. However if too many neurons are used, again oscillation take place.

In [15] a delayed input/delayed state network architecture and perceptron training scheme are described. A solution to the problem of representing analog signals by a binary neural network with feedback and delays is suggested. The adaptation mode external architecture block diagram and neural network architecture are shown in Figures 9 and 10 respectively. Delayed signals are obtained via delay elements D.

The binary neural network was trained to identify the discrete inverse dynamics of the plant. Generalized learning architecture was used.

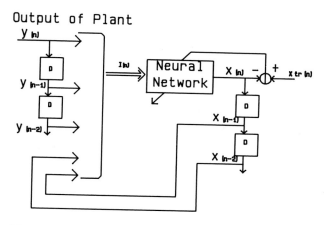

Figure 10: Neural network architecture in adaptation mode.

The neural network has one layer of N binary neurons, N being the number of quantization levels chosen to represent the analog value of the signals in the system. Distributed binary representation of analog signals serves the same purpose as the hidden units in the intermediate layers of the layered network. It supplies additional degrees of freedom, required to solve the learning problem. Thermometer representation to be explained below was chosen for the signals.

Consider an $\alpha = 8$ bit signal representation. This signal can be represented by using $2^\alpha - 1 = 255$ levels organized as a vertical column.

The data classically represented in $\alpha = 8$ bits can now be represented in this 255 level column by setting the number of levels from the bottom to 1 which corresponds to the value of 8 bit signal. As an example suppose the signal represented by 8 bits assumes the value of 250. This value is represented by thermometer representation by setting all of the 250 levels from the bottom to 1. Now suppose that 8 bit signal assumes the value of 149. This new value is represented by resetting all of the 1's from the above level down to 149th level of the column to 0's. Thus the representation of 8 bit signal is distributed to 255 levels and the variation in the 8 bit data can be observed in terms of the variations only on the upper level of the column as if it is a thermometer indicating varying temperature.

In this architecture the only layer used contains $N = 2^\alpha - 1$ neurons. Thus each neuron represents an information which corresponds to a certain level in the thermometer representation. It can be shown that [15] for a large family of plant dynamics, including all linear plants the thermometer representation guarantees existence of a valid solution to learning algorithm, and, thus, a convergence of learning algorithm to such a solution because of single layer used.

The I/O characteristic of the neural net can be expressed in matrix form as

$$X = g\{WI - T\}$$

where

$$
\begin{bmatrix} X_1(n) \\ X_2(n) \\ \vdots \\ \vdots \\ \vdots \\ X_N(n) \end{bmatrix}_{N \times 1}
= g \left\{
\begin{bmatrix} W_{11} & W_{12} \cdots W_{1N} \cdots W_{1N} \\ W_{21} & W_{22} \cdots W_{2N} \cdots W_{2N} \\ \vdots \\ \vdots \\ \vdots \\ W_{N1} & W_{N2} \cdots W_{NN} \cdots W_{NM} \end{bmatrix}_{N \times m}
\begin{bmatrix} Y_{(n)} \\ Y_{(n-1)} \\ \vdots \\ X_{(n-1)} \\ X_{(n-2)} \\ \vdots \end{bmatrix}_{m \times 1}
- \begin{bmatrix} T_1 \\ T_2 \\ \vdots \\ \vdots \\ \vdots \\ T_N \end{bmatrix}_{N \times 1}
\right\}
$$

(22)

where X, W, Y and T are output, weight, input and off set matrices of neural network respectively. In equation (23) g is nonlinearity used, and:

m is a number greater than or equal to the order of the plant

n $= 1 \cdots L$

L is the number of representations

N is the number of binary neurons which is equal to the number of quantization levels as stated before.

Simulation studies were conducted on a non-linear plant described as

(23) $$y(n) = [0.39y(n-1) - 0.3y(n-2)]^3 - x^3(n)$$

The values $N = 31, m = 4$ and $L = 200$ were chosen. The plant order 2 was over-estimated by chosing $m = 4$.

The presentations for the learning and control are shown below.

Presentation number n	Input vector			
	$Y_{(n)}$	$Y_{(n-1)}$	$Y_{(n-N)}$	$X_{(n-1)}$
1,	$Y_{(1)}$	$Y_{(0)}$	$Y_{(0)}$	$X_{(0)}$
2,	$Y_{(2)}$	$Y_{(1)}$	$Y_{(0)}$	$X_{(1)}$
$\vdots$	$\vdots$			
200,	$Y_{(200)}$	$Y_{(199)}$	$Y_{(198)}$	$X_{(199)}$

The average training error, generalization and fault tolerance abilities of the network were studied [15].

The plant's order information must be available a priori for choosing the number of delays.

If the number of degrees of freedom N of the network increases as a result of over estimation, the learning problem will be easier to solve, but the generalization ability decreases.

When over-estimation in the order of plant takes place m increases. This causes the number of inputs to be supplied to increase. The result is then the increase in the dimension of the network making it flexible, but reducing its ability to generalize.

In [23] a similar architecture to the one shown in Figure 10 has been used. This is a specialized learning architecture explained in Section 7.1. A method of modeling for a non-linear process and associated control strategy were proposed to be used in connection with tungsten arc welding process.

In another study [24] a process identification method based on neural network with memory has been suggested. The neural network with memory can be interpreted as cyclic networks. The structure is similar to the one shown in Figure 10. The network can perform on line identification of plant or inverse plant dynamics depending on the input output signals. The architecture is shown in Figure 11. Back propagation learning algorithm has been used.

In [25] use of three layer neural net trained by using present and past values in backpropagation method was proposed to identify non-linear dynamic response of pH in a continuously stirred tank reactor. A training data base was developed by using small disturbances in the form of pseudorandom binary sequence. Good agreements between the predicted actual values were obtained.

In [26] backpropagation and neurocontrol subject have been reviewed. The importance and the applications of the field have been discussed. Back propagation through time and backpropagation through random noise have been reviewed.

In [27] a technique for programming of Hopfield network [28, 29] for the purpose of system identification has been developed. Simulation studies have shown that the procedure developed is feasible on time varying and time invariant plants.

In [30] a method similar to Miller's CMAC neural network approach [31] has been compared to traditional adaptive systems methods. These are the self tuning regulator of Åström [32] and the model reference method [33]. The three control algorithms are compared under identical conditions on the same simple systems.

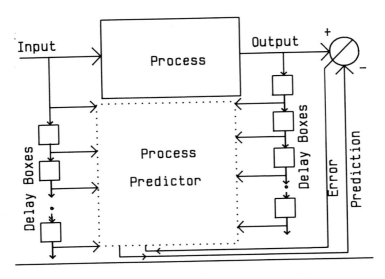

Figure 11: Neural net process predictor.

Comparisons are made concerning the stability, speed of convergence, noise rejection, memory size, the number of required calculations, and tracking performance. The results have indicated that the neural network approach exhibits desirable properties not found in the other two methods.

The inverted pendulum is a classical problem of control of an inherently unstable system. In [20] an inverted pendulum is simulated as a control task with the goal of learning to balance the pendulum with no a priori knowledge of the system dynamics. It is assumed that the performance feedback is not available on each step. It appears only as a failure signal when the pendulum falls or reaches the bounds of a horizontal track. In other applications [34] of neural networks to inverted pendulum performance feedback is assumed to be available.

To control the inverted pendulum the problems of delayed performance evaluation, learning under uncertainty and learning non-linear functions must be solved. *Reinforcement* and *temporal difference* learning methods have been presented which deal with the above issues for avoiding instability and for keeping the pendulum in balance.

In [16] use of a neural net in numeric to symbolic conversion for control has been studied. Such conversions are very important in the study of discrete event systems

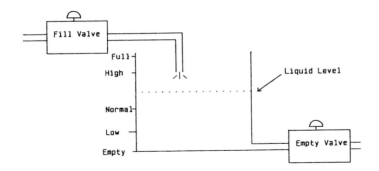

Figure 12: Level control in a surge tank.

and in intelligent controllers as explained in Section 2. Liquid level control in a surge tank shown in Figure 12 has been considered as an example. It is modeled as a discrete event system by considering the on off valve and high, low, normal levels and emptiness of the tank. Then an associated numeric to symbolic converter was specified and neural network structure for this function was studied.

In [21] use of neural networks in testing and diagnosis has been considered. It has been shown that the neural net pattern classifiers can be used to speed up the progress of diagnosis and servicing of computer controlled complicated electro mechanical systems in vehicles. A backpropagation algorithm was used. In [35] the use of backpropagation fault detection systems in on-line adaptation of nonlinear plants has been investigated. In [36] the combination of neural net and expert system technologies has been considered in general for the solution of problems in diagnosis and control. A neural net embedded in an expert system has been considered to analyze sensor data for determining machine "health".

The ability of neural networks to learn by example has been demonstrated in a continuous process control application which is shown in Figure 13 [36]. The neural net provides both real time and supervisory control. Liquid level is kept at the desired level as unmeasured output flow varies as a disturbance. The process is nonlinear and modeling is a nontrivial task. The input valve, driven by the neural net controller throttles the input flow.

Liquid level is sensed by redundant capacitive level sensors L1 and L2. The standard 4-20 miliampere sensor outputs are fed through a programmable controller analog input module and interface board to the neural net controller running on an IBM PC/AT. The control signal generated by the neural net is sent through the interface board and a 4 to 20 miliampere analog output module to drive the input valve.

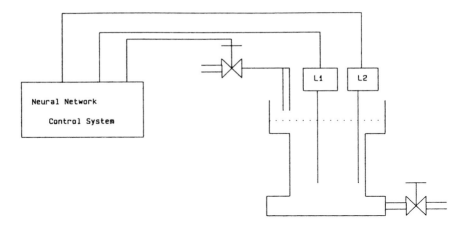

Figure 13: Level control of a tank.

The neural net has provided a stable control, and responded smoothly to changes in outflow and desired level. This capability is observed at all tank levels, including at the two abrupt transition points. The neural net on its own accommodated the nonlinearity introduced by both the abrupt transitions of the "I" shaped tank and the nonlinear characteristics of the ball type input valve.

This work demonstrates the real world capabilities of neural networks for a broad class of non-linear applications.

8 Fuzzy Logic Approach and Neural Nets

In real life control problems linguistic statements such as "high", "low", slightly increase, "OK", etc. are used rather than statements which can be written in crisp mathematical terms. In such cases the fuzzy logic approach [37, 38, 39] has many advantages. Domain knowledge which is developed by human expert is used in knowledge based systems. We propose a knowledge representation system based on neural network which is shown schematically in Figure 14 [40].

Learning is most effective when it is used in a suitable architecture. On the other hand, experiments suggest that as much a priori knowledge as possible should be built into the network for satisfactory and fast operation.

It has been reported that [20, 41] for complicated tasks a training curriculum progressing from simple to difficult parts of the task might greatly reduce overall learning time.

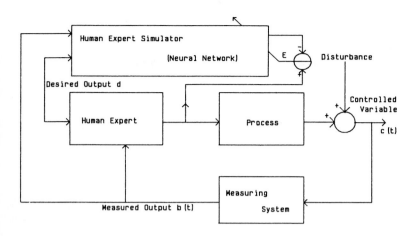

Figure 14: Domain knowledge representation by neural network.

Under the light of the above information, domain knowledge available *a priori* is decomposed into parts which can be learned by neural sectors easily. The approach proposed in [42, 43] seems to be useful in this respect. After the training of individual sectors is completed, they are connected to represent the whole domain in one network. After this initial training the network operates on-line together with the human expert as shown in Figure 14.

To the best of our knowledge such a system does not yet exist. Its advantages can be summarized as follows:

1. Unconscious but correct actions of the human operator can be formulated.

2. Expertise of various operators can be averaged objectively.

The system can be used in industry as an on-line knowledge base constructor.

9 Hardware Implementation

High computational capabilities of neural networks attract increasing attention due to the increasing availability of fast parallel architectures. Very large scale integrated, electro-optical and dedicated architectures are examples of such hardware.

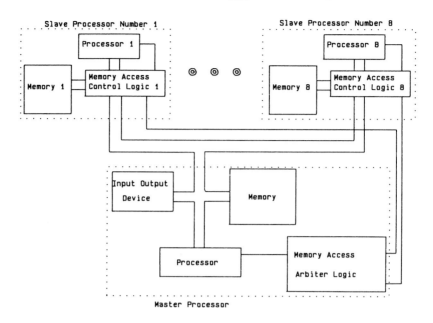

Figure 15: General block diagram of the proposed neural net simulator.

Availability of parallel architectures is expected to increase as a result of the development in microelectronics. The work of E. Pasero about an analog chip design for backpropagation network published in this volume is a recent example for the availability of suitable hardware.

As a special case we have designed a multiprocessor neural network simulator to be used in our studies [44]. Its general block diagram is shown in Figure 15. It uses off-the-shelf components and has a high performance to cost ratio which is especially important in real life applications.

The architecture consists of eight processors acting as slaves sharing a single bus for message passing. The message passing is controlled by a master processor which also performs all of the input output communication with the external environment.

The communication between the processors is carried out by broadcasting of data. In the method proposed, when the data of a slave processor is read by the master processor this data is at the same time sent to all of the slave microprocessors if necessary, during the reading cycle.

10 Future Work

There are various useful properties of neural networks which are explained throughout this work. But these properties have not yet been fully understood. The properties which are partially or qualitatively known must be investigated thoroughly [13].

There is still no clear understanding of what topology is needed for a particular task [13]. Before neuromorphic systems can interest practical end users, they must have tools and algorithms for steady state topology assignment [13].

There are other questions to be answered such as: what is the capacity of a neural network together with the learning algorithm? In other words how many patterns can be stored in a network with n processing elements? What should be done with local minima which are spurious equilibrium points [7]?

Learning methods must be further investigated especially to make better use of the abilities of neural nets for handling multi-input multi-output systems and nonlinear functions, and their potential for fast parallel implementation.

Finding signal representations which guarantee the convergence and improve the learning speed is another important goal especially in binary applications.

Another question is how the performance of learning methods can be improved for larger and more complicated tasks.

Networks trained by hint [43] may have potential applications in intelligent control of complicated processes which need human expertise.

11 Conclusions

In the present paper, neural networks, backpropagation and perceptron learning algorithms have been considered and reviewed with a view to applying them to process control.

Useful properties and disadvantages have been investigated and general conclusions concerning further research have been drawn.

It has been proposed that considering the control system as a disturbance noise filter may give a new insight to the use of neural nets in process control.

A method has been proposed where a neural net is trained by using a human expert and then can be used as a domain knowledge generator for expert systems.

Various applications of neural networks as process identifiers and controllers have been discussed.

It can be concluded that neural networks will find very useful applications in process control as a result of further research on finding suitable topology, fast learning algorithms and implementing suitable hardware.

Acknowledgments

I would like to thank Dr. Erol Gelenbe for his kind and continuing interest in our work on neural networks.

I would also like to thank my graduate student Mr. Burçak Beşer for his very constructive cooperation and assistance.

References

1. Rumelhart, D.E., McClelland J.L. and the PDP Research Group, "Parallel distributed processing, explorations in the microstructure of cognition, Vol 1: Foundations", A Bradford Book, The MIT Press, Cambridge, Mass, and London, 1986 (1988).

2. Jackson, J.H., "On localization". In Selected writings Vol. 2, Basic Books, New York, 1958. Original work 1869.

3. Luria, A.R., "Higher cortical functions in man", Basic Books, New York 1966.

4. Fleming, W.H., "Report of the panel on future directions in control theory: a mathematical perspective", Society for Industrial and Applied Mathematics, Philadelphia, 1988.

5. "Challenges to control: a collective view. Report of the workshop held at the University of Santa Clara on September 18-19, 1986", IEEE Transactions on Automatic Control, Vol. AC-32, No.4, 275-285, April 1987.

6. Gould, L.A., "Chemical process control: theory and applications", Addison Wesley Pub. Co., London, 1969.

7. Bavarian, B., "Introduction to neural networks for intelligent control", IEEE Control Systems Magazine, Vol. 8, No.2, 3-7, April 1988.

8. Gelenbe, E., "Random neural networks with negative and positive signals and product form solution", Proceedings of the Fourth International Symposium on Computer and Information Sciences, Çeşme, İzmir, Turkey, Vol.1, 603-613 October 30 - November 1, 1989, also in *Neural Computation*, Vol.1, No.4, 1989.

9. Lippmann, R.P., "An introduction to computing with neural nets", IEEE ASSP Magazine, 4-22, April 1987.

10. Lorentz, G.G., "The 13-th problem of Hilbert", American Mathematical Society, Proceedings of Symposia in Pure Mathematics, Providence, R.I, U.S.A., 419-430, 1976.

11. Wieland, A., Leighton, R., "Geometric analysis of neural network capabilities", International Conference on Neural Networks, III 385- III-391, 1987.

12. Hopfield, J.J., Tank, D.W., "Neural computation of decision optimization problems", Biol. Cybern., Vol.52, 1-12, 1985.

13. Guez, A., Eilbert, J.L., Kam, M., "Neural network architecture for control", IEEE Control Systems Magazine, 22-25, April 1988.

14. Widrow, B., Winter, R., "Neural nets for adaptive filtering and adaptive pattern recognition", IEEE Computer, 25-29, March 1988.

15. Levin, E., Gewirtzman, R., Inbar, F.G., "Neural network architecture for adaptive system modeling and control", International Joint Conference on Neural Networks, Washington D.C., II-311 - II-316, 18-22, June 1989.

16. Passino, K.M., Sartori, M.A., Antsaklis, P.J., "Neural Computing for Numeric to Symbolic Conversion in Control Systems", IEEE Control Systems Magazine, 44-51, April 1989.

17. Huang, S.C. "Supervised Learning with a Selective Update Strategy for Artificial Neural Networks", Master's Thesis, Dept. of Electrical and Computer Engineering, Univ. of Notre Dame, Notre Dame, IN, August 1988.

18. Psaltis, D., Sideris, A., Yamamura, A.A., "A multilayered neural network controller", IEEE Control Systems Magazine, Vol.8, No.2, 17-21, April 1988.

19. Almedia, L.B., "Back propagation in perceptrons with feedback", Neural Computers, Eckmiur R., Holsbwa, C.V.D., (Ed.), Springer Verlag, Heidelberg, 1988.

20. Anderson, C.W., "Learning to control an inverted pendulum using neural networks", IEEE Control Systems Magazine, 31-37, April 1989.

21. Marko, K.A., James, J., Dosdall, J., Murphy, J., "Automotive control system diagnostics using neural nets for rapid pattern classification of large data sets", International joint conference on neural networks, Washington D.C., II-13-II-16, 18-22, June 1989.

22. Shong, Lan, M., "Adaptive control of unknown dynamical systems via neural network approach", American Control Conference, 910-915, 1989.

23. Ramaswamy, K., Cook, G.E., Kristinn, A., Karsai, G., "Neural networks in GTA weld modelling and control", American Control Conference 1989.

24. Beşer, B., Tulunay, E., "Preliminary results on process prediction using perceptrons which utilizes memory", Proceedings of the Fourth International Symposium on Computer and Information Sciences, Çeşme, İzmir, Turkey, Vol.1, 431-440, 30 October - 1 November 1989.

25. Bhat, N., McAvoy, T.J., "Use of neural nets for dynamic modeling and control of chemical process systems", American Control Conference, 1342-1347, 1989.

26. Werbos, P.J., "Backpropagation and neurocontrol: A review and procpectus", International Joint Conference on Neural Networks, Washington D.C., I-209-I-216, 18-22 June 1989.

27. Chu, R., Tenorio, M., "Neural networks for system identification", American Control Conference, 916-921, 1989.

28. Hopfield, J.J., "Neural networks and physical systems with emergent collective computational abilities", Proc. Natl. Acad. Sci., Vol.79, 2554-2558, 1982.

29. Hopfield, J.J., "Neurons with graded response have collective computational properties like those of two-state neurons", Proc. Natl. Acad. Sci., Vol.81, 3088-3092, 1984.

30. Kraft, D.L., Campagna, D.P., "A comparison of CMAC neural network and traditional adaptive control systems", American Control Conference, 884-889, 1989.

31. Albus, J.S., "A new approach to manipulator control: The Cerebellar Model Articulation Controller (CMAC)", Transactions of the ASME, Journal of Dynamic Systems Measurement and Control, Vol.97, 220-227, September 1975.

32. Åström, K.J., Wittenmark, B., "On self-tuning regulators", Automatica, Vol.9, 185-199, 1973.

33. Parks, P.C., "Liapunov redesign of model reference adaptive control systems", IEEE Trans. on Automatic Control, Vol. AV-11, 362-367, 1966.

34. Tolat, V.V., Widrow, B., "An adaptive broom balancer with visual inputs", Proc. IEEE Int. Conf. on Neural Networks, San Diego, CA, II-641-II-647, July 1988.

35. Zafiriov, S.N., McAvoy, T.J., "Application of neural networks on the detection of sensor failure during the operation of a control system", American Control Conference, 1989.

36. VerDubin, W.H., "Neural nets for diagnosis and control", 3rd Annual Expert Systems Conference and Exposition, Cobo Center, Detroit, Michigan, 257-267, 4-6 April 1989.

37. Zadeh, L.A., "The concept of a linguistic variable and its application to approximate reasoning I", Information Science, Vol.8, 199-249, 1925.

38. Zadeh, L.A., "Making computers think like people", IEEE Spectrum, 26-31, August 1984.

39. Holmblad, L.P., Ostergaard, J.J., "Control of cement kiln by fuzzy logic", F.L. Smidth and Co., Copenhagen, Denmark, 1980.

40. Tulunay, E., Beşer, B., İkeda, S., "Expert knowledge-base constructor for fuzzy linguistic controller based on neural networks" Internal Report, Electrical and Electronic Engineering Department, Middle East Technical University, Ankara, Turkey, November 1989.

41. Selfridge, O.G., Sutton, R.S., Barto, A.G., "Training and Tracking in robotics", Proc. IJCAI-85, 670-672, 1985.

42. Suddarth, S.C., Lamoulie, A., "Data fusion using a back-propagation analog associative memory", Proceedings of the Fourth International Symposium on Computer and Information Sciences, Çeşme, İzmir, Turkey, Vol.1, 615-624, 30 October - 1 November 1989.

43. Suddarth, S.C., Holden, D.C.A., "Symbolic-neural systems and the use of hints for developing complex systems", Submitted to Int. Journal of Man-Machine Studies, 4 January 1990.

44. Beşer, N.B., Tulunay, E., "A multiprocessor neural network simulator", IASTED International Conference, Artificial Intelligence Applications and Neural Networks, Zurich, Switzerland, 25-27 June 1990, Accepted for presentation.